Social, Emotional, and Behavioral Supports in Schools

The Guilford Practical Intervention in the Schools Series

Kenneth W. Merrell, Founding Editor
Sandra M. Chafouleas, Series Editor

www.guilford.com/practical

This series presents the most reader-friendly resources available in key areas of evidence-based practice in school settings. Practitioners will find trustworthy guides on effective behavioral, mental health, and academic interventions, and assessment and measurement approaches. Covering all aspects of planning, implementing, and evaluating high-quality services for students, books in the series are carefully crafted for everyday utility. Features include ready-to-use reproducibles, appealing visual elements, and an oversized format. Recent titles have Web pages where purchasers can download and print the reproducible materials.

Recent Volumes

Child and Adolescent Suicidal Behavior, Second Edition:
School-Based Prevention, Assessment, and Intervention
David N. Miller

School Supports for Students in Military Families
Pamela Fenning

Safe and Healthy Schools, Second Edition: Practical Prevention Strategies
Jeffrey R. Sprague and Hill M. Walker

Clinical Interviews for Children and Adolescents, Third Edition:
Assessment to Intervention
Stephanie H. McConaughy and Sara A. Whitcomb

Executive Function Skills in the Classroom:
Overcoming Barriers, Building Strategies
Laurie Faith, Carol-Anne Bush, and Peg Dawson

The RTI Approach to Evaluating Learning Disabilities,
Second Edition
*Joseph F. Kovaleski, Amanda M. VanDerHeyden, Timothy J. Runge,
Perry A. Zirkel, and Edward S. Shapiro*

Effective Bullying Prevention: A Comprehensive Schoolwide Approach
Adam Collins and Jason Harlacher

Social Justice in Schools: A Framework for Equity in Education
Charles A. Barrett

Coaching Students with Executive Skills Challenges, Second Edition
Peg Dawson and Richard Guare

Social, Emotional, and Behavioral Supports in Schools:
Linking Assessment to Tier 2 Intervention
Sara C. McDaniel, Allison L. Bruhn, and Sara Estrapala

Family–School Success for Children with ADHD: A Guide for Intervention
Thomas J. Power, Jennifer A. Mautone, and Stephen L. Soffer

Social, Emotional, and Behavioral Supports in Schools

*Linking Assessment
to Tier 2 Intervention*

SARA C. McDANIEL
ALLISON L. BRUHN
SARA ESTRAPALA

THE GUILFORD PRESS
New York   London

LIMITED DUPLICATION LICENSE

These materials are intended for use only by qualified professionals.

The publisher grants to individual purchasers of this book nonassignable permission to reproduce all materials for which photocopying permission is specifically granted in a footnote. This license is limited to you, the individual purchaser, for personal use or use with students. This license does not grant the right to reproduce these materials for resale, redistribution, electronic display, or any other purposes (including but not limited to books, pamphlets, articles, video or audio recordings, blogs, file-sharing sites, internet or intranet sites, and handouts or slides for lectures, workshops, or webinars, whether or not a fee is charged). Permission to reproduce these materials for these and any other purposes must be obtained in writing from the Permissions Department of Guilford Publications.

The authors have checked with sources believed to be reliable in their efforts to provide information that is complete and generally in accord with the standards of practice that are accepted at the time of publication. However, in view of the possibility of human error or changes in behavioral, mental health, or medical sciences, neither the authors, nor the editor and publisher, nor any other party who has been involved in the preparation or publication of this work warrants that the information contained herein is in every respect accurate or complete, and they are not responsible for any errors or omissions or the results obtained from the use of such information. Readers are encouraged to confirm the information contained in this book with other sources.

Library of Congress Cataloging-in-Publication Data is available from the publisher.

ISBN 978-1-4625-5417-1 (paperback)
ISBN 978-1-4625-5418-8 (hardcover)

About the Authors

Sara C. McDaniel, PhD, is Professor of Special Education in the Department of Special Education and Multiple Abilities at the University of Alabama and Director of the Center for Interconnected Behavioral and Mental Health Systems (CIBMHS). The CIBMHS is a research center that engages in rigorous research in schools and focuses on supporting schools and districts in implementing positive behavioral interventions and supports (PBIS) and school-based mental health services. Dr. McDaniel conducts research and teaches in the areas of PBIS; classroom management assessment and coaching; Tier 2 social, emotional, and behavioral supports; and preventive treatments for diverse populations of students at high risk.

Allison L. Bruhn, PhD, is Professor of Special Education at the University of Iowa and Executive Director of the Scanlan Center for School Mental Health. The Center engages in professional development, research, graduate training, and clinical services to improve social, emotional, and behavioral outcomes for K–12 students and educators. Dr. Bruhn's research focuses on practical, feasible interventions and assessment for students with challenging behavior, including a mobile app (MoBeGo) she developed to improve students' self-management skills. She is committed to bridging the research-to-practice gap by engaging educational stakeholders in relationship building, professional development, research, and dissemination.

Sara Estrapala, PhD, is Assistant Research Professor in the Department of Special Education at the University of Missouri–Columbia. Her research focuses on Tier 1 and Tier 2 PBIS in high schools. She is particularly interested in studying student voice, self-regulation development, and usability and feasibility of implementation in the high school context. Dr. Estrapala has taught courses in functional behavioral assessment and in behavior and classroom management in elementary and high school settings. She is committed to translating research to practice by providing professional development for inservice and preservice teachers, writing for practitioner journals, and presenting at practitioner-focused professional conferences.

Preface

Why Tier 2? Why now? Chances are if you are reading this book, you understand the need to focus on, or even double down on, Tier 2 for social, emotional, and behavioral needs. The field of positive behavior support was founded on serving individuals with disabilities using intensive, function-based interventions, and from there it expanded to schoolwide, universal, Tier 1 positive behavioral interventions and supports (PBIS). However, with the emphasis on those two Everest-sized mountains, a huge valley was created for educators regarding what to do between universal prevention practices for all students and the intensive, individualized supports provided at Tier 3. In practice, students with unmet social, emotional, and behavioral needs may be subject to punitive discipline practices rather than receive effective targeted intervention. Or there may be an overreliance on Tier 3, which can overwhelm the entire PBIS system because there are not enough resources (e.g., personnel, time, money) to provide these highly customized interventions to every individual. Both scenarios are inherently reactive in nature, and do not help students whose support needs fall within the "valley" between Tier 1 and Tier 3. That brings us to the "Why now?" question.

When we first started focusing our research on targeted Tier 2 supports in 2011, we were addressing the aforementioned valley. We thought that without evidence-based, feasible practices and systems, educators would continue to overrely on punitive discipline, Tier 3, or even special education. More than 10 years later, the educational challenges associated with the COVID-19 pandemic, along with the youth mental health crisis that began prepandemic (2020), reignited and reaffirmed our focus on the large gap between Tier 1 and Tier 3, and the timely need to double down on Tier 2. During the pandemic, most brick-and-mortar schools closed, forcing distance learning upon educators and students. Students were isolated from their peers and many experienced harmful forms of trauma. This included food insecurity, housing insecurity, abuse in the home, neglect, family members or friends getting sick or dying from COVID-19, and increased engagement with technology and social media, which can lead to online bullying, exposure to inappropriate content, and other harms. Then, when students began transitioning back to in-person school, we tried to sound the alarm that, while educators were rightly concerned about getting back on track academically and coming up with innovative methods to make up for learning loss, students first needed their social, emotional, and behavioral needs to be assessed and addressed. Some districts and schools hired additional mental health professionals, while others purchased curricula and technology to help with assessment and intervention. But many moved on by focusing on the substantial academic deficits resulting from school closures. Although the vast majority of students returned to in-person schooling full time, the youth mental health crisis has continued to worsen. Whereas focusing on externalizing problem behaviors (e.g., fighting, cursing, skipping class) and using punitive discipline may have been the go-to solution in the past, these approaches do not address the myriad social, emotional, and behavioral issues we are seeing in schools today.

For these reasons, the answers to "Why Tier 2?" and "Why now?" could not be more clear. Schools need a systematic, feasible approach to address all student needs across the social, emotional, and behavioral continuum. Schools also need proactive approaches to identifying students with those needs, rather than relying on reactive approaches such as utilizing discipline data from office referrals garnered only after a student has done something severe enough to warrant a trip to the office. Schools need a systematic approach to integrating related service providers within the Tier 2 system to effectively match available small-group and individual interventions to emotional symptoms that can produce the same type of harmful outcomes experienced by students with more overt, disruptive behaviors. Finally, schools need to pair their punitive responses to unwanted behaviors with evidence-based, systematic Tier 2 interventions to promote new skills and maintain the use of these skills across the school day and beyond. We are hopeful that by describing our approach to systematically identifying and matching culturally and contextually appropriate Tier 2 interventions for students in need, we can begin to reduce the youth mental health issues, as well as the emerging violence and aggression, in schools.

This book begins with the basics of Tier 2—systems, practices, and data—the components essential to effective implementation. We also discuss the need to ensure Tier 1 supports are in place with fidelity and the features indicating readiness for Tier 2. We conclude Chapter 1 with the description of the four-step process to Tier 2 identification and intervention. Next, Chapter 2 covers the purpose of systematic screening and various approaches to screening to identify students with targeted social, emotional, behavioral needs. In Chapter 3, we discuss initial intervention matching. Chapters 4 through 8 provide you with in-depth information for each intervention category, including co-occurring academic needs. Chapter 9 is everyone's favorite topic—data! Just kidding, it's probably just our favorite topic. Get excited, as you will learn the ins and outs of data-based decision making in Tier 2 and making ongoing adaptations. Chapter 10 describes technical assistances and the importance of ensuring and assessing Tier 2 fidelity. Finally, in Chapter 11, we leave you with critical considerations for your local context prior to implementing this systematic Tier 2 framework. We hope this book and your subsequent implementation of a systematic Tier 2 process of matched, evidence-based Tier 2 interventions will support the students in your school or district and address the overwhelming challenges we are seeing in our schools. We firmly believe that addressing the social, emotional, and behavioral well-being of students will facilitate not only academic learning, but the life skills necessary for happiness and success.

This text, while witty and fun to read in our opinion, is not your quick summer beach read. If you are a practitioner (e.g., classroom teacher, school psychologist, administrator, district-level leader, counselor) or a preservice educator, this book is for you! Each chapter is structured to provide you with a chapter introduction and a few focus points for that chapter. At the end of each chapter is a summary and, where applicable, a resource table and example case study. Taken together, the text, tables, and figures should provide you with the materials and knowledge necessary to implement this framework across grades K–12. You will want to follow the chapters in order, as they are presented in the order in which the implementation steps exist.

Note: In this book, we use "they/them/their" when referring to a single individual. We made this choice to be inclusive of readers who do not identify with masculine/feminine pronouns.

Contents

CHAPTER 1

Social, Emotional, and Behavioral Needs and Tier 2

Logic, Purpose, and Readiness

This chapter provides an overview of positive behavioral interventions and supports (PBIS; Lewis & Sugai, 1999), foundational Tier 1 practices, and the logic behind Tier 2 supports. We emphasize the importance of ensuring effective classroom practices are in place first, before referring students to Tier 2 or in case teachers have high numbers of students who are identified for Tier 2.

CHAPTER FOCUS

- Learn how to ensure evidence-based classroom management practices within Tier 1 are differentiated to include praise, opportunities to respond, and choice.
- Understand Tier 2 readiness components that should be in place before Tier 2 training, such as teaming.
- Learn about important practical issues of communication, preparedness, and burnout related to Tier 2.
- Understand the four-step Tier 2 identification and intervention process.

PBIS AND MULTI-TIERED SYSTEMS OF SUPPORT

PBIS is a three-tiered framework addressing social, emotional, and behavioral (SEB) competencies, and has been implemented in more than 26,000 U.S. schools to date (*www.pbis.org*). This widely used framework is often integrated with academic competencies and the response-to-intervention (RTI) framework in a combined, multi-tiered framework called *multi-tiered systems of support* (MTSS; McIntosh & Goodman, 2020). Core features of MTSS across academic and SEB needs include: making data-based decisions; preventing poor student outcomes through effective instruction; providing person-centered, targeted and intensive supports when indicated; and delivering evidence-based interventions with fidelity. The framework begins with Tier 1, a preventative, universal level of instruction for all students. Tier 2 involves the addition of targeted, small-group supports for students identified with risk. Finally, Tier 3 includes intensive, individualized supports for students with serious academic or SEB needs within or outside of special education.

This book provides the reader with the tools to implement a systematic approach to implementing Tier 2 for SEB needs. This area of implementation is situated within a PBIS/MTSS framework between universal prevention (Tier 1) and intensive, individualized supports (Tier 3). In this book, we provide the reader with the rationale and background for each part of the Tier 2 identification and intervention process, as well as practical implementation cues for the practitioner. Importantly, after we review the process for identifying students who require Tier 2 supports and matching their needs to a category of intervention, in the middle chapters we overview evidence-based Tier 2 interventions that effectively address needs in that intervention category. We also know that many students will have co-occurring academic and SEB needs, so we have dedicated a chapter specifically to that issue. In the final chapter, we overview important practical considerations for the practitioner to plan for prior to implementing this framework.

SEB FOCUS

With RTI addressing the academic side of prevention and intervention, PBIS focuses on the equally important SEB side of prevention and intervention. Although practitioners may think mostly of "behavioral" needs related to discipline and disrupting instruction, it is important to note that PBIS should also address social and emotional areas of need for students. While the three are often tied together, they do represent various subskills and, therefore, require different interventions—not a one-size-fits-all intervention. Across SEB skills, there are varying underlying needs that can be addressed within Tier 2. Figure 1.1 highlights the smaller "micro skills" that weave into the larger "macro skills" and larger SEB domains that should be addressed within Tier 2. In this book, we provide strategies and interventions that address conduct (or externalizing behavior), hyperactivity/inattention, social problem-solving needs, emotional (or internalizing symptoms) needs, and co-occurring academic issues. Interventions can be adapted according to school or classroom context and student characteristics ("horizontal adaptations"; see Chapter 3), and they can be adapted for intensity based on student responsiveness ("vertical adaptations"; see Chapter 9). Adapting interventions while keeping core features in place helps educators to improve the efficiency and effectiveness of the Tier 2 practices. Taken together, the reader will gain an understanding of each area of need, the underlying skills, and matched interventions to promote those skills in the school setting.

TIER 2 LOGIC

The purpose of Tier 2 is to provide targeted, efficient, evidence-based strategies and interventions to students identified as having elevated risk, and who are not responding to Tier 1 as indicated

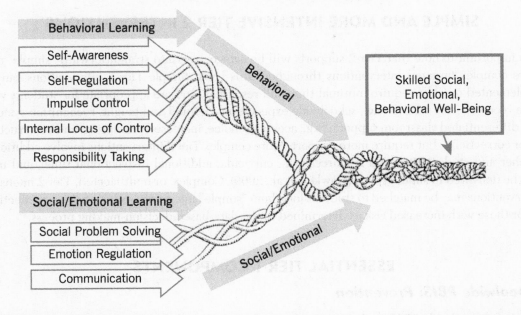

FIGURE 1.1. Braided SEB skills. Adapted from Scarborough (2001). Copyright © 2001. The Guilford Press. Used with permission.

by data (e.g., universal screener, attendance, grades, office discipline referrals [ODRs]). The catalyst for Tier 2 supports may be reactive disciplinary consequences (e.g., ODRs), but they should also be preventative or in response to an identified need without a serious disciplinary infraction occurring. The goals of implementing Tier 2 strategies and interventions are to reduce risk and to transition the student back to requiring only Tier 1 supports. If Tier 2 supports are not effective or a student's needs are more significant, teams will use a data-based decision-making process to move a student to intensive, individualized Tier 3 supports.

Tier 2 strategies and interventions should target a small number of students with similarly matched needs, be readily available, and be relatively easy to implement (i.e., not requiring a lot of personnel, time, or materials; Mitchell et al., 2015). Designed to serve approximately 15–20% of the school's population, Tier 2 systems must be in place to efficiently identify students and match effective interventions so students can quickly return to needing only schoolwide, Tier 1 strategies and practices. It is important to note that students who are identified for Tier 2 should continue to receive schoolwide supports. That is, just because a student receives Tier 2 intervention does not mean they should stop receiving Tier 1 instruction or acknowledgments for positive behaviors. Tier 2 adds to Tier 1—it does not replace it. Additionally, this framework includes problem-solving teams who use data to make decisions about possible movement to Tier 3 or special education evaluation when students are unresponsive to Tier 2 interventions. Tier 2 interventions should be short term, can be delivered in small groups, and are delivered by general educators, social workers, behavior specialists, school psychologists, counselors, or other support personnel. The foundational requirements for Tier 2 are (1) a Tier 2 problem-solving team (this can be the same as the RTI academic team, the schoolwide PBIS team, or a new team); (2) systematic assessment for identification of students in need of Tier 2; (3) reliable and valid progress monitoring; and (4) implementation of evidence-based interventions with fidelity.

SIMPLE AND MORE INTENSIVE TIER 2 INTERVENTIONS

It is important to note that Tier 2 supports will be categorized into straightforward "simple" and more complex targeted interventions throughout this book. Simple Tier 2 interventions can be implemented quickly, require minimal time and resources, and are appropriate for students who have received Tier 1 PBIS (e.g., schoolwide expectations defined and taught, recognition system) and differentiated classroom supports (e.g., access to choice, increased prompting, and constructive error corrections), but require more support. More complex Tier 2 interventions involve additional teacher and student time and resources (e.g., curricula, additional instructional time), and may also be delivered in small groups (Hawken et al., 2009). Complex, or multifaceted, Tier 2 intensive interventions may be matched to students for whom "simple" interventions have not been effective, or for those with increased risk as determined in the data-based decision-making process.

ESSENTIAL TIER 1 COMPONENTS

Schoolwide PBIS: Prevention

Tier 1, or schoolwide PBIS, is the universal tier of prevention within the three-tiered framework. This means that *all* students, regardless of risk factors, should have access to Tier 1 practices. Tier 1 requires schools to establish and teach three to five positively stated expectations, define those expectations for each setting, create and sustain a consistent recognition system and consequence system, and use schoolwide data to identify and solve problems (Lewis & Sugai, 1999). Before implementing Tier 2, it is essential to have Tier 1 in place with fidelity. That is, all key components of Tier 1 should be implemented consistently and accurately. Schools often measure fidelity using the Tiered Fidelity Inventory (TFI; Algozzine et al., 2014), which has a subscale for each of the three tiers. The cut point for implementing Tier 1 with fidelity is 70% or higher on the annual evaluation. Tier 1 is intended to serve all students in the school, and effectively prevents serious challenging behaviors for about 80% of the student population. Implementing Tier 2 without first achieving fidelity at Tier 1 may lead to an overidentification of students requiring Tier 2 supports due to a lack of consistent, fair, explicit preventative Tier 1 supports. For example, some students who are new to the building may not yet understand the schoolwide expectations and may be transferring procedures or expectations from a previous school building. These students may have a different understanding of "on time," or "respectful" behavior. As such, they may be given an ODR for a code of conduct infraction, due to a lack of understanding. Tier 1 is critical in preventing these types of skill acquisition issues. Additionally, within schoolwide or classwide supports, educators should differentiate supports for students who require minimally intensified Tier 1 supports (e.g., reteach expectations lessons, review the code of conduct, differentiate classroom supports).

Differentiated Classroom Supports

Another strategy to reduce unnecessary ODRs and overidentification for Tier 2 is to implement evidence-based differentiated classroom practices. Given a majority of ODRs occur in the classroom, it is important to remember to provide all students with differentiated strategies to support their SEB needs during instruction. Preventative, differentiated classroom supports should include providing classroom structure (e.g., predictable daily schedule and procedures), implementing feasible and predictable routines (e.g., where to turn in work, how to break into groups), teaching and reinforcing classroom expectations, developing and sustaining positive teacher–student relationships, along with six specific differentiated classroom practices.

First, classroom teachers should provide behavior-specific praise (e.g., "Great job using your inside voice," "I really appreciate you helping clean up today") when students meet classroom expectations. Rates of praise should be higher than rates of error corrections. Second, error corrections should be constructive and private, rather than public and demeaning. Third, classroom teachers should provide a high rate of varied opportunities to respond to academic instruction (e.g., call and response, response cards, private thumbs-up/thumbs-down). Fourth, when possible, classroom teachers can provide differentiated and grade-level appropriate choices for students needing additional supports (e.g., choice of pen or pencil, which task to complete first, where to sit). Fifth, students who require differentiated classroom supports also need higher rates of prompting or precorrections related to the expected classroom and schoolwide behaviors prior to the behavior expected to be displayed by that student (e.g., "Samantha, remember when we transition, we have to quickly start packing up our materials"). Precorrections or prompts help students keep the expected behavior at the forefront of their mind and reduce mistakes or unwanted behaviors. Finally, within Tier 1 differentiated classroom practices, it is important to remember that some students will require differentiated prompts, precorrects, and opportunities to review and relearn the skill they are not performing (e.g., brief reteaching of a specific routine or classwide expectation). These additional supports fall within Tier 1, effective classroom practices, and should be implemented prior to targeted, Tier 2 supports.

It is also important to note that in addition to the effective classroom practices mentioned above, instructional approaches such as pacing, grouping, differentiating academic instruction, and providing feedback should be in place prior to implementing Tier 2 supports for targeted groups of students. Student behaviors and social–emotional needs may arise because of lack of structure, instructional tasks at the frustration level, pacing that is too slow or too fast, lack of differentiated supports, and so forth. It is important to assess classroom practices, particularly when making decisions about Tier 2 intervention related to classroom-based SEB needs. Similarly, some classrooms may serve multiple students with SEB needs. If this occurs, classroom teachers may consider implementing an effective Tier 2 strategy or intervention classwide (e.g., group contingency) after ensuring there are no teacher classroom practice issues that first need to be addressed. One example is Class-Wide Function-Related Intervention Team (CW-FIT; Wills et al., 2018). In this classwide intervention, the teacher encourages prosocial behaviors with additional prompting, provides regular feedback, and increases access to contingent reinforcement for students who meet classwide expectations.

TIER 2 FOUNDATIONS: DATA, SYSTEMS, PRACTICES

In addition to implementing Tier 1 with fidelity and utilizing effective classroom practices, educators preparing to implement Tier 2 should consider the three main pillars of PBIS: data, systems, and practices.

Data

First, to develop an efficient and objective Tier 2 system, schools should be able to use a variety of data sources. This could include universal SEB screening data; attendance; ODR data; academic data (e.g., course failures, grade point average [GPA]); and potentially classroom or minor infraction data. Once Tier 2 interventions are in place, educators must have strategies for monitoring progress, which may require collecting additional SEB progress monitoring data such as Direct Behavior Ratings (DBRs; Bruhn et al., 2018; Chafouleas et al., 2013). These data are analyzed in tandem with intervention fidelity data in order to make accurate assessments about students' progress. Chapter 3 discusses these aspects of data-based decision making.

Systems

The core systems in place for Tier 2 involve personnel, resources, and professional development (Bruhn & McDaniel, 2021). While the composition and functions of the Tier 2 team will be visited later in this chapter, put simply, a problem-solving team must meet to match and assign appropriate Tier 2 strategies and interventions to students and to review progress monthly regarding each student case. Like Tier 1, buy-in from the rest of the staff is also essential. For Tier 2, buy-in will pertain to specific educator responsibilities within Tier 2 practices (i.e., screening, Tier 2 team membership, implementing strategies and interventions, monitoring progress). All staff should also have a solid understanding of the philosophy of Tier 2 strategies and interventions, how to pair consequences with instructional practices to reduce the likelihood of another infraction, and how to implement social–emotional supports to address underlying needs (e.g., disabilities, academic gaps, mental health disorders). Buy-in discussions and explaining the rationale for implementing Tier 2, and pairing consequences with instructional practices is critical to improving educators' understanding of Tier 2 and, essentially, fidelity of systems and practices. The systemic resources needed for Tier 2 include the materials for interventions and progress monitoring, data management systems, and of course, time for implementation. Finally, effective implementation requires initial and ongoing professional development to ensure educators have the knowledge, skills, and self-efficacy to intervene. You will learn more about initial training and ongoing coaching to support the initial and sustaining phases of Tier 2 implementation in Chapter 4.

Practices

As we discussed, data collected should drive decisions within the system regarding who should receive Tier 2 and how best to match and adapt Tier 2 strategies and interventions for students with an indicated SEB need. Chapter 2 provides in-depth details of available reliable and valid screeners that can be installed as a critical practice to drive Tier 2 decision making. Beyond the practice of screening, several evidence-based interventions, or practices, must be available at Tier 2. Tier 2 practices fit the targeted level of support through several core features: (1) they are implemented within a short time of the need being identified, (2) they are implemented without special education support, and (3) they can be implemented with limited resources (e.g., time, materials) and potentially in small groups (Hawken et al., 2009). Tier 2 interventions can be delivered in a flexible approach, sometimes requiring weekly meetings or completing a single form. These interventions should be reserved for students with indicated levels of need (not responding to Tier

1 implementation according to data such as a universal screener). A critical approach to improving efficiency is making precise matching decisions when determining which Tier 2 strategy or intervention to use, and how best to adapt the intervention for each student. To make data-based decisions for matching, educators should utilize available screening data that points to which area of need requires intervention.

TIER 2 READINESS: DATA, SYSTEMS, PRACTICES

In conjunction with the TFI for Tier 1, we recommend assessing your school or district's Tier 2 readiness to determine if the timing is right for implementing Tier 2 components of data, systems, and practices (see adapted Tier 2 Readiness Checklist in Figure 1.2).

Tier 2 Data Readiness

Another area of readiness to consider and planfully examine prior to requiring implementation is the readiness of Tier 2 data and systems. We have already highlighted the importance of having a reliable, valid, and useful SEB screener available to all educators. The screener should yield data pointing not only to who needs Tier 2 supports, but to which macro skills need to be addressed for intervention matching and possibly the level of intensity of supports required. Educators must also develop procedures for the screening process that explicitly state when the screener will be completed (e.g., 6 weeks after school starts); how students, families, and educators can request assistance after the screener completion time line; who will complete the screener (e.g., homeroom teacher, core academic teacher, student); how the screener will be completed (e.g., paper versus electronic) and scored (e.g., by the classroom teacher, electronically), and how those data will be shared with the Tier 2 team for students who are confirmed as having a Tier 2 need. For further reading and understanding of the screening process and logistics, we recommend *Best Practices in Universal Social, Emotional, and Behavioral Screening: An Implementation Guide* (Romer et al., 2020).

Systems Readiness

Tier 1 Fidelity

As a reminder, educators should consider whether Tier 1 is in place with fidelity first, with a minimum 70% on the Tier 1 TFI (Algozinne et al., 2014). In some cases, schools may implement both tiers simultaneously but should be on the lookout for overidentification of students for Tier 2 until Tier 1 is in place with fidelity. Second, educators should consider whether there is district, administrator, and educator buy-in for Tier 2. The district will need to provide resources for Tier 2 planning, training, and rolling out Tier 2 supports, as implementation is most effective as a districtwide effort. The local school administrator has a tremendous amount of power in determining the future success of Tier 2 implementation with their level of buy-in, similar to most new initiatives. Finally, teachers, related service providers, and other staff should understand the logic behind Tier 2 (e.g., providing instructional support to students with indicated needs, rather than punishing unwanted behaviors alone), and the tiered model prior to starting Tier 2.

Readiness Component	Response
Tier 1 TFI Score is 70% or higher.	
We consistently use data to make PBIS decisions.	
Tier 2 Team includes administrator, someone with behavioral expertise or the desire to develop it, and a grade-level teacher.	
Has the school principal committed to ensuring professional development and ongoing coaching for the whole staff related to Tier 2 PBIS for SEB needs?	
Is a plan in place to make all school faculty members aware of Tier 2 implementation and alignment with existing practices?	
Do you have a Tier 2 coordinator for your school?	
Does your school or district have a universal screener for SEB needs?	
If yes above, list below:	
Does your school have any SEB evidence-based interventions for targeted groups of students?	
List all personnel who will be able to assist with delivering Tier 2 SEB interventions (who in the building has some free time to work with students with SEB needs and is skilled at doing so?).	
Does your school have a full-time behavior interventionist or something similar?	

FIGURE 1.2. Tier 2 Readiness Checklist. Adapted from National PBIS Technical Assistance Center; *www.pbis.org/resource/tier-2-systems-readiness-guide*.

Teaming

The Tier 2 problem-solving team (PST) should aim to address co-occurring targeted needs across both academic and SEB domains. In this book, we will refer to the PST as the designated Tier 2 team, who is responsible for the problem-solving process of (a) systematically identifying students requiring supports; (b) matching evidence-based supports with student need; (c) adapting supports; and (d) progress monitoring. Educators should also consider the possibility that co-occurring academic and SEB needs may be linked. For instance, a student who reads below grade level may not feel included or supported during reading period and may respond with unwanted behavior. Or, if they perceive the work to be too hard, they may act out to get out of class. Similarly, a student with chronic emotional symptoms such as anxious feelings may miss all or parts of the school day, which can lead to gaps in learning. For these reasons, it is important to discuss cases of students in one integrated academic and behavioral meeting when possible. More information on Tier 2 teaming is presented below.

Tier 2 Practices Readiness

When planning and installing new Tier 2 data, systems, and practices, it is important to start with conducting an inventory of existing and successful evidence-based practices in each school. Educators should take a comprehensive inventory of both academic and SEB practices in place and begin to organize and categorize them into a graphic organizer like Figure 1.3.

In this way, educators can decide if they fit within Tier 1 and are available to *all* students, are better suited to Tier 2 and are available to *some* students with indicated needs, or are available to *very few* students and provide intensive, individualized support in Tier 3. Fidelity of implementation and "fit" should also be discussed during this activity. Educators can determine whether the practice is implemented with fidelity and whether it continues to be a good fit for the local school. It is common for practices to be implemented with a high level of fidelity when first introduced, then for implementation drift to occur with fidelity weaning over time (Latham, 1988). It is also possible that practices introduced to a school building prior to educator and student changes over time may no longer be the proper fit for the school currently. The inventory and subsequent sorting of interventions in the MTSS triangle should be revisited on an annual basis to determine which interventions may require more training, which are effective, which need adapting, and which require data-based de-implementing, or abandoning an intervention that is no longer effective.

After completing this activity, educators should highlight areas across all three tiers and academics and SEB supports where there is redundancy, misplacement (e.g., a Tier 2 strategy that should be moved to Tier 3), and importantly, where gaps exist. This activity will help prepare the planning team to attend to those areas and remove redundancy, reorganize, and acquire a full set of practices across the tiered system. The next step is to list all available people who can implement Tier 2 interventions for SEB needs, or your "Implementer Inventory." This list should be composed of adults (or older students for peer-mediated intervention) who are (1) available consistently as required by the various interventions and (2) skilled at building and maintaining relationships with students. Remember when drafting your "Implementer Inventory" that Tier 2 interventions must be efficient and relatively easy to implement, not requiring advanced degree work in education or a related field.

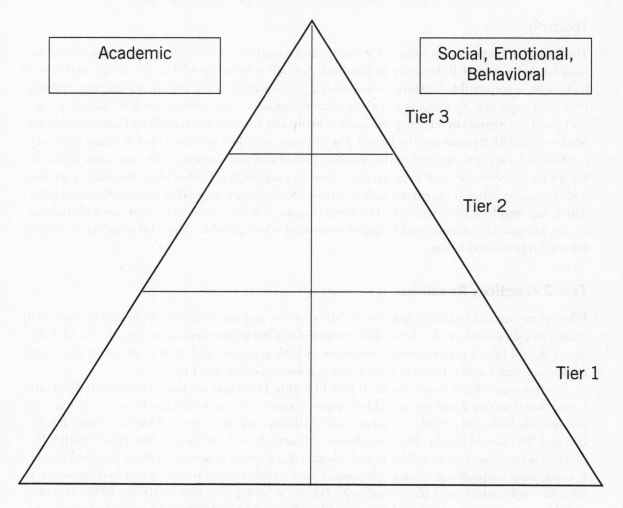

FIGURE 1.3. Double-sided MTSS triangle.

ADVANCED TIER 2 TEAMING

Beyond one integrated (i.e., academics and SEB needs) PST, it is important to develop a Tier 2 configuration that matches the needs and resources specific to each school. Many elementary schools will utilize a grade-level team as the PST. This helps with being able to discuss grade-level, age, and developmentally appropriate needs and behaviors, and often the grade-level teachers are most familiar with the students discussed. Conversely, some smaller schools use a more centralized single Tier 2 team that has a grade-level representative, administrator, and related service providers (e.g., counselor, social worker, behavior interventionist). Tier 2 teams in secondary-level school settings also vary. In secondary schools such as middle schools, where students move throughout their schedule in grade-level teams together, those team teachers can become the Tier 2 team (PST) with the representation of a counselor and administrator. In secondary schools with teams that function primarily in academic departments, intentional planning and discussion should occur in developing a Tier 2 team that includes the following: (1) administrator; (2) related service providers when possible; and (3) classroom teachers who are familiar with the students who are represented. Often, secondary schools will utilize the "homeroom" teacher as the familiar classroom teacher, but it is important to note that classroom teachers who have academic content may have a different perspective of the student across the school day than nonacademic homeroom period teachers do (Lane et al., 2021).

Meeting Frequencies, Agendas, and Roles

Typically, the Tier 2 team should meet at least monthly to discuss students receiving Tier 2 supports. In some cases where large numbers of students need to be discussed, Tier 2 teams may need to meet more than once a month to review each case. Additionally, the Tier 2 team would not meet the first month of school to discuss screening results, however they may need extended meeting times for the second meeting to process screening results after the screeners have been completed. Tier 2 teams should assign roles as needed to include a notetaker, timekeeper, and leader. Meetings should be driven by an agenda shared prior to the meeting, and notes should be comprehensive and stored in a shared location. During normal monthly meetings, Tier 2 teams will discuss student cases one by one. Student progress discussions should be guided by the Tracking and Referral Form (see Figure 1.4), or similar, which includes following standard steps: (1) review and visually represent progress monitoring data from the past month; (2) determine if progress is sufficient; (3) determine needed fading, intensifying, adapting of strategies and interventions; and (4) plan to communicate progress and changes to staff and family members. As is common with most school committees, it is important for Tier 2 membership to remain consistent across school years, with one member rolling off the committee and a new member entering the committee each year, to retain procedural knowledge on the team.

TIER 2 IDENTIFICATION AND INTERVENTION FOUR-STEP PROCESS

In this book, we detail a systematic, step-by-step process for planning and implementing Tier 2. These four steps are: (1) identifying students in need of Tier 2 and determining a category of intervention; (2) matching and adapting Tier 2 evidence-based interventions to student need; and (3) establishing data-based decision rules, and (4) data-based decision-making regarding fading, intensifying, and planning for maintenance and generalization. See Figure 1.5 for this step-by-step process.

Step 1: Identify Students in Need of Tier 2 and Areas of Need

Sometimes educators point to ODR, suspension, or attendance data to identify students who require Tier 2 supports. Educators should avoid this "wait to fail" approach in which students must first display unwanted and sometimes unsafe behavior, missing out on instructional time *before* they receive supports. Instead, using a positive, proactive approach, you should be able to identify students who need extra support without relying on reactive consequence procedures.

Individual Plan of Action (IPA): Tier 2

Student Name: _____

Student Grade: _____

Team Members: _____

_____

Initial Referral Date: _____

Referral Information

This student was referred by:

Universal screening score   ☐

Teacher referral   ☐

Caregiver referral   ☐

Student (self) referral   ☐

Other: ☐   _____

Intervention Planning

Results from the SDQ (fill in score and circle risk range):

Overall Score: _____ (normal, borderline, elevated)

Conduct: _____ (normal, borderline, elevated)

Hyperactivity: _____ (normal, borderline, elevated)

Peer problems: _____ (normal, borderline, elevated)

Prosocial: _____ (normal, borderline, elevated)

Emotional Symptoms: _____ (normal, borderline, elevated)

Student information summary (strengths, preferences, interests):

Intervention Matching

Primary Domain of Focus: _____

Least intensive strategy or intervention: _____

More intensive strategy or intervention: _____

Initial intervention to begin with: _____

Initial adaptations to include with this intervention: _____

(continued)

FIGURE 1.4. Tier 2 Tracking and Referral Form.

Secondary Domain of Focus (if applicable): _____

    Least intensive strategy or intervention: _____

    More intensive strategy or intervention: _____

Initial intervention to begin with: _____

Initial adaptations to include with this intervention: _____

Initial Decision Rules

Individual goal statement (what does mastery look like): _____

_____

Who is implementing this intervention? _____

What progress monitoring tool will you analyze each month? _____

Will you graph these data each month?   YES   NO

Who will bring these data each month to analyze? _____

What does progress toward mastery look like (rate, amount of time)? _____

What intervention will you use if the student is progressing? _____

What intervention will you use if the student is not progressing? _____

How will you plan to fade the intervention back to Tier 1? _____

_____

What are the criteria for moving to Tier 3 assessments and supports? _____

_____

Who communicates progress or nonresponse to parents and other teachers and when? _____

_____

Date of initial plan: _____

Date of intervention plan initiation: _____

Date caregiver/parent is notified: _____

Monthly Progress Update to Individual Plan of Action

Progress Update #1   **Date:** _____

    Progress Monitoring Data Summary:

        Student is responding as expected   ☐

        Student has received the intervention as planned   ☐

        Intervention has not been put in place as planned ☐

        Student is not responding as expected   ☐

    Decision Based on Data for Next Meeting:

        Stay with the intervention as planned   ☐

(continued)

FIGURE 1.4. *(continued)*

Modify the intervention (circle one)

      Fade   Intensify   Adapt: _____

Additional progress update notes: _____

Progress Update #2   *Date:* _____

    Progress Monitoring Data Summary:

        Student is responding as expected   ☐

        Student has received the intervention as planned   ☐

        Intervention has not been put in place as planned   ☐

        Student is not responding as expected   ☐

    Decision Based on Data for Next Meeting:

        Stay with the intervention as planned   ☐

        Modify the intervention (circle one)

            Fade   Intensify   Adapt: _____

Additional progress update notes: _____

Progress Update #3   *Date:* _____

    Progress Monitoring Data Summary:

        Student is responding as expected   ☐

        Student has received the intervention as planned   ☐

        Intervention has not been put in place as planned   ☐

        Student is not responding as expected   ☐

    Decision Based on Data for Next Meeting:

        Stay with the intervention as planned   ☐

        Modify the intervention (circle one)

            Fade   Intensify   Adapt: _____

Additional progress update notes: _____

Progress Update #4   *Date:* _____

    Progress Monitoring Data Summary:

        Student is responding as expected   ☐

        Student has received the intervention as planned   ☐

        Intervention has not been put in place as planned   ☐

        Student is not responding as expected   ☐

    Decision Based on Data for Next Meeting:

        Stay with the intervention as planned   ☐

        Modify the intervention (circle one)

            Fade   Intensify   Adapt: _____

Additional progress update notes: _____

FIGURE 1.4. *(continued)*

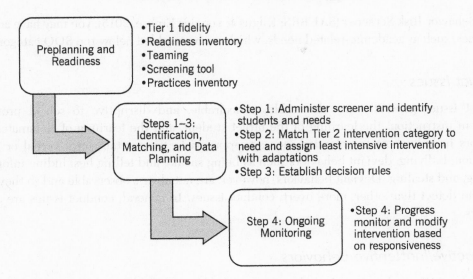

- Tier 1 fidelity
- Readiness inventory
- Teaming
- Screening tool
- Practices inventory

Preplanning and Readiness

Steps 1–3: Identification, Matching, and Data Planning

- Step 1: Administer screener and identify students and needs
- Step 2: Match Tier 2 intervention category to need and assign least intensive intervention with adaptations
- Step 3: Establish decision rules

Step 4: Ongoing Monitoring

- Step 4: Progress monitor and modify intervention based on responsiveness

FIGURE 1.5. Tier 2 step-by-step process.

Another option educators consider is a teacher nomination approach. In application, teachers would be trained to identify social–emotional–behavioral needs. The teachers would then be able to "refer" students to Tier 2 based on their observations. This process requires consistency and follow-through at the school level in addition to the necessary training component, so teachers know what types of behavior are appropriate for referral. Students with SEB needs who require Tier 2 supports must demonstrate various symptoms and characteristics. Several concerns remain in using only teacher nomination for Tier 2 identification. First, teachers may not notice "invisible," or less obvious, internalizing symptoms. Second, teachers can have issues with bias and personal expectations of behaviors that are not aligned with school norms. Third, teachers may not use the nomination process consistently, and students who move throughout the day may not demonstrate behavioral needs in each class period. Fourth, this strategy for identifying also relies on the wait to fail, reactive approach. Finally, even though teachers may attend training on how to identify Tier 2 needs, that information may be interpreted differently depending on teacher background.

Though not perfect, the primary way to counteract the wait to fail perspective of identification is to conduct universal SEB screening as described in Chapter 2. This aligns with typical academic screening in which every student is rated each year to determine who is at risk. There are several validated systematic screeners that may already be in place.

Before we describe the specific steps to gathering, analyzing, and using need-specific information, we first discuss different types of needs that fit within Tier 2. One reason Tier 2 practices should include multiple and varying practices available is that not all interventions are aimed at addressing the same needs. For the same reason, it is important to detect precise needs beyond "internalizing" or "externalizing" behaviors, as these behaviors can be further delineated into more specific issues or categories. The five categories of needs below and matched practice highlighted are: conduct issues, hyperactivity and inattention, social skills, emotional symptoms, and co-occurring academic and SEB needs from the Strengths and Difficulties Questionnaire (SDQ; Goodman, 1997). If you are using an alternate screener such as the Social, Academic, and Emotional Behavior Risk Screener (SAEBRS; Kilgus & von der Embse, 2015), you may have additional categories, such as academic-related needs, which we have added below the SDQ categories.

Conduct Issues

Conduct issues generally are observable, measurable, and disruptive to school procedures, classroom instruction, the learning of the target student, and the learning of classmates. These behaviors include short or extended, non-age-appropriate temper tantrums; verbal or physical aggression; bullying; deviant behaviors such as being sneaky and telling lies, hiding information, cheating, and stealing. Deviant behaviors, however, are not always observable and so they may be harder to detect than other, more overt, conduct issues. In general, conduct issues are directed at others.

Hyperactive/Inattentive Behaviors

Next, hyperactive and inattentive behaviors can also be very disruptive to classroom instruction. These behaviors are most frequently noticed during classroom instruction, rather than throughout the whole day in common areas such as hallways. These typically academic-related behaviors include restlessness, overactivity (for age/development), difficulty sitting still for periods of time required for instruction or task completion, fidgeting, being easily distracted by typical classroom behaviors (e.g., pen clicking, sharpening pencils, chatting peers), wandering, and poor focus. These behaviors are similar to what we think of with attention-deficit disorder (ADD) and attention-deficit/hyperactivity disorder (ADHD), but this level of behavior may be less intensive, and we do not use this Tier 2 designation to diagnose students with ADD or ADHD.

Social Skills

Social skills needs typically relate to a student's inability to appropriately interact with others. This can be with a specific group of people, like peers or adults only, or can be general, where they are demonstrated across peers, adults, and younger children. In this category, we focus on students who have conflict with peers. It is important to distinguish who the student has issues associating with, so you can address that specific need during instruction. Students may have issues that include being solitary, arguing, refusing to compromise or cooperate, having few or no same-age friends, choosing to play alone, being picked on by others, failing to share with peers, getting along better with adults and even younger children, and lacking consideration for others' feelings (Goodman, 1997).

Emotional Symptoms

This category aligns with internalizing behaviors that are generally not disruptive, or even obvious. Symptoms may include somatic complaints (e.g., headaches, stomachaches), frequent requests to see the nurse, and excessive worrying or anxiety. Symptoms can also include social anxiety (e.g., being in the cafeteria or nervousness in new situations), phobias (e.g., fears of thunder or lightning or loss of confidence after disappointment or rejection), test anxiety, and difficulty with personal relationships (e.g., starting friendships or social isolation). Students who exhibit these symptoms may withdraw from situations that trigger their anxiety symptoms. They may also demonstrate persistent sadness or depressive symptoms.

Co-occurring Academic Needs

This category of intervention can be identified using the SAEBRS or regularly collected academic data like work completion, GPA, or course failures. These data can help to identify students who have needs in both an academic area and an SEB area (e.g., academic and social skills, or academic and inattention). The SEB needs may impact academic learning or vice versa. For instance, a student may have an unmet academic need that reduces their motivation to complete tasks and stay in class and that student may display disruptive behavior in an effort to be removed from class, distract the teacher, or not be required to complete academic work. This category does not serve as a specific academic diagnostic assessment but can point the PST toward a previously unidentified area of need or impact.

Step 2 requires educators to examine screening data beyond the initial confirmation for Tier 2 in the total score and analyze subscale data available to determine which category of need to focus on. After inspecting need information across the five categories, the team may notice that scores are elevated in more than one category. There are a few options to consider in this scenario. The first option is to prioritize the one social, emotional, or behavioral need that most disrupts the student's learning or the learning of others. Another option is to look for internalizing behaviors and address those before the other four categories due to the potential for unaddressed emotional symptoms worsening to harmful behaviors (e.g., self-harm, substance abuse). Third, it may be necessary to identify the first behavior that needs to be addressed that can put in motion change in other areas. For instance, it is sometimes important to address inattentive behaviors in the classroom before you can work on social behaviors such as working in a group and sharing. The final option is to combine interventions across more than one category, which we will discuss as we move through the intervention descriptions.

Step 2: Match and Adapt Tier 2 Evidence-Based Interventions to Student Need

Next, once the team determines what a student needs to address with Tier 2 intervention, the team should identify a category of interventions and then match and tailor an intervention. Each category is aligned with a need type and each category has several intervention options within it. The intervention options become important for matching the intensity of required intervention. Emotional symptom needs match to cognitive-behavioral therapies. Conduct issues match to the category of Check-In/Check-Out (CICO) variations. Hyperactivity and inattentive behaviors match to the category of self-regulation strategies. Social skills needs match to the social problem-solving category. Each intervention category has critical components that are designed to change the type of behavior identified for improvement. For instance, self-regulation strategies work to improve how students think about their behavior, track their own behavior, and set goals for their behavior. Chapter 3 overviews how to make initial matches to intervention. Chapters 4 through 8 highlight intervention categories and evidence-based interventions.

Step 3: Establish Data-Based Decision Rules

The third step requires the Tier 2 team to plan beyond the initial intervention that was selected in Step 2. In this step, the team must complete an entire action plan for each student. This includes gathering and discussing more information about the student to include strengths, preferences, and home contexts. In creating decision rules and establishing the full action plan the family should be included in communication and planning. The team will need to work with the family and other school staff to establish communication protocols that match the contextual needs of the family and the school.

Next, the team should revisit the Tier 2 "Implementer Inventory" and determine which person will facilitate the decided-upon Tier 2 intervention. This person may also require training and oversight to implement the intervention with fidelity. Next, the team will determine what criteria for success looks like (e.g., grade-level, age-appropriate attention holding). From there, the team will determine the pace of progress toward that criteria (e.g., documented improvement in Daily Progress Report score by 15% each month) that is expected. Next, the team will plan for responses if the student does not meet this pace of improvement. In some cases, students may need a different intervention, an adaptation, or an additional intervention. Then the team will discuss and plan for data-driven maintenance and generalization and fading of the intervention to require only Tier 1 supports. This is discussed in more depth in Chapter 3.

Step 4: Make Data-Based Decisions Regarding Fading, Intensifying, and Planning for Maintenance and Generalization

The Tier 2 team will make monthly decisions with the available progress monitoring data. The decision options for students who are responding positively (e.g., less off-task behavior, improved social interactions) to implemented supports are to maintain the same support, fade the support, or withdraw support and return to Tier 1, universal supports alone. Generally, teams should fade supports while also programming for maintenance and generalization of new skills to all school settings prior to withdrawing support and returning to only Tier 1 support. The decision options for students who are deemed unresponsive to Tier 2 supports are equally complex. First, the team should ensure that the intervention was implemented with fidelity, because a child cannot benefit from an intervention they did not receive. If fidelity or adherence to procedures was not achieved, the team should focus on how to improve the implementation of the strategy or intervention. Second, the team should consider the context for students not displaying improvement. It is possible that the classroom context, school climate, or other scenarios (e.g., peer bullying, changes at home, sports participation) may be preventing improvement. Third, the team should consider that in some student cases, we should expect first for the level of behavior to not improve dramatically, but also not worsen as a signal of improvement itself. In other words, when a student's behavior is not as volatile or variable, but instead levels out to a predictable and manageable level while not getting worse, this can be considered to be a sign of improvement. For students in crisis, particularly, displaying more consistent levels of behavior is indeed progress. Fourth, the team should thoroughly analyze whether the student requires adaptation or modification to specifically tailor the intervention to match student strengths and preferences, and to be more culturally responsive. Finally, teams should consider whether to intensify the current intervention or move to a new, more intense intervention. More information regarding these decisions is available in Chapter 9.

PRACTICAL EXAMPLES AND POTENTIAL PITFALLS

In many schools across the United States, when PBIS or instructional coaches step in to assist a school with "behavior" or "discipline" challenges, the team will start with discussing what interventions and supports are available at each tier. The conversation will be guided by a coach who asks, "What does everyone get?"; "What do some students get?"; and "What do very few students get?" They will also discuss what data drives those decisions. In our experience, many schools implement Tier 1 PBIS well, and understand the importance of gathering and using schoolwide data. Often the special education teachers will step up and describe their available intensive, individualized supports. What is left is an empty space of what is available at Tier 2 for students with targeted needs. This gap can easily (and incorrectly) lead to an increased reliance on punitive, exclusionary discipline as the response to students with targeted needs, when no systematic approach is available.

Second, when schools have a Tier 2 process in place for identifying students and even a Tier 2 team that reviews student data, another common occurrence is that when the PBIS coach asks "what interventions do you have available at Tier 2," the school will list a single intervention that all students who require Tier 2 receive, such as social skills training. This one-size-fits-all approach limits the ability to match intervention to specific Tier 2 needs, making it more likely that many students will not have their needs met by an intervention that was not designed for them.

Finally, many schools focus only or primarily on disruptive or defiant behaviors that interfere with instruction and lead to ODRs. In these schools, educators are utilizing a reactive approach and failing to address the social and emotional needs of students in their schools that may be less obvious or interfere less with instruction. The culture and climate in these schools may also reflect this focus. The culture may be punitive, with adults exerting and expecting control over students. The school may also have limited focus on strengths and positive behaviors.

Practitioners studying this framework and Tier 2 SEB needs should ensure that there is buy-in for Tier 2, a willingness to implement more than one intervention, and a focus on all three SEB areas of need. A school that is willing to move beyond a one-size-fits-all approach (given adequate support) is one that is likely to see positive changes. For additional considerations, make sure to read through Chapter 11 regarding avoiding deficit thinking, making contextual and culturally responsive adaptations, and building on strengths.

CONCLUSION

In this chapter we detailed the rationale for using a multi-tiered framework to prevent and address SEB needs, focusing on the targeted, Tier 2 level. Additional details described the nuances of SEB areas of need in schools. Finally, we overviewed the four-step Tier 2 process for setting up the system, identifying and planning, and progress monitoring and adapting for effective, efficient Tier 2 intervention. These steps are described in more detail in the following chapters.

CHAPTER 2

Tier 2 Identification of Students' Strengths and Needs

This chapter focuses on the first step of the Tier 2 process, which is identification of students in need of Tier 2 support, and their areas of need.

> ### CHAPTER FOCUS
> - Learn about various universal SEB screeners; procedural steps; and real-world application.
> - Learn how to use these screeners to identify students for Tier 2, while also using other forms of data for identification such as teacher or family referral, academic measures, attendance, and office discipline referrals.
> - Understand subscales of each screener and how to use subscale data to identify an area or category of need, as well as areas of strength, and learn how to match Tier 2 interventions to need and intensity.

ASSESSMENT PRACTICES

In effective models of prevention and intervention like PBIS, data-based decision making is a critical component for ensuring a continuum of supports are available to meet students' needs (Lloyd et al., 2019). Schools and districts gather and utilize data to drive a variety of decisions related to allocating resources, providing instruction and intervention, and determining how a student or school, as a whole, is performing. Some examples include academic performance data, family satisfaction data, classroom-level reading performance, direct observation of student behavior, and attendance data. In all cases, valid and reliable measures should be used to ensure the effectiveness and efficiency of assessment practices. That is, the measures schools use should have evidence they produce accurate and consistent results. In the area of SEB needs, we mainly rely on teacher perception of student performance or needs through screening or diagnostic measures completed by the teacher. Screeners are typically administered to all students, while diagnostic measures are administered to individual students. Second, screeners should be brief and relatively easy to complete, while diagnostic measures may have more items and multiple gates or steps. Third, the information these two types of assessment practice yield vary. Screeners tend to inform educators of the big picture by identifying students who may need additional support in broad areas due to increased risk levels. Diagnostics, on the other hand, are typically administered after identifying that risk exists, in order to drill down on specific areas of strength or areas for improvement.

In the following sections, we describe how universal screening can be used in our systematic approach to Tier 2 implementation. In the next chapter, we describe another type of ongoing assessment method called progress monitoring, which is used when students are receiving intervention and PSTs need to determine if the intervention is working for the student. But for now, let's focus on screening.

TIER 2 INITIAL IDENTIFICATION

The first critical step to a systematic Tier 2 plan is to objectively, proactively identify students who need targeted support beyond what is provided at a foundational level in Tier 1. This process mirrors academic measurement processes such as end-of-year standardized testing, or in a specific grade such as a third-grade writing exam, or three times throughout the year with benchmark curriculum-based assessments. Universal screening for SEB needs is just as important to school success as academic testing, as kids are more likely to engage in academic instruction when they feel emotionally safe, use appropriate social skills, and display positive behaviors. Using an objective, systematic screening process will assist educators in determining which students need supports that can promote academic learning and overall psychological wellness. The term "universal" indicates that this is a data collection process that that place for *all* students, not just some selected students. Meaning, every student enrolled in school should be assessed, just like they are for attendance and academic skills. As an initial identification tool, universal screening data should be analyzed for total or overall scores that fall within a risk category. Many universal screeners report three bands, or levels, of risk: no risk, moderate risk, serious risk. While they may use different terms for these three bands, the overall scores that fall within the "no risk" band can be referred back to Tier 1, contextually relevant and differentiated supports. Overall scores that fall within the "moderate" or "serious risk" scores can be referred for consideration for Tier 2 supports. It is important to note that this is referral for discussion for possible Tier 2 supports. The next and final step in identification then, is to confirm this need with other data available. Schools may want to confirm the Tier 2 need with office referral data, attendance data, grades, or teacher confirmation. It is also important to consider that with one teacher completing a 20- to 30-item screener on numerous students, some overall scores may not look like they are in the risk level for Tier 2 consideration, and those cases should also be brought up for discussion.

SCREENING: THREE PROCEDURAL STEPS

Step 1: Identify the Respondent

Regardless of the specific reliable, valid, and useful screener chosen, educators should follow specific and systematic steps for completing screeners and utilizing screener data. First, many screeners have options for who completes the screener. For instance, screeners often have different versions for parent/caregiver report, student self-report, and educator report. For this process we focus primarily on educator-completed screener data. While it would be incredibly useful to have parent/caregiver perspectives, it is difficult to rely only on parent/caregiver screeners that may not be completed and returned to the school. It is also possible SEB needs look different at home and in the community. For example, the student may have an area of strength in the community regarding taking care of or playing with younger children, but at school the student demonstrates difficulty with sharing or resolving conflict with same-age peers. For parent/caregiver information, we encourage educators to consider sending home a survey of student strengths, interests, preferences, and needs or possibly inviting the caregiver to Tier 2 meetings to discuss strengths, issues, and progress. Many schools consider using student-completed screeners, especially for secondary-age students. These data could also be informative and useful, as they may highlight something an educator has not had the chance to observe. That said, it is important to remember that students are still developing self-evaluation skills and their understanding of expectations and age- and developmentally appropriate skills may not be aligned with those of classroom teachers. For these reasons, we recommend focusing on data from a teacher-completed universal screener and using parent/caregiver or student data as a supplement on an as-needed basis.

The next decision point will be to determine which teacher will complete the assessment. In elementary buildings, typically the classroom teacher who serves the student for most of the day will complete the screener on the student. This approach changes when students begin moving to numerous classroom teachers throughout the day, which is common in sixth through twelfth grades. In this case, it is possible for the administrator to choose one class period in the day (e.g., third period) and have the classroom teacher complete the screener on whomever is in their class during that period. It is important to use an academic period and not homeroom or specials for this, given the co-occurrence of academic and SEB needs. One issue that commonly comes up with the approach of choosing one academic period is when a student demonstrates different needs across class periods, possibly due to different academic content, classroom structure, peer composition, or teacher–student relationships. In this case, it may be useful for a second teacher to also complete the screener. There are a couple of options when more than one teacher completes the screener. One, they can average their scores together or, two, they can complete the screener together and try to come to agreement on each item. In these two approaches, only one final screening score is produced. A third alternative is to have both teachers complete the screener independently and then have decision rules about how students are identified for Tier 2 support (e.g., both teachers' scores must indicate Tier 2 is needed, at least one teachers' score must indicate Tier 2 is needed, or if there is a discrepancy between teachers' scores then a third teacher is asked to rate the student).

Step 2: Determine the Administration Time Frame

Next, schools will need a systematic process for when to complete the universal screeners. At the start of the school year, students are often working to build new relationships and reconnect with old friends, while also relearning (or learning for the first time) rules and procedures. The school may be focusing heavily on teaching schoolwide (Tier 1) expectations (e.g., Be Respectful, Be Safe) and practicing procedures so that they become routines. As the first month progresses, academic demands begin to increase as teachers learn more about their students. So, we recommend educators do not complete universal screening within this "get to know you" phase of the beginning of the year, typically the first 4–6 weeks, and instead wait until they have known the student for at least 1 month if not more. In addition, most screeners have recommendations on how long the respondent should know the student before completing the instrument, which typically falls within the 4- to 6-week time line. As an example, many schools open a screening window of time from September 15 through September 30 (of course, this depends on when the school year starts). This provides educators with enough time to orient to the new school year, get to know the student, and 2 weeks for a classroom teacher to complete the screener. Administrators can provide detailed time frames for when screening can begin and how long teachers have to complete the screening (e.g., 2 weeks after screening opens). Alternatively, administrators could provide all teachers time during a schoolwide faculty meeting (e.g., after school). When this initial screening phase closes, it is important to remember that schools must have processes available for the student, family, and educators to refer the student for a repeated screener in a "referral for assistance" procedure. For example, if the student is not identified as a student needing Tier 2 in September during universal screening, but begins to display different behaviors or needs in December (prior to the next screening time point in January, for instance), there should be processes in place that the student themselves can request assistance, that their family can request assistance, and that any educator can request assistance for the student throughout the year. Oftentimes, the student will be provided an email address or Google form that they can use to request support. Family members are also given a "how to contact the counselor" or "how to ask for help for your student" summary in home newsletters, and educators will be told to complete a referral form for a student potentially requiring additional support.

Step 3: Develop Systems for Scoring and Storing Data

Next, educators must plan for an efficient scoring process and data storage for screening data. Many screeners have strategies for scoring completed screeners electronically, which reduces the time-consuming procedures of hand scoring. Scoring screeners by hand may require reverse coding (e.g., some items a "3" is a "1") and summing individual items to determine subscale scores (e.g., items 2, 7, 12, 16). Taken together, these procedures can be very time consuming and introduce opportunities for error; thus, electronic scoring is encouraged when possible. Electronic scoring also lends itself to efficient data storage within a screening system (e.g., Fastbridge; *www.illumina-teed.com/products/fastbridge/social-emotional-behavior-assessment/saebrs*) or computer program (e.g., Excel). In Excel, for instance, teams can input formulas that make reverse coding and summing items automatic upon entering item-level scores. As an example, a PST chose to list student identification numbers for all students who scored outside of the "typical" range in September. In the next column, the team indicated the overall or total score. In the next five columns, the team indicated the scores across hyperactivity, conduct, emotional symptoms, peer problems, and prosocial skills. In all of the cells with numbers, the team color-coded the numbers to reflect the level of need (e.g., red indicated high level of need, yellow indicated moderate level of need, green indicated an area of strength). Regardless of the scoring method used, it is important to remember to protect student privacy. This can be done by using student identification numbers that can be linked to student names (with names stored separately) and make sure data are stored on a safe, encrypted, password-protected server. If a school uses hand scoring, then whomever is doing the scoring will need to be trained. It may be that each teacher scores their own screeners, or maybe the Tier 2 team completes the hand scoring.

The selected screener should have an overall or total score that typically represents all items on the screener. This is the score used to confirm or deny the need for Tier 2 intervention because it is a broad, overall score. Many screeners provide cut points that correspond to risk bands (e.g., no risk, low risk, moderate risk, high risk; normal, borderline, abnormal). These cut points and risk bands are determined by researchers developing the tool during psychometric testing, and the cut points and scoring ranges in the provided screening manuals should be followed accurately. Educators should identify anyone with a total or overall score in an elevated or moderate risk range for Tier 2, and these student ID numbers or names should be referred to the Tier 2 team for further consideration. Those with higher risk scores may move directly to Tier 3 in some cases, or Tier 2 interventions may be tried with some adaptations and increased intensity (see Chapter 3 for more details on this process). This is a team decision that should be made cautiously because many students respond well to Tier 2 intervention and do not require intensive and costly Tier 3 supports.

VARIOUS SCREENERS

When choosing a universal screener, there are four important considerations: (1) valid, reliable SEB screener, (2) feasibility or number of items, (3) information yielded that can be used in a problem-solving process, and (4) grade-level/contextual appropriateness. First, it is important to choose a universal screener that is reliable, valid, and useful. Published, peer-reviewed psychometric studies analyze and confirm the extent to which screening tools are reliable and valid. In other words, are they measuring what we want them to measure, and do they measure that thing consistently over time and contexts? Reliability refers to the consistency of the measure, while validity refers to the accuracy of the measure. It is important to use a screener that produces similar results at different times and with different observers. Similarly, it is important to use a screener that is comparable to other validated screeners of similar constructs. For example, let's say you had been having some heart issues recently and you found two screeners purported to assess risk for heart disease. You take both screeners, but only one screener indicates you are at high risk. Which one do you trust? Ideally, these screeners would come to the same conclusion. With SEB screeners, researchers repeatedly test and compare them to ensure they can be trusted, though this is not to say there won't be some minor differences.

Next, it is important to choose a universal screener, and not a diagnostic measurement tool. A universal screener should be brief and provide fundamental information, not diagnoses. Teachers do not have time to complete 100-item assessments for every student in their class, nor is that level of data needed at the universal level. Instead, they must be able to assess their entire class (approximately 25 students) within about 45–60 minutes maximum. For example, the BASC (Behavior Assessment System for Children; Kamphaus & Reynolds, 2015) is a lengthy behavioral diagnostic tool with more than 100 items. Its companion assessment, the BESS (Behavioral and Emotional Screening System; Kamphaus & Reynolds, 2015) is a much briefer version that yields basic information regarding risk and areas of need. Any screener that is more than a few items and fewer than 30 should be feasible for most educators and contexts.

Next, pay careful attention to what data or important information the universal screener yields. Most, if not all, screeners will yield a total score that many times corresponds to a SEB risk band (e.g., no risk, low risk, moderate to high risk). While the total score is important for establishing who is at risk and to what level (e.g., who needs Tier 2 support), screeners used in a systematic problem-solving process to match students to an appropriate intervention should also yield several subscale scores for the various SEB domain macro skills (i.e., conduct, emotional, hyperactive/inattention, social, academic). Some screeners, such as the Student Risk Screening Scale—Internalizing and Externalizing (SRSS-IE; Lane & Menzies, 2009), yield a total score but only two subscales (i.e., "internalizing" or "externalizing"), which may help identify students for broader categories of interventions but cannot be used to pinpoint more specific areas of need (e.g., anxiety, emotional dysregulation, deviance, disruption) for matching Tier 2 interventions. When schools are limited on time or Tier 2 resources, a screener that simply identifies internalizing and externalizing issues (e.g., SRSS-IE, Systematic Screening for Behavior Disorders [Walker & Severson, 1992]) may be recommended universally followed by a more specific screener that identifies macro skills for students initially identified with internalizing or externalizing risk. For example, a school may screen all 500 kids and find that 50 have externalizing risk and 25 have internalizing risk. These 75 students may go on to be screened for specific emotional symptoms, hyperactivity, inattention, conduct issues, social skills, and academic difficulties. The BESS, SDQ, and SAEBRS all yield rich subscale data that can be used in a problem-solving process to match interventions with the area of need. All three screeners yield a subscale score and a risk band that can be used to identify that area either as an area of strength, a neutral or developmentally appropriate level, or an area of need. These universal screening data can be confirmed or triangulated with other available data to help in the matching process, such as attendance, grade, and office referral data.

Fourth, your school or district should pay careful attention to the grade level and contextual appropriateness of the screener. Because the screeners must be reliable and valid, they have been validated with a certain grade range. Sometimes items are reworded for different ages or grades. It is important to find a screener that can be used across K–12 grades, even if different forms may be used in elementary and secondary grade levels.

Remaining considerations for potential universal screeners include cost, completion format (e.g., paper vs. electronic), informants (e.g., teacher, self, and family), and scoring system (e.g., reverse-coded items, difficult to score or interpret screeners). In Table 2.1, we have provided a brief comparison of some recommended screeners. The following section focuses on three screeners— BASC (Kamphaus & Reynolds, 2015), SDQ (Goodman, 1997), and SAEBRS (Kilgus & von der Embse, 2015)—because all three screeners are valid and reliable, are feasible, yield important subscale scores for matching, and are appropriate for various grade levels.

SEB SCREENERS MEETING CRITERIA

Below, we overview the BESS, SDQ, and SAEBRS with regard to the above four critical criteria in choosing a universal SEB screener.

TABLE 2.1. Comparison of Universal SEB Screeners

	Number of items	Number of subscales	Informants	Cost
Social, Academic, Emotional, Behavioral Risk Screener	19	4	Teacher, parent, self	Yes
Strengths and Difficulties Questionnaire	25	5	Teacher, parent, self	Free
Behavioral and Emotional Screening System	25–30	3	Teacher, parent, self	Yes
Direct Behavior Rating—Single Item Scale	3 (repeated)	3	Teacher	Free
Behavior Screening Checklist	12	3	Teacher	Free
ADD-H Comprehensive Teacher Rating Scale—Second Edition	24	4	Teacher, parent, self	Yes

Behavioral and Emotional Screening System

The BESS is a valid, reliable universal SEB screener. It is currently in its third iteration (BESS-3; Kamphaus & Reynolds, 2015). The number of items required to complete within the instrument is within the feasible range. The self-report, or student form, has 28 items and the teacher form has 20 items. In total, the screener should take between 5 and 10 minutes. The BESS also has a parent- or family-report instrument. The scores yield overall information about behavioral or emotional risk. Beyond those, there are the following subscales: internalizing, externalizing/self-regulation problems, adaptive skills/personal adjustment problems. This instrument is validated for children ages 3–18. The BESS has an electronic system that scores the responses and produces an electronic and easy-to-use score report for initial identification and intervention matching. It is also available in Spanish.

Strengths and Difficulties Questionnaire

The SDQ (Goodman, 1997) is valid and reliable. The SDQ has a total of 25 teacher-rated items and three rating anchors: "not true," "somewhat true," and "certainly true." The SDQ has both a three-band (normal, borderline, abnormal) and four-band (close to average, slightly low/slightly raised, low/high, very low/very high) scoring system. Ratings yield both a total risk score and individual subscale scores. The five subscales on the SDQ are emotional symptoms, conduct issues, hyper-activity/inattention, peer problems, and prosocial behavior. Of these, the first four are difficulties and prosocial behavior is the strength. The four difficulties are summed to produce the total risk (or total difficulties) score, which is used to confirm the need for Tier 2 supports. If a student scores in the "normal" of "close to average" range for total difficulties, they are not confirmed for Tier 2 supports. Conversely, if the student scores in the borderline or abnormal range (three-band scoring) or the slightly raised, high, or very high range, the student may be benefit from Tier 2 supports and should be considered for intervention. The SDQ has two different forms. One is for

4- to 10-year-old students and the other is for 11- to 17-year-old students. There are also alternative forms for parent report and self-report that are not necessary for this process, but as previously stated, can be used as a supplement to the process. The SDQ has also been interpreted in over 30 languages. You can find a summary of the SDQ and other screeners here: *https://pbismissouri.org/wp-content/uploads/2018/09/Compendium-Version-2.pdf.*

Social, Academic, and Emotional Behavior Risk Screener

The SAEBRS (Kilgus & von der Embse, 2014) is a valid, reliable SEB screener. It includes 19 items and is intended to provide educators with assessment data across a wide range of subscales and includes a parent, teacher, and student report. It includes a total score and three large subscales (i.e., social behavior, academic behavior, and emotional behavior). The social behavior subscale is made up of externalizing behaviors and social skills. The academic behavior subscale is made up of attentional issues and academic enablers. The emotional behavior subscale is made up of internalizing behaviors and emotional competence. The SAEBRS can be administrated up to five times per year, but should not be used as a progress monitoring tool. The norm-referenced SAEBRS is completed online and generates a comprehensive score report for the PST. The SAEBRS is validated for students in grades 2–12.

OTHER IDENTIFICATION DATA

The TFI (Algozinne et al., 2014) indicates multiple data sources should be used to make decisions regarding Tier 2 identification. Perhaps the most commonly used piece of data used for Tier 2 identification is the ODR, as these data are collected by nearly every school. Schoolwide data can help us identify students with multiple ODRs or suspensions. Oftentimes, a few students visit the office numerous times, driving up ODR numbers. This group of students who earn more than one major ODR per year could be nominated for Tier 2, yet this is still a reactive procedure for identifying for Tier 2. And while ODRs may do an excellent job of capturing students who have disruptive or conduct issues associated with externalizing issues, students who have internalizing issues such as anxiety may not accumulate any ODRs (McDaniel et al., 2015). This is why we recommend relying heavily on screening data as a more holistic approach to identification. Since attendance is frequently tied to behavior and academic performance, identification can also include inspecting attendance data. Teams could consider the number of tardies and/or numbers of unexcused absences when considering students who require additional support.

Schoolwide data are convenient and relatively easy to analyze. However, cautions should be noted in using only schoolwide ODR, suspension, and attendance data. First, as we noted, schoolwide ODR data typically only pick up students with externalizing behaviors. These behaviors are observable and often the most disruptive to instruction. While these are important behaviors that can be particularly problematic in classrooms, more and more students are requiring targeted mental health supports for internalizing, less obvious needs. Internalizing issues tend to be more difficult to detect in schools and classrooms and, thus, they are often overlooked. Second, sometimes teachers and administrators inadvertently demonstrate bias in assigning ODRs and suspensions. In this case, two students could demonstrate the same misbehavior and one student may earn an office referral, while the other student is reminded of the rules and is not sent to the office. ODR disproportionality is a common problem in schools across the nation but can be addressed with explicit strategies (McIntosh et al., 2018). Along the same lines, across faculty within a school, some teachers and administrators may assign ODRs more frequently than others, which causes inconsistency in the ODR data. ODRs also can be very subjective depending on the school's code of conduct—again leading to bias and inconsistency. Subjectivity in the code of conduct leaves room for different interpretations of violations. Finally, particularly for students with internalizing or emotional symptoms, other data may be used to identify students potentially requiring additional support. Consider using school nurse visits, lack of work or homework completion, and high rates of minor, classroom-managed behaviors in addition to ODR, suspension, and attendance data when making decisions. Further, for teachers who have students complete journaling tasks, reading those for signs of distress may also be important. Similarly, some students with emotional difficulties may reach out directly to a trusted adult or peer to let them know they need some additional help. Finally, some schools or classrooms may also have daily or weekly data points such as point charts, weekly check-in prompts for wellness, or teacher-completed weekly ratings (i.e., direct behavior ratings). These also may be included in the identification process.

IDENTIFYING AREAS OF NEED

As a reminder, the focus of this book is on the subscale macro skills: emotional symptoms, conduct issues, hyperactive/inattention, social skills, and co-occurring academic needs. The above reviewed screeners provide subscale scores for these areas that can drive intervention matching after identifying a prioritized category of need on which to focus. That is, after the total score has indicated risk, the Tier 2 team can drill down further into the screening data to figure out what interventions will be best suited for the student. We address these interventions in Chapters 4 through 8. For instance, Olivia (a middle school student) had an overall SDQ score of 26, indicating a need for Tier 2. Drilling down from there, she had the following scores: emotional needs: 6, conduct: 8, hyperactivity: 6, peer problems: 6, and prosocial: 10. The PST had a discussion about these scores. The 10 in prosocial was highlighted as a strength. With three categories scoring a 6, they decided to focus on the 8 in conduct issues, given this indicated the highest risk. This was verified with ODR data reflecting Olivia had earned two detention assignments and one in-school suspension the prior year, as ODR data tend to capture conduct issues.

Chapter 11 addresses what to do when students are identified across numerous areas of need. In a team decision/matching meeting, the school may follow a simple three-step approach. First, the team will review all total scores and ensure that they are only matching interventions for students with elevated total scores. Next, the team may decide to go student-by-student to indicate the one area of need to address. This will require the team to discuss which area of need is interfering most with instruction and safety, and which area to start with that will make the biggest impact for each student. The students with the same identified area (e.g., conduct) are then compiled together until the entire group of students is reviewed. The third step is to go one area at a time to match interventions within that area to each student in that group. In this process, the team should consider which interventions can be implemented as small-group interventions with students in that same group.

CASE EXAMPLE

The Heflin County School District recently analyzed referrals to outside mental health providers and office referral and suspension data. They noticed a 30% increase in mental health referrals after the COVID-19 pandemic, and a 45% increase in suspensions. With this increase, they decided to take a proactive approach rather than waiting on students to demonstrate a particular level of need, and begin a systematic universal screening process for SEB needs. The district school psychologist was included on the instrument review panel, as were four classroom teachers, a family member, and three administrators. The school psychologist, Mrs. Garza, was familiar with the BASC, and therefore the BESS as a screener version of the BASC diagnostic. She encouraged the team to look at the items and information it yields, to see if it fits the district needs. Mr. Johnson recently completed his Education Specialist degree and in his advanced behavior management course learned about both the SDQ and the SAEBRS. After their initial inventory of possible screeners that were reliable and valid, the team landed on these three as good possibilities. Next, they reviewed the final three criteria: feasibility, subscale scores for matching, and grade level. The district quickly decided that all three instruments were feasible and had similar numbers of items and procedures for scoring and interpreting scores. One difference they noted at this stage was cost. The BESS and SAEBRS cost money, while the SDQ was available at no cost. Next, all three instruments yield important subscale information that could be used for problem solving and matching. During this discussion they decided that the BESS did not provide as detailed subscale information as they needed specific to social needs. Finally, they looked at grade-level appropriateness, and read through items to determine contextual appropriateness for the Heflin community. With the SAEBRS not being validated until second grade, the overall discussion led the team to choose the SDQ instrument. The other piece of information that helped sway the team was cost. The district hadn't identified funds for this new task so the cost-free nature of the SDQ ensured that the new process would be sustainable over the coming years.

CONCLUSION

This second chapter provided an in-depth review of the rationale for using a systematic process for screening and identifying students with targeted SEB needs. We also emphasized the ways in which without a systematic process, students may be under- or overidentified. Next, we reviewed the primary domains of need within the SEB umbrella and the symptoms of those needs.

In this chapter, we move to matching students to an initial appropriate Tier 2 intervention and more nuanced methods for ensuring they respond positively, as well as implementing interventions and problem solving for what to do if the intervention is not working. This requires Tier 2 team members to adapt interventions initially and on an ongoing basis once the intervention is in place. The latter is covered in depth in Chapter 9.

CHAPTER FOCUS

- Understand how to assign an initial intervention match based on available data.
- Understand how to gather information about contextual and student factors to make initial adaptations.

INITIAL INTERVENTION MATCHING

In Chapter 2, we discussed various SEB screeners that can be useful in problem solving beyond simply identifying students who may benefit from Tier 2 supports. The three screeners we highlighted, the BESS, SAEBRS, and SDQ, all yield subscale scores that align with various SEB needs in the SEB rope. In this chapter, we discuss how to use these subscale scores to (1) drill down to find an area of need to focus on, and (2) match interventions to that need based on level of intensity. In Chapter 2, we discussed Olivia's SDQ scores from the September administration. You will remember that the team also utilized ODR data to verify the focus on the conduct area of need for Olivia. This process should be systematic and efficient. In developing this framework, we reviewed the large literature base of Tier 2 evidence-based interventions used across the field. Next, we developed a list of interventions that were effective for students and that included a theory of change that addressed a core SEB need area (e.g., self-regulation for inattentive issues). Last, we organized the Tier 2 interventions in order of intensity based on the time required, the personnel, and curriculum needed to implement the intervention to fidelity. Table 3.1 is a resulting table of broad areas of need, matched categories of intervention, and single strategies and interventions.

INTEGRATION OF DATA BEYOND SCREENING FOR MATCHING

As was noted in Chapter 2, initial intervention matches can be driven by available screener sub-scale data. In the SDQ example, the team may decide to find the subscale with the highest score and start intervention in that category. However, it is important to note that other information may also be available to confirm or triangulate needs in this area. For the hyperactivity/inattention area of intervention, the team may want to consider academic grades. If students are not focused and organized during academic instruction, their grades may reflect a need in this area as well. In the conduct area of need, the team could consider ODR data to include classroom-managed behavioral needs. The team may consider number of ODRs, number of suspensions (in and out of school), and placement in alternative school. A need in this area would likely be reflected in aligned discipline data. In the emotional symptom area of need, the team may discuss with the counselor, psychologist, or social worker the number of visits to the nurse and counselors. Students with emotional symptoms may have frequent somatic complaints (e.g., stomachaches, headaches), and may need to visit frequently with the counselor or even the administrative team. In

TABLE 3.1. Example SEB Needs and Matched Interventions

Areas of need	Intervention category	Interventions
Conduct problems	Check-in/check-out variations	• Check-In/Check-Out • Check and Connect • Check, Connect, Expect
Hyperactivity/inattention	Self-regulation	• Goal-setting strategies • Self-monitoring • Self-graphing
Social skills	Social-problem-solving activities	• Social/behavior contracts • Problem-solving activities • Restorative meeting or circle • Social skills or social–emotional training
Emotional	Cognitive-behavioral therapy	• Small-group therapy or counseling • Individual therapy or counseling
Academic	Explicit academic and academic-supporting activities	• Supplemental explicit instruction • Breaks are Better (BrB) • Homework, Organization, and Planning Skills (HOPS)

the social-problem-solving area, the team may want to consider social-specific conflict or aggressions in the ODR data. The team may notice that ODRs are commonly documented after peer-to-peer conflict, conflict with authority or administrators, or social problems in classroom-managed behaviors (e.g., poor communication, lack of sportsmanship). Similarly, a co-occurring academic area of need will be reflected across both the universal SEB screener and academic data such as grades, attendance, and proficiency data. In Chapters 4–8 we will continue to describe ways in which to integrate multiple forms of information and data to confirm the area of need, make precise intervention matching decisions, and help provide context for intervention planning decisions (e.g., time of day, goals).

Beyond Table 3.1, with a list of interventions and categories, we provide Figure 3.1, the Tier 2 matrix, to help you organize the interventions you have available at your school, by SEB category, and in order of intensity. To make use of this figure, first take an inventory of evidence-based interventions you have at your school already and determine with which category of need each intervention can be matched. Next, insert those interventions into the matrix and fill in gaps where you do not have existing interventions available in order of intensity. We conceptualize intensity organization by considering (1) the time the student needs to be involved in the intervention, (2) the time an adult needs to be involved in the intervention, and (3) the resources (e.g., curriculum, training) required to implement the intervention. (An example of a completed matrix is also included as Figure 3.2.) For example, if your school does not have any interventions to support emotional symptoms, it may be necessary to contract with a community partner who can provide small-group counseling, particularly if there is not a school counselor, social worker, or other related mental health provider available. The purpose of creating this Tier 2 matrix is to help the PST, and really the whole school, understand what interventions are available to support students with varying needs.

STRATEGIES AND INTERVENTIONS BY NEED CATEGORY

Below is a brief description of each category to orient you, and interventions that are described in detail in Chapters 4–8.

Conduct

Students with conduct needs at Tier 2 can have varying types of issues to address. For instance, some students may have minor verbal aggression/inappropriate language issues, such as a student who argues with authority and demonstrates disrespectful language when given feedback. However, students who require support in this category may also demonstrate more dangerous, disruptive behaviors such as fighting, elopement or leaving the classroom, and throwing school materials. The order of intervention intensity in this category accounts for how much student time is primarily involved. Since we want our students spending time in class learning, we want to start first with interventions that do not take them out of the learning environment. Check-In/Check-Out (CICO) is an intervention that does not require time out of class. Next, Check and Connect is a more intensive version of CICO. Finally, Check, Connect, and Expect is the most intensive intervention in this category because it requires a full-time behavior coach and time out of class. Chapter 5 covers these more in depth with real-world application examples.

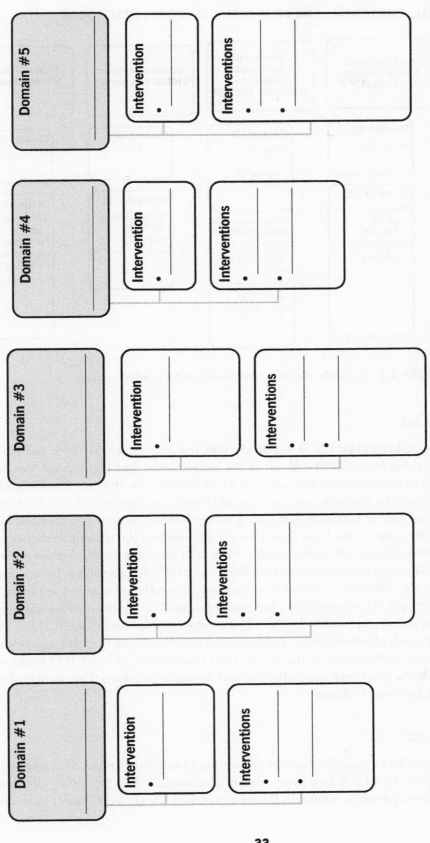

FIGURE 3.1. Fillable matrix of SEB interventions.

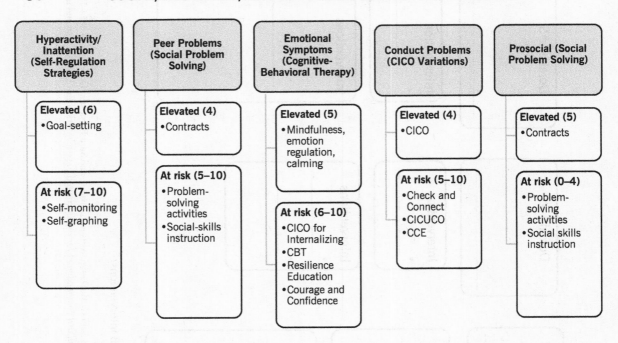

FIGURE 3.2. Example of a completed matrix of SEB interventions.

Check-In/Check-Out

An example Tier 2 team knows that CICO is a simple, effective intervention at Tier 2 and started their Tier 2 process using basic CICO with all of the students who had highlighted "conduct" needs. They decided to intensify from the basic CICO intervention for students requiring additional support. For example, students may need an additional check-in with their CICO mentor, or a modified goal-setting approach. CICO is a research-based intervention that has been implemented across the country for more than 15 years and involves the student beginning and ending the day checking in and out with a mentor, while also receiving feedback from teachers throughout the day. The evidence suggests that students receiving this intervention have reduced classroom behaviors (e.g., disruption, off-task)—particularly when those behaviors are attention driven (Park & Blair, 2020). When considering behavioral function (i.e., what is driving motivation for the occurrence or maintenance of the behavior?), it is important to know that CICO has been effective for students with attention-driven and escape-driven behaviors, though escape-driven behaviors require some modifications to the typical CICO procedures. While CICO works well with elementary students, it has been more effective with secondary students (Park & Blair, 2020) and can be modified for young children.

Check and Connect

An example high school Tier 2 team has been implementing Check and Connect for 3 years without a full Tier 2 framework. In this case every student identified for Tier 2 received Check and Connect. With the new systematic approach, the team matched Check and Connect to students with conduct and attendance needs. Check and Connect is similar to CICO, but it is design for secondary students for dropout prevention. Instead of regular feedback sessions with a teacher, the student meets weekly with a mentor to review academic and behavioral data, discuss goals, and problem-solve setbacks.

Check, Connect, and Expect

The last level of intensity in this category is Check, Connect, and Expect. An example elementary school has a full-time behavior "coach," Mr. Lee. Mr. Lee uses the Check, Connect, Expect intervention in his work with a small group of students. In the past, he has only worked with students with four or more office referrals but Mr. Lee noticed that by the time he got to work with these students, their behaviors were very ingrained. Placed within the systematic Tier 2 approach, he was able to expand the number of students he worked with, and work with them sooner. Check, Connect, Expect follows the same basic CICO procedures, but adds in social skills and problem-solving lessons. In one level, students self-monitor with their daily progress report. This intervention also has a level system where students eventually "graduate" out of the program once they demonstrate mastery. The focus in this intervention is a positive coach who builds relationships with students and implements all components. The coach also pushes into the classroom frequently to check on their students.

Hyperactivity/Inattention

The order of intensity of interventions for this category starts with simple goal-setting activities, followed by self-monitoring strategies during single periods of the day, then self-monitoring with self-graphing. The self-regulation category is a common area for students to display unexpected behaviors, particularly those that disrupt instruction. For that reason, many students who demonstrate disruptive behaviors during instruction are removed from the classroom. The purpose of Tier 2 interventions in this category is to help students who struggle to pay attention and remain focused on their work in assigned areas to (1) be aware of their behavior; (2) realize that their behavior is not aligned with being on task and engaged; and (3) regulate their behavior to match classroom expectations.

Goal Setting

At an example middle school, the counselor created a goal-setting worksheet with the school's mascot and aligned to their Tier 1 expectations. The Tier 2 team knows that this is the simplest Tier 2 strategy for students with hyperactive or inattentive needs and the counselor taught the team to modify the goal-setting sheet to focus on such behaviors (e.g., staying in seat, raising hand, listening to instruction). The Tier 2 team decided to match this goal-setting sheet weekly (one weekly goal) for students in a slightly elevated range, and to shift to a daily goal-setting sheet for students with elevated levels of need. There are several important components to evidence-based goal-setting activities. To apply this intervention and adhere to these components, it is important to consider the following when planning and teaching goal setting to students. These are reviewed in detail in Chapter 6.

1. Who is the goal important to? It cannot be a goal that is only important to the adults in the building. Goal setting is more likely to be effective when students have bought into the behaviors they are trying to change (Estrapala et al., 2022).

2. How do you prioritize goals? In this category, we try to tackle one behavioral need at a time, and not more than one. In this way, we prioritize the behaviors displayed that stand in the way of students receiving instruction as the "first in the chain" of multiple behaviors.

3. Should the goal be student- or teacher-created? Depending on the age of the student, it is possible that the adult and student work together to discuss behaviors the student would like to change. Some students can come up with their own behavior goals, while other students will require assistance from teachers to create appropriate goals. Goal areas are important but improvement rates (how long it will take to achieve a certain level of improvement) are also important to consider. Some students may have unrealistic ideas about the rate of their improvement to expect.

4. Should goal-setting activities focus on schoolwide PBIS goals? There is some discussion about whether Tier 2 behavioral goals should be focused on the three to five positively stated Tier 1, or schoolwide, behaviors; or if they should be more specific. Using one of the Tier 1 expectations for behavior helps to tie-in the importance of the Tier 1 plan. However, these expectations are broad. One solution is to use the examples of the broad expectation for behaviors. For instance, if the schoolwide broad expectation is "Be Responsible," an example behavior demonstrating responsibility might be "turn your work in on time." Either way, the adult and student can decide if the goal should focus on broad Tier 1 expectations or more specific behaviors such as "raising your hand" or "staying in your seat."

Self-Monitoring

If goal-setting has been implemented without response, or if a student's behavior requires a more intensive intervention, the Tier 2 team should consider a self-monitoring intervention. An example middle school team met after a month of goal-setting implementation for students with identified hyperactivity/inattention needs. The team identified four students who were not responding to goal setting alone and determined that each of these students would be matched to a self-monitoring intervention. The Tier 2 team asked classroom teachers on each student's team to identify the time of day or period that was most difficult for the student. As a result, each of these four students began a self-monitoring intervention for that one class period for the next month before the next progress meeting. Self-monitoring fits within the self-regulation category. The goal is to promote independent, self-sufficient students who can manage their own behaviors without the assistance of others, shifting from an external to an internal locus of control. This requires students learn to (1) recognize their behavior, (2) identify the behavior as incorrect, and (3) adjust the behavior to align with prosocial expectations. During self-monitoring sessions, students think about their behavior and record the extent to which it is occurring. This type of intervention is appropriate for low-intensity behaviors (e.g., out of seat, hand raising, talking out, off task). The behaviors in this category are typically targeted for intervention within the classroom, not outside of the classroom. Although this intervention is focused on the student developing skills for themselves (hence, self-regulation), the teacher will need to be involved to varying degrees. The teacher should set up this intervention, train the student to self-monitor, facilitate it daily, check in with the student on accuracy, and provide feedback (and possibly reinforcement).

Self-Graphing

Out of the four students who began self-monitoring during the November middle school Tier 2 meeting, one student was not demonstrating progress. As a result, the Tier 2 team added self-graphing for this student. Self-graphing falls under the self-regulation umbrella and is a simple strategy that can help alleviate some teacher responsibility and help reinforce the locus of control for the student. Self-graphing can be used in conjunction with academic, behavioral, and social interventions and is often an added component to goal setting and self-monitoring. For instance, students may be self-monitoring the number of times they raise their hand during class. After calculating the total, they could graph this number on a sheet of paper or electronically (e.g., Excel). The graph provides a form of visual performance feedback that can be especially motivating to students.

Social Problem Solving

In this category, the least intensive intervention is behavioral contracting, then problem-solving activities, and finally social skills instruction as the most intensive. This continuum of intervention options highlights one of the reasons we do not use a "one-size-fits-all" approach to Tier 2. While social skills instruction would address multiple issues in this category, it is also the most intensive. This is because it takes time for the interventionist to deliver and requires students to take time away from instruction, as it generally occurs outside of the classroom (e.g., with the school counselor). So, it may be more practical or feasible to start with something requiring fewer resources.

Behavior Contracts

Penhill Elementary school has a strong Tier 1 PBIS system in place. As a result, the Tier 2 team knew that a simple, individual-centered modification to their Tier 1 system would provide behavior contracts for students with social-problem-solving needs at Tier 2. The Tier 1 and Tier 2 teams worked together to focus on their "Solve Problems Peacefully" Tier 1 expectation for the behavior contracts. They matched all students with peer problems to this simple Tier 2 intervention. Behavior contracts, sometimes referred to as contingency contracts, are an evidence-based strategy for improving targeted behavior. The contract is a written agreement between two individuals (usually the student and a teacher) that specifies a behavior, the context and criteria for the behavior, and a reward for meeting criteria (Cooper et al., 2007). Because we are in the social skills category of interventions, contracts should focus on social competencies. These social behaviors could be derived from items on the screener indicating the student needs additional support (e.g., playing with friends, sharing). You could use behavior contracts in other categories, focusing on other types of behavior, too. For a behavior contract, the teacher will meet with the student to explicitly define what behavior they want to see, teach the steps to the behavior, and provide a good rationale for why demonstrating that behavior is important. The contract should be achievable, though you can increase the rigor of the contract over time. Together with the student, the teacher will set a time line for meeting the contract and agree on contingent reinforcement, or what good thing will happen if the student holds up their end of the "bargain." The contract needs to be something the student is interested in participating in, so including some opportunities for the student to be involved in planning is important (e.g., giving the student different options for reinforcement).

Problem-Solving Activities

The Tier 2 team at Southland Middle School knew that eight students with Tier 2 needs had specific needs related to responding to adult authority or correction. These students also frequently received ODRs related to these behaviors. For these students, the team added the ABC-GO (McDaniel & Flower, 2015) intervention to any future ODRs. We offer this example of a problem-solving activity in Chapter 6 then highlight other options that might already be available in your school. One important note is that problem-solving activities should be the only type of reactive strategy in which a problem has to happen first and the intervention is accessed after the problem/incident happens. This intervention helps make better use of time when processing an office referral or detention. This also can help students understand the patterns of their behavior and can be tied to individual target behaviors or schoolwide expectations. For adolescents, peer mediation rather than adult conflict resolution circles is an excellent approach. If you have other reactive, problem-solving strategies and interventions available in your school, you can assign those in this category. For instance, many schools have restorative discipline practices or restorative justice circles, peer mediation processes, and conflict management practices already available.

Social Skills Training

Before implementing a systematic Tier 2 process, Highlands High School assigned all students with targeted needs to their social skills groups for that grade level. With the new process in place, they decided to wait to match social skills groups for students who did not respond to behavior contracts or problem-solving activities. They also decided to compose groups of students who had similar social skills needs. The most intensive intervention within this category is social skills training or instruction. There are two basic types of social skills needs: acquisition and performance. Acquisition needs require explicit instruction for students who do not understand the basic steps to displaying prosocial behavior. That is, they haven't yet acquired the social skills. Or, perhaps they have acquired them, but they are not fluent or consistently using them. Performance needs happen when the student understands what the correct social behavior is and how to demonstrate it, but chooses not to in natural contexts. In both cases, students require more repetition and feedback to increase the fluency and accuracy of using the skill. Social skills training has several core components: explicit instruction of the skill, modeling, role play, feedback, and programming for generalization. Generally, this training occurs outside of class, with students participating in small groups with a school counselor or other related service provider.

Emotional Symptoms

This area of need can lead to deleterious and self-harming behaviors and should not be overlooked, though it can be hard to recognize. Many students who have emotional symptoms needs have chronic and slowly or quickly building symptoms (e.g., fatigue, crying, apathy, weight loss, weight gain, self-harm, drug abuse). This category requires a bit of additional information to determine the specific appropriate intervention, though all recommended interventions in this book are grounded in cognitive-behavioral therapy (CBT). CBT is generally a short-term support focused on changing how a student thinks, helping develop coping skills, and building resilience. Interventions are generally small groups and may address anxiety (e.g., Brief Coping Cat), depression (e.g.,

Penn Resilience Program), or trauma responses, depending on students' needs. Ideally, interventions are delivered by a trained school-based mental health professional such as a counselor. Critical to the effectiveness of these interventions is building a relationship between the student and the interventionist and creating a warm, welcoming, safe group for students to share thoughts and feelings.

Academic

Specific academic needs such as oral-reading fluency and math computation can be addressed within the academic side of the MTSS. However, some academic needs that are related to SEB issues, and especially behavioral issues, can be addressed within an integrated Tier 2 system. The SAEBRS does a nice job of helping educators to identify when students have academic-adjacent areas of need and require planning for that area. The interventions that match this category start with broad academic instructional strategies such as providing advanced organizers, preferred seating, additional time on assignments, and repeated instruction. Small-group academic instruction may also be necessary and, if not content-area focused, can include topics such as studying skills, homework management, time management, and requesting help from the teacher. Still, some students will need more intensive academic supports, which can be delivered through dedicated reading or math time, in a supplemental set of sessions to work on explicit skills, or even after school or during study hall.

STUDENT- AND CONTEXT-CENTERED ADAPTATIONS

Above, you learned about matching students to Tier 2 interventions based on their needs according to screening data and what the Tier 2 team decides is appropriate for their local context. This is a critical first step to ensuring students are supported in the most efficient and effective ways. The logic of initial matching is similar to what educators do when trying to determine the types of academic interventions students need when they are not performing at grade level. This is just a first decision for the team to get them started on the intervention needed and available. For instance, third-grade students who are still reading slowly and making multiple errors while reading aloud may be matched to a fluency intervention, whereas a student who reads fluently but exhibits some struggles with understanding the text may be provided an intervention focused on improving comprehension. Remembering Olivia and her SDQ scores, the team first verified her need for Tier 2, then verified the focus on conduct needs based on the conduct score of 8 and her multiple minor and major discipline incidents. Based on these data, the team's initial intervention decision for Olivia was to match her to Check-In/Check-Up/Check-Out (CICUCO; described in more detail in Chapter 4). The team used their school's Tier 2 matrix to make this initial decision, but realized they needed to run through possible intervention adaptations that would help motivate Olivia to participate. These are the "initial adaptations" to the intervention.

Beyond data-based intervention matching, PSTs may consider whether initial, simple modifications to the intervention are necessary prior to beginning implementation. Majeika and colleagues (2020) referred to these as "horizontal adaptations." We use that term interchangeably with "initial adaptations," which are relatively easy adjustments based on student-level or school-level factors. Before considering these factors, however, *we strongly recommend that the core components of interventions (described in the following chapters) remain intact.* For example, core components of CICO include daily check-in and check-out sessions with a mentor, an attainable goal on the daily progress report (DPR), three to five expectations listed on the DPR, a DPR form that is carried by the student from class to class, teacher feedback after each class, reinforcement for meeting the goal, and home–school communication (Majeika et al., 2020). These core components have malleable features that can be altered if student or contextual factors indicate a change may improve implementation, and in turn, student outcomes. The remaining focus of this chapter is on making data-based decisions beyond the initial intervention decision. In the following sections, we guide you to consider adaptations that may increase student and teacher buy-in, which is likely to result in better implementation and positive student response to the intervention.

STUDENT FACTORS INFORMING ADAPTATIONS

While initial adaptations are not necessary for all students receiving Tier 2 interventions, the Tier 2 team should, at least, consider relevant factors that may impact responsiveness prior to implementation (Majeika et al., 2020; Sterret et al., 2020). Student-level factors (e.g., culture, race, gender, function of behavior) are those within the student themselves—traits or characteristics— that the student has little control over in most cases. These may include disability, culture, gender, sexual orientation, race, socioeconomic status, function of behavior, family characteristics, and interpersonal relationships (Majeika et al., 2020). The ultimate questions for Tier 2 teams considering student-specific, person-centered planning are:

1. Is there anything about the student that may impact their ability to benefit from intervention?
2. Would a small, initial change based on this student factor increase the likelihood of success?
3. Can we reasonably make this change and still implement core components with fidelity?

If the answers to those three questions are "yes," then making initial student-centered adaptations is a good idea. For example, the Tier 2 team is discussing students with social-problem-solving needs and comes to a student named Naomi. Naomi is in eighth grade and the PST team members know her well. Since arriving at the middle school 3 years ago, Naomi has not had a steady group friends. She has made a friend here and there, but generally those friendships have ended in misunderstandings and mistrust. She does not respond well to male teachers or administrators, but gets along well with her volleyball coach (a female) and her bus driver (also a female). As a result, the team thought of ways to integrate this information into the behavior contract she would have. Since Naomi sees her volleyball coach and bus driver daily, this seemed like a feasible adaptation. Her bus driver would hold her in the morning as the last student to exit the bus and remind her of what she needed to do to meet her contract. If she met her weekly contract, she would have a 1:1 volleyball lesson with her coach.

Sometimes, Tier 2 teams may need to gather a little information about the student. For instance, if the student has already had a functional behavior assessment (FBA; perhaps as part of an individualized education plan process), then it would be helpful for the team to have access to the results of that FBA to guide intervention planning. If the intervention involves a family component (e.g., sending CICO progress reports home for feedback), then understanding the extent to which the family is available and communicative may be important. Maybe the team knows that a caregiver doesn't respond to email, but often answers text messages; they could make an adjustment to communicate via text rather than email. Relatedly, if the child is living in a volatile home where a poor score on a DPR or disappointing test grade could result in severe punishment, the family component may need to be adjusted or even eliminated (even if it is a core component). Race, gender, and sexual orientation may also play into intervention decisions—particularly those that involve adult or peer mentors. Some students may respond more favorably to mentors with similar characteristics. For students with a disability (e.g., dyslexia), they have likely developed relationships with a special educator, paraprofessional, or related service provider (e.g., school psychologist, counselor, behavior specialist, speech/language therapist, occupational therapist). Having a trusted adult involved in intervention delivery may be a key factor in intervention success. Consider our previously discussed student, Olivia. The team needed to decide who a good CICUCO mentor would be. For this discussion, they reviewed her discipline log and academic grades. They noticed that Olivia is in band and is most successful in band. They also knew that the band director, Mrs. Lopez, is available midday for the check-up procedures. Based on the existing relationship and availability, they assigned Mrs. Lopez as the mentor.

CONTEXTUAL FACTORS INFORMING ADAPTATIONS

After we consider student-centered adaptations, we should remember that the student navigates within the educational context of the school. Contextual factors, unlike student factors, are those factors that exist in the school or classroom environment. Generally, these factors are related to resource availability (e.g., time, money, personnel), but may also include things such as school values, physical space, scheduling, instructional routines and delivery, and technology. For instance, the school may have a Tier 1 plan in place that has an acknowledgement system grounded in praise and recognition but no tangible items, because the school is opposed to rewarding students with material things or because tangible items are not viewed as developmentally appropriate, such as in secondary schools. However, if reinforcement is built into the Tier 2 intervention and the student does not like public praise or recognition but is willing to work for a different type of reinforcement, then the team will need to problem-solve to determine what type of reinforcer (e.g., free homework pass, extra recess, lunch with a preferred adult) aligns with school values and is preferred for the student.

Resource availability may be a particularly important contextual factor that requires careful consideration. While Tier 2 interventions are designed to require minimal amount of time and money to implement, they often still need people, space, and materials to be carried out in an efficient and effective manner. Social skills instruction, for example, requires a validated curriculum, an adult to deliver instruction and, ideally, a private space to meet. Schools with fewer resources may not be able to afford an expensive, research-validated social skills curriculum. If they decide to pull lessons from the internet or create their own lessons, they need to ensure the core evidence-based features are still foundational to the lessons (e.g., explicit instruction, modeling, role play, teacher feedback, generalization programming).

Technology also plays a more prominent role in (and out of) schools, especially in light of the COVID-19 pandemic. Some students may be enrolled in "online school" either temporarily or permanently, while also requiring Tier 2 supports. As 2020 and beyond have shown us, many interventions were not initially designed to be delivered remotely (Hirsch et al., 2022), but educators have been resilient and found ways to adapt to the context and demands of the day. This might be delivering social skills instruction through Zoom or completing cloud-based electronic DPRs. Prior to the pandemic, self-monitoring interventions were already being implemented using technology. As Bruhn and Wills (2018) pointed out, using mobile apps to deliver self-monitoring interventions has improved the efficiency of these interventions. No longer do teachers have to create and print out forms or calculate and graph data because several mobile self-monitoring apps do that form them. Two examples, I-Connect (Wills & Mason, 2014) and MoBeGo (Bruhn et al., 2022), have been evaluated through rigorous research and demonstrated strong improvements in on-task and disruptive behaviors. These apps may be a helpful initial adaptation to traditional paper-and-pencil methods from a standpoint of both teacher efficiency and student buy-in, given students' status as digital natives (Bruhn & Wills, 2018).

Like the consideration for student factors, Tier 2 teams should ask the following questions about contextual factors:

1. Is there anything about the school or classroom context that may impact their ability to benefit from intervention?
2. Would a small, initial change based on this contextual factor increase the likelihood of success?
3. Can we reasonably make this change and still implement core components with fidelity?

Again, if the answer to all of these is "yes," then an initial adaptation is needed prior to implementation. This does not mean that adaptations cannot be made later—we simply encourage them initially as a way to increase the likelihood of success rather than waiting, which would be less efficient. For Naomi, the team reviewed contextual factors at their school. The team reviewed her middle school schedule and noted that out of her six teachers, two are male. In PE, it was easy to shift Naomi to second period and therefore, have her PE and science teachers be females. They decided to revisit this schedule change once Naomi was responding to the intervention to make sure she could get along well with male teachers. This change also removed her from one particular peer who she had a physical altercation with the year before. As with the teacher change, the team decided to reintroduce this student within Naomi's day after she was responding to the intervention. For Olivia, who was matched to CICUCO, the team knows that all middle school students are embarrassed about carrying a paper form around. Since the school is 1:1 with tablets, the team decided that Oliva and her teachers would complete the CICUCO DPR on the tablet, as it is a little less obvious. This small, initial change could increase the likelihood that Olivia will participate, and thus benefit from the intervention. In Table 3.2, we have included a list of core (unchangeable) components from several interventions, the malleable features (those that are eligible for initial adaptation), and examples of initial adaptations.

CONCLUSION

The data-based decision-making process is not an easy one, especially since there aren't any hard and fast rules to help you plan. That's why we rely on the basic question about considering small

TABLE 3.2. Examples of Core Components and Initial Adaptations

Core components	Malleable features	Examples of adaptations
	Check-In/Check-Out	
• Check-in and check-out sessions • Three to give behavioral expectations listed on DPR • Daily goal of 80% • DPR carried in each class • Teacher feedback after class • Reinforcement for meeting goal • Home–school communication	• Role of mentor • Incorporate other programs • Topography of expectations • Number of expectations • Goal of 80% of points on DPR • Format of DPR • Schedule of feedback • Schedule of reinforcement • Type of reinforcement • Access to DPR	• Peer mentor • Add in social skills lessons; homework-check program • Function-based replacement behaviors • Reduce to two expectations • Increase or decrease goal based on performance • Electronic form • Increase (e.g., every hour) or decrease (e.g., twice per day) • Midday opportunity for reinforcement; weekly goal • Reinforcement menu • Email or text DPR to caregiver
	Self-monitoring	
• Identify target behaviors • Self-monitoring form • Set regular, timed intervals • Assess and record extent to which behavior occurred • Feedback	• Skills targeted • Format of form • Alter length of intervals • Format of cue system • Person who provides feedback • Pair feedback with tangible reinforcement • Use of accuracy matching	• Function-based target skills • Post-it note, checklist, mobile app • Increase length to fade and decrease to intensify • Digital timer, teacher cue, mobile app • Peer buddy • Token economy, tickets, access to an activity • Teacher also records data and compares with student recorded data
	Social skills training	
• Explicit instruction in target skills • Modeling • Role play • Teacher feedback • Generalization	• Role of instructor (e.g., peer) • Skills targeted • Role modeler • Format of practice • Schedule of feedback • Reinforcement • Encouraging skill use	• Use a peer instructor • Select specific lessons from curriculum; target function-based replacement behaviors • Use peer models • Digital apps that allow for application in various scenarios • Increase to intensify and decrease to fade • Pair feedback with tangible reinforcement • Use DPR for targeted social skills and monitor in multiple settings Work with teachers to incorporate intervention language into classroom interactions

(continued)

TABLE 3.2. *(continued)*

Core components	Malleable features	Examples of adaptations
CBT-based interventions		
• Small group • Mental health provider • Identifying	• Composition • Demographic match	• Grouping based on age, cognitive development, gender, race/ethnicity • Matching provider based on key demographic variables to prevent cultural mismatch

adaptations that may increase the likelihood of success, while still implementing core features with fidelity. Because of this, the Tier 2 team has a lot of flexibility related to making these initial tweaks. We encourage you to access additional training and professional-learning supports, as well as rely on district coaches (or other experts) as you work to become fluent data-based decision-makers. In the next few chapters, we go more in depth about each intervention category. And, in Chapter 9, we return to data-based decision making as we examine how to make further adaptations based on fidelity data and student response data.

CHAPTER 4

Evidence-Based Interventions for Conduct Issues

Chapter 4 describes in detail evidence-based interventions for the conduct need area. Conduct issues are commonly identified by teachers and administrators for targeted support, as they are typically listed in a school's "code of conduct" or handbook. These behaviors can lead to unsafe or disruptive learning environments, creating an important area of focus within Tier 2. To match to intervention in this area, you may use screener subscale data (e.g., SDQ "conduct" score), in addition to ODR data and teacher or family referral information.

> ## CHAPTER FOCUS
> - Learn about the varying symptoms of conduct needs.
> - Understand how to implement Check-In/Check-Out.
> - Learn how to intensify CICO to include Check-In/Check-Up/Check-Out.
> - Understand how to implement Check and Connect.
> - Understand how to implement Check, Connect, and Expect.

CONDUCT NEEDS INTERVENTIONS

Most teachers have experienced a student who argues with peers or adults, refuses to engage in class activities, and disrupts instruction. Perhaps this student has even destroyed school property, or is excessively truant. Some students display more cover conduct issues like lying, cheating, or stealing. Despite you systematically implementing evidence-based classroom management strategies, the student may continue to exhibit these harmful externalizing behaviors that lead to disrupted

45

learning and increased instances of exclusionary discipline (e.g., suspension, referral to alternative school). Students who display these behaviors typically demonstrate elevated risk in the "conduct" category of the SDQ or externalizing behaviors on the social-behavior scale on the SAEBRS and higher than typical rates of office discipline referrals. When the Tier 2 PST reviews screening and ODR data, the team would match these students to Tier 2 interventions such as Check-In/Check-Out (CICO; Hawken et al., 2020); Check-In/Check-Up/Check-Out (CICUCO; Swoszowski et al., 2015); Check and Connect (Sinclair et al., 1998); and Check, Connect, and Expect (CCE; Cheney et al., 2009). For example, at Princeton Elementary School, the Tier 2 team uses primarily the SDQ subscale scores to determine which students are in need of supports in the conduct domain. After the team identifies all students with scores outside of the typical range, the members discuss discipline data to locate students who have had major office referrals (e.g., fighting) or more than four minor office referrals (e.g., being disrespectful to teachers, not following instructions). With this additional information, they determine which students would be best matched to intervention in the conduct category. The PST identifies Hank, a second-grade boy who scored "high" in the conduct category of the SDQ, has had one major office referral for shoving a desk, and two minor referrals for refusing to follow teacher directions. Given these data, the team matches Hank to an intervention to help him build stronger, positive relationships with adults at school.

Students with conduct-related issues often receive high rates of negative attention and corrective feedback from adults and peers, which may inadvertently maintain or increase the rates of externalizing behaviors displayed by these students. To reverse these patterns of negative attention and externalizing behaviors, CICO, CICUCO, Check and Connect, and CCE interventions are designed to provide students with high rates of structured feedback and positive adult attention. Structured feedback is when an adult mentor discusses a student's behavior with the student on a predetermined, regular, and repeated schedule. The feedback typically targets a particular behavioral or academic domain in which the student struggles, such as respecting peers and adults, maintaining positive relationships, attendance, or work completion; or, the feedback can be tied specifically to schoolwide expectations. During feedback sessions, a trusted adult mentor engages in a conversation with the student to celebrate successes and problem-solve setbacks regarding their behavior for the day and may set formal or informal goals to work toward. These feedback sessions are intended (1) to show students their participation within the school community is important, (2) to show students the adults care about their success and well-being, and (3) to discuss with students the challenges they may be facing before these escalate into a crisis situation.

Feedback can be a simple and immensely powerful tool for shaping student behavior (Markelz et al., 2021; Royer et al., 2019), yet delivering effective affirmative or corrective feedback is more nuanced than simply saying "good job" or "not quite." First, feedback should include a specific description of the behavior that earned the corrective or affirmative statement. That is, when praising a student, tell the student exactly what they did right (e.g., "Thanks for pushing in your chair, Angelo! Way to show safety in the classroom!"). When correcting a student's behavior, tell them what they did wrong and how to fix it (e.g., "Henry, it is disrespectful to shout out answers. Remember to raise your hand to speak in class"). Second, feedback is most impactful when it is provided in quick succession to the behavior, as the student can directly associate what it felt like and what they were thinking during the behavior with the feedback being provided. Third, students should receive a higher ratio of positive feedback to corrective feedback, and some experts recommend a ratio of 3:1, praise to reprimand (Caldarella et al., 2020). One strategy for always maintaining a high ratio of positive to corrective feedback is to use the sandwich method. That is, begin with a positive observation of the student's behavior (e.g., "I like the way you walked into the class quietly today"), followed by the corrective feedback (e.g., "However, you started talking to your neighbor as soon as you got to your desk. Remember, you're supposed to start the bell ringer when you sit down"), and end with another positive statement (e.g., "I always enjoy reading your creative responses to the bell ringers"). That is, you "sandwich" the corrective statement between the positive statements.

In addition, although determining the function (e.g., escape an academic demand, or gain peer attention) of a student's behavior is typically reserved for Tier 3 interventions, it might be helpful for the PST to consider function when referring students to feedback interventions. This is because interventions that focus on providing structured feedback and attention are best suited for students whose function of unexpected behavior is to access adult attention (Maggin et al., 2015). In other words, many of these students have a predictable pattern of their behavior followed by a response that will likely provide adult or peer attention, positive or negative, and the possibility that they will be removed from class. Thus, the PST may want to review the student's Tier 2 referral data for consequence patterns that follow the student's externalizing behavior. For example, most ODR forms include descriptions of the consequences, and students with multiple ODRs should have sufficient data to determine consequence patterns related to receiving attention and/ or escaping tasks. Consider our previously mentioned student Hank from Princeton Elementary School. The PST examined Hank's ODR data a little closer and learned that whenever his classroom teacher gave him a redirection (e.g., raise your hand to speak, share with your partner), Hank would talk back and disrupt the entire class. On one occasion, the teacher redirected Hank to push in his chair before lining up, and Hank shoved his desk across the room. The PST noticed a pattern in these data: Whenever Hank was publicly redirected, he acted out, and was removed from the class. Given this new knowledge, the PST matches Hank to CICUCO, a moderately intensive feedback intervention.

Further, although the interventions covered in this chapter might include some instructional components, they are primarily directed at providing quality adult attention, and not providing intensive instruction on appropriate replacement behaviors.

In this chapter, we describe four evidence-based interventions that can improve school-based conduct issues: CICO, CICUCO, Check and Connect, and CCE. These interventions are organized from least to most intensive in terms of interventionist and student time required, complexity, and materials needed. We will describe (1) persons involved, (2) design and implementation steps, (3) data collection and progress monitoring, and (4) data-based individualization. Key considerations, resources, and a case study are also included. It is important to note that Chapter 11 asks us also to consider the classroom and school contexts in an effort to determine if they are conditions that are setting students up for demonstrating conduct needs or externalizing problem behaviors. Chapter 11 also asks us to focus on areas of strength: Perhaps students with this area of need may not have a strength in conduct, but they may have a strength in social problem solving, such as helping others or getting along well with younger students. These strengths should be highlighted with the student and leveraged into intervention adaptations across the intervention category.

CHECK-IN/CHECK-OUT

CICO, also known as the "Behavior Education Program," is the most prolific and well-researched Tier 2 intervention implemented in schools (Hawken et al., 2020). Unfortunately, many schools do not implement CICO as it was designed—as an intervention focused on providing structured, positive adult feedback throughout the school day—and instead, intervention teams might attach a "points sheet" to a student, without providing quality adult attention, and call it CICO. When CICO is implemented as designed, students will engage in multiple daily feedback sessions with a facilitator (i.e., mentor) and their classroom teacher, and feedback is guided by data collected on a daily progress report (DPR).

The DPR includes three to five positively stated behaviors, typically tied to schoolwide expectations, and a three- to five-point rating scale (e.g., 0–2, 1–5). Older students can typically use a numbered rating scale (Figure 4.1) and younger students might benefit from a rating scale with symbols or emojis rather than numbers (Figure 4.2). The students' feedback schedule, Figure 4.3, is the same each day: (1) bring the signed home note from the previous day, (2) check-in with a facilitator in the morning, (3) receive feedback from their teachers throughout the day, (4) check-out with the facilitator at the end of the day, and (5) bring a home note to their caregivers to sign and return the next day. (A blank template version is also provided as Figure 4.4.) Additional components might include communication with the students' at-home caregivers and contingent reinforcement. Further, facilitators typically manage 5–10 students, and facilitators can be any adult in the school who is trained in CICO procedures. However, facilitators should not also be the student's teacher. Students should receive feedback from at least two different adults throughout the day.

Name: _____

Date: _____

	1 = never 2 = rarely 3 = often 4 = always											
	Be	**Respectful**			**Be**	**Responsible**			**Be**	**Safe**		
Period 1	1	2	3	4	1	2	3	4	1	2	3	4
Period 2	1	2	3	4	1	2	3	4	1	2	3	4
Period 3	1	2	3	4	1	2	3	4	1	2	3	4
Period 4	1	2	3	4	1	2	3	4	1	2	3	4
Period 5	1	2	3	4	1	2	3	4	1	2	3	4
Period 6	1	2	3	4	1	2	3	4	1	2	3	4
Period 7	1	2	3	4	1	2	3	4	1	2	3	4
Totals												

Today's Goal: _____

Did I reach my goal?   **YES**   **NO**

FIGURE 4.1. CICO DPR.

Name: _____

Date: _____

Rarely = 1	Sometimes = 2	Always = 3
☹	😐	☺

	Be Respectful			Be Responsible			Be Safe		
Reading	☹	😐	☺	☹	😐	☺	☹	😐	☺
Math	☹	😐	☺	☹	😐	☺	☹	😐	☺
Science	☹	😐	☺	☹	😐	☺	☹	😐	☺
Social Studies	☹	😐	☺	☹	😐	☺	☹	😐	☺
Writing	☹	😐	☺	☹	😐	☺	☹	😐	☺
Totals									

Today's Goal: _____

Did I reach my goal?   **Yes**   **No**

FIGURE 4.2. CICO DPR for early childhood.

Implementing CICO

Prior to involving the student in any feedback sessions, teachers should collect 3–5 days of baseline data using the DPR. This will provide data on the student's behavior prior to intervention to set initial points goals and will help the teacher learn the routine of observing specific student behaviors at regular moments throughout the day.

After baseline, at the start of each day, the student will "check in" with a facilitator or coach who will provide a new DPR to the student. The facilitator will typically review the behavioral expectations, discuss a point goal for the day, and precorrect any anticipated problems the student might face that day, such as assemblies, fire drills, or tests.

Next, the student brings the DPR to their classroom, where their teacher provides feedback throughout the day on how well the student performs the behavioral expectations included on the DPR. Students in elementary schools will receive feedback from their classroom teacher after each content area lesson or during natural transitions, and secondary students will receive feed-

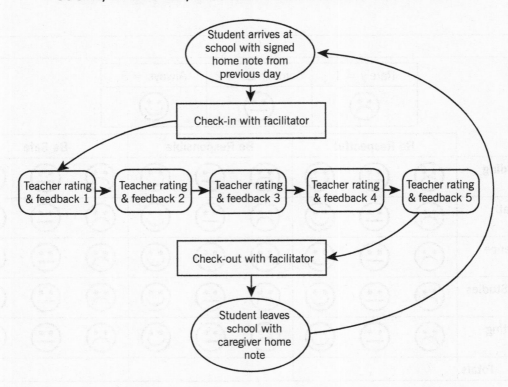

FIGURE 4.3. Example of a completed CICO schedule.

back at the end of each class period from each of their teachers. Secondary students are typically responsible for bringing their DPR from class to class and initiating the feedback session with their teacher, whereas initiating feedback sessions in elementary classroom can be done by either the student or the teacher. Feedback sessions throughout the day are brief (i.e., 30–60 seconds); the teacher quickly rates the students' performance associated with each expectation on their DPR, provides behavior-specific praise or constructive feedback, and encourages them to continue following their behavioral expectations. These DPR rating and feedback sessions typically occur at least five times per day.

Finally, at the end of the school day, the student returns to the facilitator with the completed DPR to "check out." The check-out session includes totaling the points earned on the DPR, determining whether the student met their goal, and delivering positive or corrective feedback based on their performance. Facilitators may also provide contingent reinforcement for students who meet their goal or reteach the behavioral expectations the student failed to demonstrate that day and problem-solve how to do better next time. Last, some CICO variations also include participation with at-home caregivers, which includes sending a note home with the student that summarizes their behavior for the day. However, the PST should consider the student's home life before including this component. For example, some caregivers might be overly harsh with their child if they bring home a DPR with negative ratings, or they may be unable to sign and return the DPR the next day. In these instances, it would be best to eliminate the home-note portion of the CICO intervention.

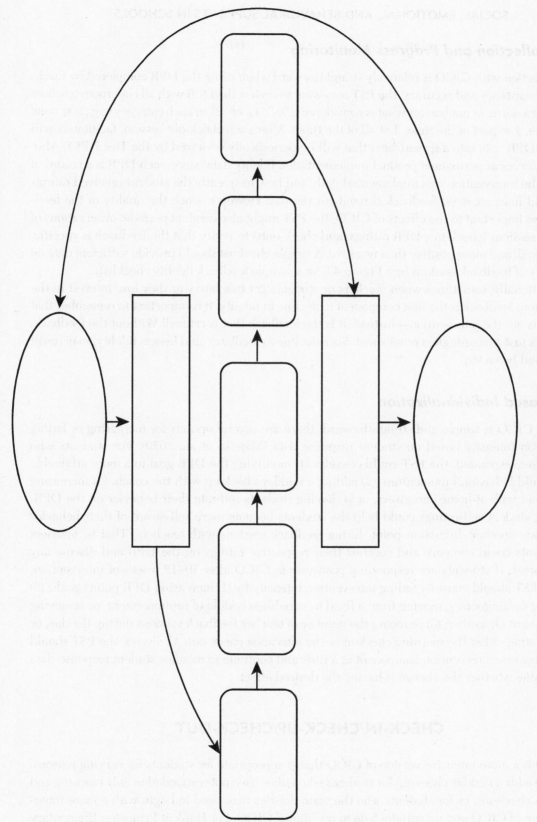

FIGURE 4.4. CICO schedule.

Data Collection and Progress Monitoring

Data collection with CICO is relatively straightforward when using the DPR completed by teachers. For consistency and accuracy, the PST may want to review the DPR with all classroom teachers and create a norm, or anchor, for what is considered a "0," "1," or "2" in each category (e.g., 0 = none of the time, 1 = part of the time, 2 = all of the time). After each check-out session, facilitators will enter the DPR data into a spreadsheet that will be periodically reviewed by the Tier 2 PST. Also, the DPR serves as permanent product implementation fidelity data, since each DPR is a record of whether the intervention was implemented daily and how frequently the student received ratings and should have received feedback throughout the day. However, since the quality of the feedback is also important to the effects of CICO, the PST might also conduct periodic observations of feedback sessions (check-ins, DPR ratings, and check-outs) to verify that the feedback is specific, instructional, and more positive than negative. A simple checklist should provide sufficient data on the quality of feedback sessions (see Figure 4.5 for a sample feedback fidelity checklist).

Additionally, sometimes when teachers or students get in a hurry or they lose interest in the intervention, feedback is the first component to decline in fidelity. It is important to remember that the DPR is not the intervention—instead, it is the feedback that is critical! Without the feedback, the DPR is just a meaningless point sheet. So, a decline in feedback (and hence, fidelity) may result in worsened behavior.

Data-Based Individualization

Although CICO is simple and straightforward, there are several options for increasing or fading intervention intensity based on student response data (Majeika et al., 2020). For students who have not yet responded, the PST could consider (1) modifying the DPR goal to a more attainable goal to build behavioral momentum, (2) adding a midday check-up with the coach, (3) increasing involvement with at-home caregivers, or (4) having students self-rate their behavior on the DPR. Including student self-ratings could help the students become more self-aware of their behavior and provide another discussion point during feedback sessions with teachers. That is, teachers and students could compare and contrast their respective ratings on the DPR and discuss any discrepancies. If students are responding positively to CICO after 10–12 weeks of intervention, then the PST should consider fading intervention intensity by (1) increasing DPR points goals; (2) increasing contingencies, moving from a fixed to variable schedule of reinforcement, or removing reinforcement altogether; (3) reducing the number of teacher feedback sessions during the day; or (4) eliminating either the morning check-in or the afternoon check-out. As always, the PST should only change one intervention component at a time and continue to monitor student response data to determine whether the change is having the desired effect.

CHECK-IN/CHECK-UP/CHECK-OUT

CICUCO is a more intensive version of CICO that is appropriate for students for varying reasons. CICUCO adds a midday check-up for students who either have not responded to only morning and afternoon check-ins, or for students who the team decides may need to begin with a more intensive version of CICO and potentially fade to traditional CICO. For Hank at Princeton Elementary

CICO Feedback Implementation Fidelity Checklist

Check-In			
Greeted student.	Yes	No	NA
Collected signed home note.	Yes	No	NA
Praised student for bringing the signed home note back to school.	Yes	No	NA
Review expectations on DPR.	Yes	No	NA
Precorrected any challenges the student might face that day (e.g., tests, fire alarms, assemblies).	Yes	No	NA
Reminded the student of their daily goal.	Yes	No	NA
Ended with a positive, encouraging statement.	Yes	No	NA
Maintained a positive tone throughout.	Yes	No	NA
Teacher Feedback			
Prompted student to begin DPR rating session.	Yes	No	NA
Verbally stated and marked the rating the student earned for each expectation on the DPR.	Yes	No	NA
Verbally provided behavior-specific praise for any 2 rating.	Yes	No	NA
Verbally provided specific corrective feedback, followed by encouragement, for any 0 or 1 ratings.	Yes	No	NA
Ended the session with a positive, encouraging statement.	Yes	No	NA
Maintained a positive tone throughout.	Yes	No	NA
Check-Out			
Greeted student.	Yes	No	NA
Totaled DPR points earned.	Yes	No	NA
Helped student identify if goal was met.	Yes	No	NA
Provided reinforcement (if applicable).	Yes	No	NA
Provided behavior-specific praise if goal was met.	Yes	No	NA
Provided corrective feedback if goal was not met, followed by encouragement.	Yes	No	NA
Prepared home note and sent with student.	Yes	No	NA
Maintained positive tone.	Yes	No	NA

Total number of Yes circled = _____

Total number possible (exclude NA) = _____

Percent implementation (total Yes / total possible × 100) = _____

FIGURE 4.5. CICO Implementation Fidelity Checklist.

School, the Tier 2 PST started with CICUCO. This decision was based on the intensity of his demonstrated behaviors and the increased opportunity for feedback provided from the midday check-up.

The adaptation of adding a midday check-up is helpful for younger students who require less time between a demonstrated prosocial behavior (e.g., saying something respectful) and the contingent reinforcement that should follow (e.g., tangible sticker). That is, a small token can be provided midday (e.g., sticker, stamp) to help strengthen the association between their behavior and reinforcement. Further, it may be difficult for students with more frequent, engrained behaviors to wait an entire school day to be provided with contingent reinforcement. Some students may require that reinforcement twice a day—at midday, for meeting expectations in the morning, and again in the afternoon, similar to younger students. For students who tend to perseverate on negative feedback, it may be useful to add the midday check-up in order to provide students with an opportunity to "start over" on their day. If they did not meet their morning goal, they can restart their day and aim for meeting their afternoon goal. And for students who are motivated by the attention of their CICO facilitator, or for whom the connection with that person is very important, it may be useful to have a midday check-up where the student and facilitator can spend extra time together processing their day, checking in on goal progress, and providing praise and precorrections/reminders.

Other than scheduling a midday time where the student and facilitator can meet, the only other intervention change for this intensification is to modify the DPR to include a midday check-in within the point area, and/or a midday goal and contingent reinforcement area. This way, the student and facilitator can calculate the midday total, check off whether the morning goal was attained, and whether the student earned the agreed upon contingent reinforcement. It is important to note that intensifying any interventions may add increased levels of complexity and difficulty with procedures. For instance, in order to add a midday check-up, the facilitator must be available around lunchtime to check-in with the student. In some cases, this will not be possible, or be too complex to be sustained.

CHECK AND CONNECT

Check and Connect is another evidence-based feedback intervention; in contrast to CICO, it has been extensively researched in middle and high schools with very promising findings on dropout prevention, increased attendance, and increased academic social and academic engagement (Maynard et al., 2014; Powers et al., 2017). The primary differences between Check and Connect and CICO are, in Check and Connect (1) students engage with a mentor to monitor various data sources (e.g., grades, tardies), and (2) there is a strong family involvement component. In other words, a student "checks" with a mentor to review academic and behavioral data, and "connects" with a mentor who provides individualized attention, fosters positive relationships between the school and family members, and presents relevant school or community-based supports. At Peterson High School, students often had co-occurring discipline issues (e.g., ODRs) and attendance issues. This made Check and Connect a great match for their Tier 2 "conduct" intervention.

Selecting Mentors

Since the impact of the Check and Connect intervention relies heavily on mentors and students developing a strong relationship, selecting the best mentors is critical. First, mentors should have a vested interest in the personal well-being of all students and be able to maintain a kind and empathetic demeanor when facing challenging interpersonal conflicts. Second, mentors can be dedicated school, district, or regional employees whose primary responsibility is serving as a mentor for Check and Connect or other similar behavioral interventions. Teachers, administrators, counselors, paraprofessionals, or other interested school staff members could serve as mentors as their time allows. Community volunteers, such as local college students, civic institutions (e.g., Big Brothers, Big Sisters; social workers, retired teachers) may also be mentors. Third, mentors should be fully trained in Check and Connect procedures, such as how to collect and review student data, strategies for working with families, and knowledge of available school and community resources for providing additional SEB supports for students. Figure 4.6 provides an example of one school's selection of mentors, matching with mentees and scheduling.

Implementing Check and Connect

Once mentors have been selected and trained, students referred to Check and Connect should be matched to an appropriate mentor. Considerations for matching students to mentors include student and mentor scheduling availability and student preference. For example, does the student prefer to work with males rather than females, and does the student have a problematic history with one of the mentors? It might also be beneficial for students to pick their mentor from a list of available mentors.

Next, mentors should establish a regular schedule to meet with each student and to check in with their family, which typically starts as once per week. During these brief meetings, mentors

Intervention	Mentor	Students/Mentee	Meeting notes	Group name
Check-In/ Check-Out	Dr. Swain	John B. Elisa T. Anwar N.	Meet in principal's office 7:45 am and 2:50 pm	Principal's priority
Check-In/ Check-Out	Ms. Lieber	Aniah R. Brayden M. Luke N.	Meet in cafeteria during breakfast and front lobby at 2:50	Lieber's Library Group
Check-In/ Check-Up/ Check-Out	Coach Hostin	James P. Henry R. Zamir T. Miles P.	Meet in conference room at 7:45, lunch visits with shared lunchtimes, meet in basketball gym before practice	Athlete's corner
Check-In/ Check-Up/ Check-Out	Mrs. Roe	Jessica R. Rilee B. Brooklyn T. Jackson E.	Meet in counselor's office at 7:45, lunch bunch in counselor's office at 11:35, meet in counselor's office at 2:50	Roe's Girls Group
Check, Connect, Expect	Mr. Miguel	Tania P.—Basic Zaiden R.—Basic Kinsely T.—Basic+ Olivia P.—Basic+ Emma T.—Basic+ Owen A.—Self-Monitor Noah R.—Self-Monitor Honour A.—Self-Monitor	Meet in Mr. Miguel's office 7:45, Mr. Miguel checks throughout the day for each student, one class period, pullout social skills and problem-solving groups Tuesday and Thursday and 2:50 check-out	Mr. Miguel's Stars

FIGURE 4.6. Example of school mentor selection and scheduling.

teach students how to access the student's academic and behavioral data, record the data on a monitoring form, and review the data to determine whether the student is making progress. Academic data sources often include the number of Ds or Fs earned in the past week, number of missing assignments, cumulative grade-point average, and credits earned. Behavioral data may include the number of tardies, skipped classes, unexcused absences, excused absences, behavior referrals, detentions, or suspensions. To aid in determining data patterns, mentors should track data on a spreadsheet or table (Figure 4.7), and consider teaching students to graph their data (Figure 4.8), or use the Check and Connect application (see Table 4.2 on p. 60).

After gathering and reviewing data, the mentor and student celebrate successes and discuss areas where the student continues to struggle. This portion also leads to communicating with families—through phone calls, notes, meetings, or emails—as well as with school staff or other

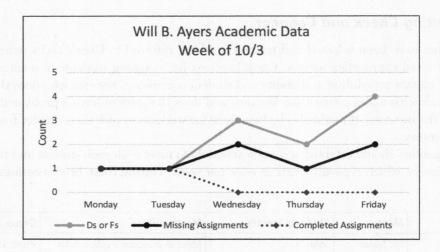

FIGURE 4.7. Example of academic data tracking report.

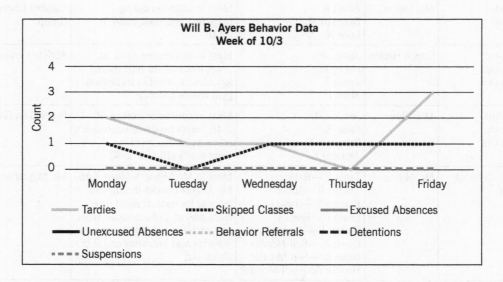

FIGURE 4.8. Example of behavior data tracking report.

outside agencies. The developers of Check and Connect also provide lesson plans and worksheets to guide mentors through engaging in effective mentoring meetings with students (*https://checkand-connect.umn.edu/default.html*). For example, lesson plans may include a progression of topics (e.g., skipping school, failing classes) and questions (e.g., What is the difference between an excused and unexcused absence? What are acceptable and unacceptable reasons for missing school? What are some consequences for missing school?) aimed at helping students understand the consequences of their actions and how to develop a plan to improve their behavior. Mentors and students might also follow up at future mentoring meetings on particular topics where a student is struggling.

Data Collection and Monitoring

Data collection with Check and Connect is very straightforward, since the intervention itself is about collecting and reviewing academic and behavioral data with students. Tracking implementation fidelity data is also relatively simple, since mentors should use worksheets or spreadsheets to facilitate data collection and review, which will provide a permanent product for fidelity evaluation. This will provide a record of when meetings occur, the information discussed in the meetings, what data were accessed and reviewed, and the family communication strategy implemented (e.g., note sent home, email, phone call, meeting scheduled). However, similar to CICO, the PST might consider periodically conducting fidelity observations of mentoring sessions to determine the quality of conversations, feedback, and support provided by mentors.

Data-Based Individualization

Check and Connect is conceptualized as a two-tier intervention. Tier one, the basic level, includes weekly data review and communicating with students and families, and is often sufficient to enable SEB and academic improvement. However, students who are not showing improvements might benefit from a more intensive intervention, tier two. Methods for intensifying intervention include meeting with mentors more frequently, increased communication with families, explicit problem-solving instruction, or adding an auxiliary intervention, such as self-regulation, social skills groups, tutoring, or counseling. Students often engage in goal-setting exercises directed at either academic or social/behavioral domains (strategies for teaching goal setting are covered in Chapter 6). Another option is combining Check and Connect with CICO, which is discussed in the upcoming CCE section.

Finally, most research on Check and Connect has revealed that extended involvement with Check and Connect (i.e., at least 1 year) will yield the best results related to dropout prevention and improved academics and behavior (Powers et al., 2017). As such, even when students demonstrate consistent improvements, the PST may fade intensive supports or reduce the frequency of mentoring meetings, but they should still maintain regular, periodic mentoring meetings and occasional communication with families.

CHECK, CONNECT, AND EXPECT

As mentioned above, CCE is similar to CICO and Check and Connect but it is the most intensive out of all of the options, as it includes extended mentoring, a full-time "behavior coach" or mentor who pushes into the classroom, pullout lessons, and frequent, daily teacher feedback. In addition, CCE is organized into three levels of support: Basic (similar to CICO), Basic Plus (most intensive), and Self-Monitoring (McDaniel et al., 2011). Students are assigned to a support level based on their baseline DPR data, and can move between levels based on their response to intervention.

At the Basic level, students participate in daily check-in and check-out meetings with a mentor, or coach, and engage in repeated feedback with their teacher on a DPR. Check-in and check-out meetings with coaches, similar to CICO, include setting points goals, reviewing DPR data, and determining goal attainment. DPR data and goal-attainment information are also shared with families, and contingent reinforcement may also be provided for students who reach their goals. When students fail to make progress at the Basic level, they move on to Basic Plus.

Basic Plus, as the name implies, includes all the intervention supports provided at the Basic level, with the addition of pullout problem-solving instruction and social skills lessons. These can be individual or small group. Typically, coaches will target specific areas where the student is struggling based on their DPR data. Further, coaches can facilitate skill generalization to the classroom by communicating with the student's teacher on the exact problem-solving methods and social skills taught during mentorship meetings. CCE coaches may even push into the classroom to support a student or check in with a student during the day. As teachers become aware of the issues and skills addressed during coaching meetings, they can reinforce and correct the student's behaviors using the same language and strategies used by the coach.

The Self-Monitoring level is for students who have responded positively to the Basic level, and includes reduced frequency of check-ins or check-outs with coaches. At this level, students are taught to self-monitor their own behavior, with the student presenting the coach with the ratings for discussion, faded to the student keeping track of their own ratings independently. At this point, the student becomes a CCE "graduate," which is a reinforcing, positive aspect of CCE.

The tiered structure of CCE can have a substantive impact on the types of services provided to students with conduct issues, particularly for schools that have other systematic feedback interventions already in place. For example, at McNott Middle School, the principal decided to make a change to her existing discipline plan. For years, she employed a full-time in-school suspension room teacher who monitored students after they received a major discipline infraction and were assigned in-school suspension. Instead, she decided to shift that person to be a full-time "behavior coach" to implement Check, Connect, and Expect. She used substitutes for in-school suspension on the rare occasion that was still needed after implementing CCE for one semester. The CCE behavior coach was assigned to students who were not responding to the initial CICO or CICUCO interventions, and those with infractions that would have otherwise been assigned alternative school (e.g., drug use, multiple fighting offenses). The behavior coach was able to work with their small group of students daily and prevent further major disciplinary incidents. Since CCE is a leveled intervention, the students were able to move back and forth from more intensive supports to less intensive supports within CCE.

KEY CONSIDERATIONS

Several key considerations described in detail in Chapter 11 apply to the interventions and adaptions of the interventions included in this chapter. Before matching students to CICO, CICUCO, Check and Connect, or CCE, the PST should consider important student characteristics, incorporating student voice, and overall resource requirements. First, in addition to considering function of behavior and skill versus performance issues, the PST should also consider the student's grade level. Evidence supporting CICO includes research conducted across K–12 grades (Maggin et al., 2015; Mitchell et al., 2017), CCE is primarily based on research across grades K–8 (Cheney et al., 2009; McDaniel et al., 2016; Stage & Galanti, 2017), and Check and Connect has been primarily tested in high schools to reduce risks associated with school dropout (e.g., attendance, academic completion, school engagement; U.S. Department of Education, 2015). Second, the PST should consider soliciting input from students across various intervention design decisions. For example, students could help identify unexpected behaviors that they should address, operationally define the behaviors tracked on DPRs or data sources used in Check and Connect, determine goal criteria, select reinforcers, and choose their mentor. Also, the PST should consider the individual resource requirements for each intervention, and whether their school or district can support implementation (see Table 4.1). In addition, the PST should designate a building coordinator who will provide general oversight across all mentors and students. This individual can help consolidate performance data across all students and ensure that caseloads are spread evenly across mentors. Table 4.1 provides a comparison across interventions. In most schools, the conduct category is the highest subscale category for scores in an at-risk range. This will mean that numerous students who need support in this area, will also need support in one or more other areas of need. Chapter 11 offers suggestions for handling the issue of multiple areas of need.

TABLE 4.1. Comparison across Interventions

	CICO and CICUCO	Check and Connect	CCE
Persons involved	Facilitators—conducts daily check-in and check-out sessions Teachers—rates student behavior on DPR throughout the day	Mentors—conducts weekly meetings with students	Coaches—conducts daily check-in and check-out sessions Provides problem-solving or social skills instruction Teachers—rates student behavior on DPR throughout the day
Materials needed	DPR	Spreadsheet or Table to store student academic and behavior data Problem-solving or goal-setting lesson plans	DPR Problem-solving or social skills lesson plans
Feedback schedule	Every day, multiple times throughout the day	Weekly	Every day, multiple times throughout the day
Data tracked	Behavior ratings included on DPR	Academic and behavioral data typically collected in schools	Behavior ratings included on DPR
Student grade level	K–12	9–12	K–8

RESOURCES

Table 4.2 provides resources related to interventions for conduct issues.

TABLE 4.2. Resources

https://checkandconnect.umn.edu/model/default.html

This website is hosted by the University of Minnesota and provides a suite of training, monitoring, and implementation tools for Check and Connect.

Hawken, L. S., Crone, D. A., Bundock, K., & Horner, R. (2020). *Responding to problem behavior in schools: The Check-In, Check-Out intervention* (3rd ed.). Guilford Press.

This book includes an in-depth review of the research supporting CICO, several implementation guides with adaptations for various contexts (e.g., high school, alternative school, early childhood), and supporting materials.

McDaniel, S., Flower, A., & Cheney, D. (2011). Put me in, coach! A powerful and efficient Tier 2 behavioral intervention for alternative settings. *Beyond Behavior, 20,* 18–24.

This article presents strategies for implementing CCE in alternative education settings.

www.youtube.com/watch?v=BO3cEpp1JTY

Video explaining Check and Connect implementation

www.pbiscaltac.org/resources/targeted%20group%20interventions/N.%20Check%20Connect%20Expect.pdf

Example of Check, Connect, and Expect

www.pbis.org/resource/check-in-check-out-a-targeted-intervention

CICO guidance from PBIS.org

http://pbismissouri.org/wp-content/uploads/2017/06/5.0-MO-SW-PBS-Tier-2-Workbook-Ch-5-CICO.pdf

CICO description

CASE EXAMPLE

Cassidy was a typically developing third-grade student at Hawkins Elementary School, located in an affluent suburb of Indiana. She was meeting grade-level standards across academic subjects, but she frequently engaged in disruptive behaviors such as wandering around the classroom, refusing to begin her assignments, and occasionally arguing with her classmates or teachers when her behavior was redirected. As a result, she earned poor grades and had few friends. Recently, Hawkins Elementary implemented a schoolwide behavioral screener, the Strength and Difficulties Questionnaire (SDQ), and Cassidy's teacher rated her at slightly raised for hyperactivity and high for externalizing/conduct subdomains. Thus, given her persistent externalizing behaviors impeding her learning and the learning of other classmates, and elevated SDQ scores, the school's Tier 2 PST matched Cassidy to CICO. Her initial daily CICO goal was set at 65% based on teacher ratings conducted by the PST prior to starting her on the procedures. The PST team decided to raise the goal 10% each time Cassidy was able to meet or exceed her goal for 5 school days.

The PST decided to use the schoolwide expectations on Cassidy's DPR: Be Respectful, Be Responsible, and Be Safe, and operationally defined these expectations to address the specific conduct issues she exhibits in class. Next, Cassidy was matched with the Hawkins art teacher, Ms. Ryder, as the two always got along well when Cassidy took art during the Fall quarter. Finally, after meeting with Cassidy's family and learning their concern that they rarely received positive feedback from the school, the PST also included weekly home notes that describe Cassidy's progress and a minimum of one success daily.

After 2 weeks of intervention, Cassidy demonstrated several improvements in her classroom behavior. She thrived on the positive adult attention with Ms. Ryder; she no longer argued with her classroom teacher, who was now also pointing out positive behaviors she saw; and she showed renewed interest in interacting with her classmates during group and partner activities. Unfortunately, Cassidy still struggled to accept feedback from peers. For example, twice in the past 2 weeks she shouted at classmates who contradicted her and then refused to work for the next 30 minutes while she calmed down. Cassidy's teacher had already tried having her meet with the counselor to discuss physical signs that she is getting angry, and increased her own rates of precorrections for Cassidy when she assigned group work. She continued to precorrect Cassidy during feedback sessions and praised her profusely after any positive interaction with her classmates. Two weeks later, Cassidy still had no major outbursts during class and met her 65% goal criteria. Even though Cassidy demonstrated consistent improvements across all her DPR behaviors, the PST decided not to begin fading intervention until she met 80% consistently. The team wanted Cassidy to continue repairing relationships with her peers, and felt that fading intervention too quickly could jeopardize her progress. As such, the PST decided to continue monitoring her DPR data and decided to review her progress in another 2 weeks.

CONCLUSION

Conduct needs can lead to disrupted learning for the student with the need, but also disrupted learning for all students in the learning environment. These needs can also lead to unsafe learning environments. This chapter overviews the symptoms of conduct needs and why students with these needs are matched to systematic feedback interventions. This is followed by in-depth descriptions of the following interventions in order of intensity: Check-In/Check-Out; Check-In/Check-Up/Check-Out; Check and Connect; and Check, Connect, and Expect. Finally, each intervention description also includes available data that can be used to monitor progress.

CHAPTER 5

Evidence-Based Interventions for Self-Regulation Issues

Do you ever stop to consider why you opened this book and started reading? What are you hoping to accomplish with this knowledge? Did you have to schedule time in your calendar to spend time reading this book? Chances are, if you're reading this right now, you have engaged in some self-regulated behaviors that brought you to this chapter. That is, you likely have a personal or professional goal to learn about Tier 2, and you are regulating your attention and behavior to reach this goal. Self-regulation is a process in which individuals can set meaningful goals, plan a course of action to meet these goals, predict potential barriers to reaching their goals, and reflect on whether their behavior is helping them reach their goals (Arslan, 2014). This chapter details Tier 2 self-regulation interventions that address targeted inattention and hyperactivity issues.

CHAPTER FOCUS

- Learn the signs of inattention and hyperactivity needs.
- Understand self-regulation as an umbrella of interventions.
- Learn how to use goal setting as a Tier 2 intervention.
- Understand how to implement self-monitoring.
- Learn how to integrate self-graphing with goal setting or self-monitoring.

SELF-REGULATION

In school, students use self-regulation to simultaneously understand what is expected of them, control their impulses, and direct their behavior at achieving expectations. These expectations can be set by others or themselves, and can relate to SEB goals or academic goals. Students may struggle with self-regulation when they experience a discrepancy between expectations and environmental triggers, such as being asked to complete a math worksheet while also sitting next to their best friend. Self-regulation needs may be due to developmental age, executive-functioning level, and/or the lack of opportunity to learn and practice key self-regulation behaviors (Gardner et al., 2008). Students might engage in externalizing behaviors (e.g., noncompliance, disruptions, impulsivity) or internalizing behaviors (e.g., academic disengagement, anxiety, depression, social withdrawal), thus it is important that teachers and educators promote self-regulation development. In addition, behaviors that are high frequency (e.g., occur often) and low intensity (e.g., inattention, chatting with peers) are well-suited for self-regulation interventions, as are academic-related behaviors (e.g., task completion). On the other hand, low-frequency and intense behaviors such as fighting, and covert behaviors like cheating or lying, are inappropriate for self-regulation interventions.

To apply the matching framework described in this book, the Tier 2 PST should implement a screener with a self-regulation (or similar) subscale such as the SDQ, SAEBRS, or BESS. Since many behaviors associated with self-regulation issues are nondisruptive, such as poor work completion, staring out the window, or coming to class unprepared, and do not often warrant major or minor ODRs, the Tier 2 PST should not rely on ODRs for identification. Rather, academic performance may be a sign of an issue like inattentiveness, particularly if students are not completing work in a timely manner. Students may turn in partially completed work or turn in work late, or they may be missing essential components of assignment—as these issues may stem from a lack of self-regulation. Other data sources (in addition to screening) might include teacher notes or classroom logs or checklists. For example, at Simpson Middle School, all minor behavior classroom problems are entered into a log completed by the teacher, and only major disruptions (e.g., fighting, bullying) are reported to the office. Grade-level classroom teachers discuss students with multiple classroom discipline logs during grade-level meetings, and determine strategies used to support the student (e.g., move their seat, provide graphic organizers, reduce classroom noise, revisit classroom expectations). The Tier 2 team at Simpson Middle School uses these logs, in addition to screening data, when matching students to appropriate Tier 2 interventions, and this process is particularly effective for matching students to self-regulation interventions.

Self-regulation interventions involve explicitly teaching strategies related to self-instruction, goal setting, self-monitoring, self-graphing, and self-evaluation, and can include a combination of strategies or target an individual strategy. Self-regulation strategies can be implemented in isolation or combined into a self-regulation package. The PST can determine the self-regulation strategy or combination of strategies based on intervention matching and adaptation procedures described in Chapter 3. Each strategy should include (1) explicitly teaching the student how to set goals, self-monitor, and self-graph; and (2) structured practice across various school settings. We also recommend students receive regular adult (or peer) feedback on their use of the self-regulation strategy and its impact on their behavior. They may also consider using contingent reinforcement.

In addition, self-regulation interventions should include opportunities for students to provide input on intervention design decisions. Students can provide input across various self-regulation intervention components, such as determining the issue and replacement behaviors, setting goals, establishing self-monitoring procedures, selecting reinforcers, and self-evaluating their performance. Student input is important because it can enhance buy-in (i.e., willingness to engage in the intervention), and help establish a personally meaningful intervention, which may improve intervention effectiveness (Bandura & Locke, 2003). Further, for students with self-regulation needs, it is essential they are taught how to make their own self-regulation decisions in order to actually "self" regulate. Educators who choose to utilize student input should carefully consider within which components of the intervention to include students' input and determine whether the student possesses the prerequisite skills necessary to make informed decisions. For example, younger students could be provided simple choice-making opportunities, like choosing between an audio or tactile prompt for self-monitoring, and older, more self-aware students could help operationally define the behaviors they will self-monitor. Additional suggestions for including student input are included throughout this chapter. Other issues to consider in this category of intervention are highlighted in Chapter 11. For example, it is important that interventions for self-regulation are instructional and therapeutic, designed not to control but to cooperate with a student. Further, it may be necessary to make adaptations to academic-related self-regulation interventions in secondary settings given the movement of students between several periods a day and across large school buildings. Finally, Chapter 11 asks us to explicitly plan for and promote generalization. It is not enough to improve time on task in one class period out of seven per day. The new self-regulation skills acquired with Tier 2 intervention should be practiced across all academic settings, and perhaps at home in collaboration with the family to ensure homework is attended to and completed.

In this chapter, we describe three evidence-based interventions that can improve behavioral self-regulation: goal setting, self-monitoring, and self-graphing. These interventions are organized from least to most intensive in terms of educator and student time required, complexity, and materials needed, as well as the order in which they can be combined into a multicomponent intervention package. We describe (1) core intervention components; (2) steps for designing the interventions; (3) strategies to enhance student involvement; and (4) implementation methods. Finally, we present a case example to highlight intervention in this area.

GOAL SETTING

Goals are the foundation for all self-regulation interventions because all self-regulated behaviors are directed at achieving goals. Goals can stand alone as their own intervention, be included within a multicomponent self-regulation intervention (e.g., self-monitoring, self-graphing), or be added to an existing intervention to incorporate student input (e.g., CICO) or to enhance skill generalization (e.g., social skills groups). For example, students who are placed in CICO can help determine the behaviors they should include and set points goals on their daily progress report. When goals are used in multicomponent interventions or added to an existing intervention, they can be written by the educator, the student, or as a collaborative decision between the educator and student. However, the stand-alone goal-setting intervention is most effective when students are directly involved in establishing and writing their own goals (Bruhn et al., 2016). Once these goals are written, students should regularly review their goal statements and engage in informal progress monitoring and feedback sessions with an educator. This can help students refocus their attention on key behaviors they are improving and help them determine whether their actions are enabling goal attainment (Barbrack & Maher, 1984; Estrapala et al., 2022; Kelly & Shogren, 2014).

In addition, research has shown that goals that include specific attainment criteria are more motivating and provide the necessary information for systematically monitoring goal attainment.

In other words, goals are most effective when they are SMART (i.e., specific, measurable, achievable, relevant, and time-bound; Bovend'Eerdt et al., 2009). For goals to be Specific, they must include the other components (e.g., MART). Measurable goals mean they include a data source and a criterion, such as earning at least nine points on CICO daily progress report, arriving to class on time 3 days in a row, or spending at least 10 minutes engaging in an academic activity. Achievable goals are those that are appropriately challenging and can be reasonably attained within the allotted time period. Relevant goals explicitly relate to the student's area of SEB need and educational context. Finally, goals must include the amount of Time the student has to achieve the goal criteria (e.g., by the end of the class period, day, week). The amount of time included on goal statements will depend on how the goals are used with the student; however, short-term goals are generally more effective than long-term goals.

At Baybridge Elementary School, one of the Tier 1 PBIS expectations is to "Be Responsible." The Tier 2 team aligned all self-regulation Tier 2 interventions with this schoolwide expectation so students knew promoting their self-regulation demonstrated responsibility. They also specifically aligned their goal-setting worksheet the "Responsibility Review" with this expectation. Students receiving the goal-setting intervention worked with an assigned adult (e.g., school counselor, instructional coach, paraprofessional) to determine the specific behaviors to improve in the classroom and what achievable goals they could set for those behaviors. The adult and student discussed whether the goals were specific enough and how they would be able to observe and measure the behaviors. Next, they checked with the student's classroom teacher to make sure the goals were relevant to the teacher's expectations and classroom instruction. The adult and student worked together to determine any additional supports that were needed, such as reminders or visual cues to promote goal attainment; they also set a time frame for reaching their established goal. In this way, their "Responsibility Review" was S (specific), M (measurable), A (achievable), R (relevant), and T (timely). Examples and non-examples of SMART goals are provided in Table 5.1. Finally, goals will be more effective when students focus only on one goal at a time. It might be helpful to write multiple goal statements or incorporate multiple goal-related behaviors and allow the student to prioritize which goal or behavior they find the most motivating or important.

TABLE 5.1. Examples and Non-Examples of SMART Goals

Examples	Non-examples
I will meaningfully participate in the discussion at least three times by the end of class.	I will be actively engaged in class.
I will complete at least 10 math problems by the end of math class today.	I will be productive.
I will pay attention while the teacher is presenting by keeping my eyes on the screen or my notes and ask questions when I am confused at least 80% of the time.	I will pay attention.
I will come to class with my Chromebook charged every day this week.	I will be prepared for class.

STEPS FOR WRITING BEHAVIORAL GOALS

As mentioned above, stand-alone goal interventions should directly involve students in collaborative goal statement writing. Students could be included in (1) identifying and defining goal behaviors, (2) determining measurable goal criteria, and (3) determining the time frame. Depending on the student's developmental capabilities and self-awareness, they can be included in the entire goal-writing process or just in one or two portions, or the educator could draft a couple of goal statements and allow the student to pick the one they find most motivating or important. Further, educators might find it helpful to use the template in Figure 5.1 to help students write goals that include all the necessary information. We find that including information in goal statements that is specific, measurable, and attainable will ensure that goals are SMART.

Next, we will cover three steps that educators can use to enable their students to help write specific, measurable, and attainable behavioral goals.

Step 1: Identify Goal Behaviors

To ensure that goals are Specific and Relevant, all goals should include positively stated, age- and developmentally appropriate behaviors (e.g., increasing time on task to 2 minutes for a 6-year old, increasing time on task to 10 minutes for a 9-year old). Positively stated behaviors are those that students should do (e.g., follow directions), rather than those they should not do (e.g., don't argue). Appropriate behaviors, as opposed to unexpected behaviors, are those that will enable the student to experience SEB success and academic success. In addition, the behaviors written into goal statements can be based on school- or classwide expectations and can include student input. For example, the educator can suggest the student should work on staying on task in class, and the student can offer examples in their own words, like raising their hand to participate rather than blurting out answers.

Alternatively, students can take the self-report versions of a behavioral screener (see Chapter 2) to help them identify behaviors to write into their goal. This might also include color coding results based on subscale for no area of concern (e.g., green), small area of need (e.g., yellow), or primary area of need (e.g., red), or simplifying assessment score reports with student-friendly language and eliminating irrelevant subscales (e.g., academic achievement). Or educators can teach the student to review their baseline or Tier 2 eligibility data to help pinpoint a specific need area to focus on in their goal. Students and educators could also examine grades, assignment completion, and other academic-related indicators that could help point to a goal area. Importantly, adults

Template
I will (*behavior*) at least (*number of times, percent of time*) by (*time frame*).
Example
I will *read* at least *5 pages of my reading homework* by *the end of study hall*.

FIGURE 5.1. Goal template.

working with students on this portion of the goal-writing process should remember that directly addressing their student's behavioral needs can trigger feelings of anxiety and shame in the student. As such, they should maintain an empathetic and positive affect throughout the conversation and reassure the student that the purpose of this activity is not punitive, but instead is meant to help them be successful in school.

Once the student identifies a behavior they would like to address, the educator should help the student identify and define appropriate replacement behaviors to write into their goal statements. These replacement behaviors should be written positively, oriented to what they want to *increase*, rather than *decrease*. When students interact with goals that include positive, personal, and socially appropriate language, they will be reminded exactly what behaviors they are working on and feel motivated to continue improving. Further, educators should encourage students to write observable and measurable examples (e.g., participating in discussions, finishing worksheets during class time, talking when appropriate) and non-examples (e.g., checking phone, sleeping, chatting with friends) in their own words. This should help the student visualize their behavior and remember what they should be doing.

Step 2: Determine Measurement

Again, it is important that behaviors chosen can be observed and measured, because this will facilitate establishing goal criteria, collecting behavioral data, and monitoring progress (i.e., Measurable in SMART). To keep things simple, determine whether the behavior is short and discrete (e.g., number of problems completed) or if the behavior is continuous (time spent on-task). Short, discrete behaviors can be counted (i.e., frequency) and continuous behaviors can be timed with a stopwatch (i.e., duration). Sometimes, it will make sense to convert the frequency or duration into a percentage. For example, a student who would like to raise their grade might measure the percentage of assignments completed (e.g., assignments completed divided by the assignments given, multiplied by 100). Or, students who are working on sustaining attention during whole-group instruction might consider estimating the amount of time they were on-task. Students might struggle with determining the appropriate form of measurement (e.g., percent completion, time spent on task, number of questions answered), so it is OK to recommend a measurement type.

Step 3: Establish Goal Criteria and Time Frame

For goals to be motivating and appropriately challenging (i.e., Achievable in SMART), it is important to carefully consider goal criteria. Have you ever tried to work toward a New Year's resolution that was out of reach (e.g., setting the goal of working out 7 days a week)? The fitness industry sees a spike in engagement after the New Year, and we all know the spike then wanes across the spring and summer. Instead of making small, achievable (maybe even easy) goals, we often set our goals way too high, then fail to meet them and experience frustration and disappointment (and sometimes continued gym payments for the rest of the year). To determine the initial goal criteria, educators could use the data the PST used to identify and match the student to their goal-setting intervention, or collect baseline data for 3–5 days prior to beginning intervention using a method described in Chapter 3. The initial goal should be set minimally (e.g., 10%) higher than the baseline average. Remember, these goals are meant to be achievable, not impossible. We want students to achieve their goals and success. This creates behavioral momentum and a reinforcement pattern (i.e., set a goal, reach it, raise the goal, reach it, and so on). This step cannot be perceived as another failure or "gotcha." When a goal is set substantially higher than the student's current level of performance, they may find it unrealistic and frustrating, and, thus, not even attempt to change their behavior. To involve students in setting goal criteria, educators can show the student their baseline data and ask them what they think is a reasonable starting goal criterion, and remind them that they are looking for small, incremental improvements achievable over a short amount of time.

Next, the educator should ask the student when they should be able to reach their criterion, and we recommend daily or weekly time frames to allow the student multiple opportunities to revise their goals once they begin progress monitoring (i.e., Time-bound in SMART). Once the student has identified their goal behavior, form of measurement, criterion, and time frame, they can write their statement using the template in Figure 5.1.

Finally, once the initial goal is set and the student agrees to work toward achieving their goal, the goal criteria should be periodically updated based on student performance. For example, students who are continually achieving or exceeding their goal could receive another 10% criterion increase, and students who continually fall below their goal could have a 10% criterion decrease. Any changes to goal criteria should also be discussed with the student to determine what actions are either helping or hindering their goal attainment. Once students meet acceptable levels of behavior, goals can be rewritten with different behaviors or across different contexts.

IMPLEMENTING GOALS

After the student collaborates with an educator to write their specific and measurable goal, they should be instructed to work toward goal attainment. That is, if the student has decided to improve their on-task behavior, then they should be instructed to practice the replacement behaviors written into their goal (e.g., watching the teacher during demonstrations, asking questions when confused) during class. Educators and students might also find it helpful to problem-solve potential challenges to achieving their goals and make environmental changes. That is, if the student struggles with on-task behavior because they cannot see what their teacher is doing, then they can request a seating change.

Next, the purpose of this type of goal-setting intervention is teaching the student to analyze their own history of maladaptive behavior patterns, to speculate how their behavior may interfere with their future learning, and to identify specific changes they can make to reverse their behavior patterns. In goal-setting interventions alone, students are not explicitly required to systematically collect data on goal progress. That will be reserved for self-monitoring and self-graphing. Instead, students should be reminded of their goal each day and asked to think about whether their behavior is supporting overall goal attainment. This can be facilitated through daily or weekly journaling or by asking students to complete a simple direct behavior rating (DBR) at the end of the day or class period. The DBR can include three standard behaviors (e.g., academically engaged, respectful, disruptive) or be customized to more closely align with the goal-oriented behaviors (Chafouleas et al., 2010).

Finally, the educator who has worked with the student through goal setting should establish periodic feedback sessions to discuss goal attainment with the student. These sessions should occur at least weekly, and the educator and student can review the student's journals or DBRs, grades, attendance, and other relevant data and discuss whether the student feels they are making improvements. If the student's classroom teacher is collecting concurrent DBRs (described next), then they can compare the teacher's data to how the student feels they are improving. Students who are demonstrating clear improvements might increase their goal criterion, or, write a new goal. Students who continue to struggle to make changes might benefit from adding self-monitoring.

Data Collection and Progress Monitoring

Across all Tier 2 interventions, the easiest and fastest way to monitor progress is to use data that are already collected within the intervention (see Chapter 3). CICO is a good example of this. Within the intervention a daily progress report (DPR) is used for student feedback and can also be used as progress monitoring data. Since stand-alone goal-setting interventions do not include any educator-collected intervention-based progress monitoring data, teachers could collect daily DBRs during the time frame specified in the goal statements. Teachers can collect DBRs using the three standard behaviors (e.g., academically engaged, respectful, disruptive) or include more specific behaviors written into the student's goal. Teachers should collect DBRs daily throughout intervention implementation.

Aside from the feedback sessions with the student, the PST should evaluate teacher DBR data at least weekly to determine whether the student is making adequate behavioral progress. Students who demonstrate continuous improvements can iteratively fade intervention components (e.g., increase goal criteria, eliminate feedback sessions, eliminate DBRs or journaling). Students who fail to improve with goal setting alone might benefit from increasing intervention intensity by adding self-monitoring.

SELF-MONITORING

Students who are unsuccessful with a stand-alone goal-setting intervention, or who have more intense self-regulatory needs, might benefit from a more intensive self-monitoring intervention. At Stocktown High School, the Tier 2 team decided that all students identified with a Tier 2 level need in hyperactivity or inattention on the SDQ would start with a goal-setting intervention. After two monthly data meetings reviewing progress, they noticed that four ninth graders were not making progress toward their classroom off-task behaviors. Based on this information, they asked the classroom teachers who reported the highest levels of off-task behaviors to join them during their next meeting. The discussion with the classroom teachers led to the team assigning self-monitoring during the most difficult time of day for the next month, until their next data meeting.

Self-monitoring as an intervention requires an individual to observe and record whether they are or have been engaging in a particular behavior at a given time. This intervention is slightly more intense than a goal-setting intervention because after the goal is set, a specific plan for monitoring discrete goal-oriented behaviors is designed, with or without student input, and then implemented by the student. Self-monitoring can take a variety of forms, ranging from completing simple checklists to implementing an interval-based prompting and recording system. The type of self-monitoring intervention implemented should relate to the student's specific strengths, self-regulation needs, and academic needs.

Checklists

A student who can maintain their attention to complete a single task, yet struggles with organizing and prioritizing their time, would benefit from maintaining a daily planner or checklist. In this case, the student would write out specific tasks assigned to them each day, rank the tasks from most to least important, and cross off each task when it is complete. This process can occur once per day or during each class period/academic subject, and can include adult feedback or reinforcement for completing tasks. However, many students referred to Tier 2 for self-regulatory issues need to improve maintaining attention and/or exhibit frequent impulsive and disruptive behaviors, and would benefit from an interval-based self-monitoring system described below.

Interval-Based Self-Monitoring

Interval-based self-monitoring is when an individual is repeatedly prompted to observe and record their behavior after a short amount of time has elapsed (i.e., less than 5 minutes) during a specific learning activity or time of day (i.e., overall self-monitoring session; see Figure 5.2).

This process requires the student to learn and practice self-awareness of their goal-oriented behaviors (i.e., what it looks and feels like to be on task) and to record their own data on how frequently they engage in these behaviors. In addition, interval-based self-monitoring can include "in the moment" self-monitoring in which students determine whether they are currently engaging in a behavior (e.g., asking themselves "Am I on task?"). In retrospective (i.e., reflective) self-monitoring, students determine whether they were engaging in the behavior across the previous interval (e.g., "Was I on task for the last 5 minutes?"; Bruhn & Wills, 2018). Further, these self-monitoring interventions can include feedback, reinforcement, or matching components. Since there are many options to consider when designing interval-based self-monitoring interventions, it is important that educators understand research-based recommendations related to designing or including various intervention components.

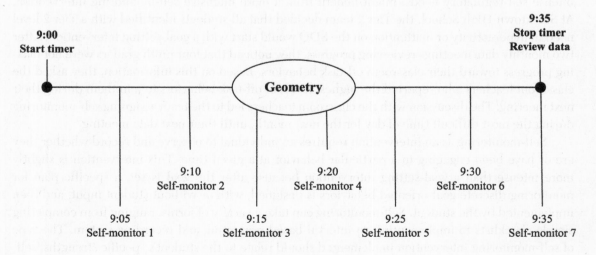

FIGURE 5.2. Example of a self-monitoring time line.

Implementing Interval-Based Self-Monitoring

Step 1: Identify Behavior to Monitor

First, educators should use the same behaviors written into their student's goals in the self-monitoring plan. However, the behavior should be rephrased as a question the student will ask themselves when prompted to self-monitor. For example, for a student whose goal behavior includes being safe around others, their self-monitoring behavior question could be "Have I been safe?," or phrased more specifically, "Have I kept my hands and feet to myself?" The level of specificity depends on how well the student understands general behavioral expectations, like those used in school or classwide expectations, or whether they would benefit from self-monitoring explicit example behaviors associated with each expectation. This can be determined through asking the student to define the expectations or through role playing. If the student struggles to define or demonstrate the individual behaviors associated with a general expectation like "be responsible," "be respectful," or "be safe," then their self-monitoring questions should be more explicit. To involve students in this component of designing self-monitoring interventions, the educator could ask the student, "What question could you ask yourself during class to determine whether you are being safe?," and help the student write an appropriately detailed question. Or, the educator could write out two behavior questions and have the student choose which one makes the most sense to them.

Step 2: Determine Recording Method

Educators can choose between technology-based or traditional paper-and-pencil self-monitoring implementation. This decision can be made based on available resources and student preference. Traditional paper-and-pencil self-monitoring will require a self-monitoring form and a cueing device. The form should include an operational definition of the behavior students will self-monitor, the self-monitoring question, and space for the student to record their self-monitoring data.

In addition, there are options for the response type, or how the student actually answers their self-monitoring question when prompted. Students can choose between a yes/no response type or a simple rating scale (e.g., 0, 1, 2, 3). Yes/no responses are well suited for in-the-moment self-monitoring (e.g., Am I on task?) and rating scales are appropriate for retrospective self-monitoring when students are averaging their behavior across an entire interval. If a student selects a rating scale, it is important to clearly define what each rating means within the context of the behavior the student is self-monitoring. For example, if a student is self-monitoring "Have I been working to the best of my ability?," then the rating scale could be defined as 0 = never, 1 = sometimes, 2 = often, and 3 = always. For younger students, they may prefer using a smiley face emoji and sad face emoji, or even colors (e.g., red, yellow, green). Next, the educator should clearly link examples and non-examples to each rating. That is, if the student is often on-task but rushes through their assignments, then they could rate themselves a 1 or a 2, but if they work slowly and carefully, then they might rate themselves a 3. Once the rating scale is clearly explained and defined, the educator should role-play different scenarios with the student. This will help the student link their behavior to each possible rating. Teachers can also complete concurrent ratings on the same schedule to use as a point of comparison or to help students more accurately rate their behavior.

Step 3: Program Cueing Method

Cueing device options include kitchen timers, smartphone applications, or a dedicated device called a MotivAider or GymBoss, and each of these options presents pros and cons for self-monitoring. Kitchen timers are low cost, however they must be reset after each interval and the audible chime may be distracting for some students. Smartphone applications require students to use their own smartphone in the classroom, which might violate some schools' cell-phone policies or be distracting. On the other hand, there are numerous applications available, free or paid, which can automatically reset after each interval has elapsed, and can provide customizable audible or tactile cues. Finally, the MotivAider and GymBoss are small electronic devices that can be clipped to a belt or placed in a pocket, provide a tactile vibration, and automatically reset when the interval has elapsed. These devices are easy to program and unobtrusive in use; however, costs range from $19.95 to $64.50 each.

Alternatively, technology-based self-monitoring can integrate cueing and recording responses within a single smartphone, tablet, or computer application, and two evidence-based options have recently emerged as viable options. First, MoBeGo (Bruhn et al., 2022) is a free iPad application allowing users to program and implement self-monitoring interventions for multiple students. This particular self-monitoring intervention includes both teacher and student self-monitoring, where teachers and students independently rate the student on a four-point scale on the extent to which the student engaged in classroom-appropriate behaviors (Figure 5.3). Additional features include fully customizable interval lengths and behaviors, real-time graphs of student response data, and automatically calculated goal recommendations based on student data.

The second free, evidence-based self-monitoring application, I-Connect (iconnect.ku.edu), is available across Android and Apple smartphones and tables as well as personal computers. I-Connect, similar to MoBeGo, includes customizable behaviors and interval lengths, and automatically graphs self-monitoring data. However, I-Connect utilizes a yes/no response type and does not include teacher ratings. Instead, teachers and other stakeholders can access student data using the I-Connect website and their username.

Step 4: Determine Interval and Session Length

The educator should determine when the student should implement the self-monitoring intervention (session) and how frequently the student should be prompted with the self-monitoring question (interval length). The self-monitoring session typically encompasses a single academic subject (e.g., reading, math, history), learning activity (e.g., whole-group instruction, independent work), or class period where the student exhibits the greatest challenges with self-regulation (e.g., low academic engagement, high rates of disruptive behavior). The overall duration of the session should be long enough for the student to self-monitor their behavior several times, typically ranging from 10 to 60 minutes. Research in interval-based self-monitoring has indicated that shorter intervals often result in faster improvements in student behavior, and experts recommend interval lengths of 5 minutes or less depending on the classroom context, session duration, and student need (Bruhn et al., 2022). That is, it may be unrealistic and overwhelming for a student to self-monitor every 30 seconds during a 60-minute reading block. Instead, the educator might select a portion of the reading block, like 15 minutes of independent practice, and ask the student to self-monitor every 3 minutes or so. Intervals can be variable (e.g., on average every 3 minutes) or fixed (e.g., exactly

Maria's Self-Monitoring Form

Behavior: <u>Be Responsible</u>

I will show <u>responsibility</u> during science by watching the teacher during demonstrations, working on my lab assignment during class, and cleaning up after myself. I am not showing responsibility when I use my phone inappropriately, chat with my friends, and leave a mess.

Interval: 5 minutes

0 = no, never   1 = rarely   2 = often   3 = yes, always

5:00 min	Have I been responsible?	0	1	2	3
10:00 min	Have I been responsible?	0	1	2	3
15:00 min	Have I been responsible?	0	1	2	3
20:00 min	Have I been responsible?	0	1	2	3

Tim's Self-Monitoring Form

Behavior: <u>Be Safe</u>

I will <u>be safe</u> when I keep my hands and feet to myself. I am not safe when I hit or touch my classmates.

Interval: 3 minutes

	Yes	**No**
Am I being safe?	👍	👎
Am I being safe?	👍	👎
Am I being safe?	👍	👎
Am I being safe?	👍	👎

FIGURE 5.3. Sample self-monitoring forms.

every 3 minutes). Moving from a fixed to variable interval schedule is one way to program for maintenance once a student is responding positively. See Figure 5.2 for a sample self-monitoring session divided into intervals.

Step 5: Establish Feedback and Contingent Reinforcement Procedures

The educator should determine whether they will include structured feedback and/or reinforcement, and if so, establish a clear plan for when and how to deliver feedback and reinforcement. Feedback can be corrective, affirmative, instructive, or be based on student accuracy of self-monitoring data and can be delivered after each interval or at the end of a self-monitoring session. Reinforcement can be contingent on reaching a predetermined goal, monitoring accurately (as compared to parallel teacher data), or for simply following the self-monitoring procedures accordingly. Selecting appropriate reinforcements is critical to their effectiveness. Options for selecting reinforcers include observing the student and noting any tangibles or activities they enjoy, providing the student with a survey, or simply asking them what they would like to earn when they reach their goal. Preparing multiple reinforcements (e.g., iPad time, snacks, extra credit) and providing a menu of options from which the student can choose can also increase reinforcement effectiveness

(Cannella-Malone et al., 2013). It is also important to remember that activities or items a student finds enjoyable might change over time, so periodically swapping out items on the menu can keep the student motivated longer. Regardless, it is important to know research has shown feedback and reinforcement can significantly enhance the effectiveness of self-monitoring interventions (Bruhn et al., 2022).

Step 6: Teach the Student to Self-Monitor

Finally, once all self-monitoring materials are prepared, the educator should teach the student how to self-monitor using explicit instruction techniques (e.g., model, lead, test; Archer & Hughes, 2011). This means the educator describes and models each of the behaviors the student will self-monitor and demonstrates how to use the self-monitoring technology or materials. Next, the educator should describe classroom scenarios where the student and educator can role-play examples and non-examples of the self-monitoring behavior and practice self-monitoring. Finally, the educator should describe another scenario or two and ask the student to self-monitor, to determine whether the student can self-monitor independently with 100% accuracy. The student should also understand the contingencies associated with earning reinforcements, meaning they know that they have to reach their daily or weekly goal to earn their prize.

Progress Monitoring

Finally, as with all Tier 2 interventions, the PST should continually monitor data to determine student response and any subsequent adaptations. Educators can monitor responsiveness using the student's self-monitoring data. However, educators must first verify that students can accurately observe and record their behaviors before relying on student data for progress monitoring purposes (Bruhn et al., 2020). That is, can the student self-monitor accurately? To answer this question, teachers should collect concurrent self-monitoring data using the same procedures that the student uses (e.g., MoBeGo), or collect daily DBRs. Next, the teacher should compare their data to the student's, and if the student can accurately self-monitor for several days in a row, then the teacher can reduce the frequency of collecting concurrent self-monitoring or progress report data to once per week. Then they can use the student's self-monitoring data for ongoing progress monitoring and data-based decision making. On the other hand, if the student cannot self-monitor accurately, even after reteaching behavioral definitions and additional role play, it is essential the teacher continues to collect their own intervention data to determine student responsiveness. Finally, teachers and educators should not be concerned with students who struggle to self-monitor accurately if the teacher data indicate that students are making progress.

Concurrent to monitoring behavior response data, educators should maintain a record of intervention decisions regarding the self-monitoring behavior, response type, interval length, and feedback and reinforcement (see Table 5.2).

This record will aid in monitoring implementation fidelity and provide options for systematically fading or intensifying intervention based on student response (Bruhn et al., 2020). Self-monitoring and fidelity data, as well as the record of adaptations, should be collected and stored on a secured shared server, so teachers and the PST can have easy access to monitor data. In addition, some technology-based self-monitoring applications, like I-Connect, have a web-portal where parents or other stakeholders can view self-monitoring data in real-time.

TABLE 5.2. Intervention Design Decisions

Date	Goal	Interval length	Feedback	Reinforcement	Response or nonresponse?
9/30	Be safe 95% of time	3 minutes	At the end of session	None	Response—goal met 3 consecutive days
10/7	Be safe 95% of time	5 minutes	At the end of session	None	Mixed—goal met 2/5 days
10/14	Be safe 95% of time	5 minutes	At the end of session	None	Response—goal met 4/5 days

SELF-GRAPHING

At Stocktown High School, the Tier 2 team was excited to see that out of the four students who received self-monitoring in one class period for the last month, three received positive reports from classroom teachers. Student self-monitoring data also highlighted increased time on-task. However, one student, Javon, did not respond well, and the team decided to try adding self-graphing. They knew that Javon loved working on his Chromebook doodling and creating art, so they worked with him to find a way that he could visually represent his graphed self-monitoring data.

The last strategy to improve student self-regulation and behavior is self-graphing, which involves students reviewing and graphing their behavioral data either electronically (e.g., Excel, Google Sheets) or with graph paper, and serves as a visual aid for feedback and self-evaluation. Researchers have suggested that visual representations of data can increase goal-oriented motivation (Covington, 2000). Student self-graphing also can reduce educator responsibility and increase the student's self-awareness (Briesch et al., 2019; Bruhn et al., 2016). The data students graph can include self-monitored behavioral data (e.g., percentage of time spent on task, number of questions asked), academic performance data (e.g., number of pages read, percentage of math problems correct), or other intervention-based measures (e.g., CICO points earned). In the context of self-regulation interventions, self-monitoring data are often graphed daily and compared to the student's behavioral goal (see Figures 5.1 and 5.3).

To implement the self-graphing component of self-regulation interventions, it is important for educators to first teach students how to consolidate their daily self-monitoring data into a single number. This could include summing the number of points earned or the number of "yeses" circled (see Figure 5.3), or calculating a percentage (e.g., total yeses divided by number of intervals, multiplied by 100). Then, educators and students together should determine whether the student should graph their data on paper or electronically. This could be based on student preference and fluency with technology, or available resources. Then, educators allow the student to design the look of their graph. This can include choosing between a line or bar graph, font type, and graph colors, and for paper graphs, students might choose between markers, crayons, or stickers to represent their data. Educators should teach the student how to either enter their data into their graphing software or how to accurately draw their data on graph paper. Younger students who do not yet possess the counting skills necessary for graphing could simply color in a predrawn bar graph. Figure 5.4 provides an example.

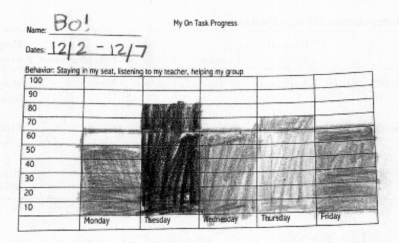

FIGURE 5.4. Example of self-graphing.

Once students know how to accurately graph their data, they should engage in self-graphing analysis daily and immediately following their self-monitoring session. This will provide an opportunity for them to self-evaluate their performance and determine whether they are on track for meeting their goals, the pace of their progress, and/or the direction of data. Educators can help with creating a goal or aim line, can help graph average progress over time, and can help evaluate the trend over time toward improvement or lack of improvement. Self-graphing sessions also provide an opportunity for educators to deliver corrective or affirmative feedback in close succession to the student's self-monitoring session, which is when feedback is most effective. Finally, self-evaluation sessions are also a natural opportunity to provide contingent reinforcement for students who reach their goal. Once students can independently and accurately self-graph their data, they may enjoy accessing their reinforcement independent of the educator. In addition, students might fade self-graphing sessions to every other day or once per week if they have met their goal criterion for several days in a row. It is also worth noting that although many technology-based self-monitoring applications automatically graph student data, students can still benefit from debriefing sessions with an educator where they observe and evaluate their data.

KEY CONSIDERATIONS

As the Tier 2 PST and educator determine the self-regulation strategy or combination of strategies to implement for each student, it is important to carefully document each intervention design decision and monitor implementation fidelity (see IPA example provided in Chapter 4). Given the many components, options, and flexibility across each intervention type, it may be helpful for educators to maintain a spreadsheet or table to track all initial decisions and subsequent adaptations (see Table 5.2).

As data-based adaptations are made, be sure to update any associated fidelity tracking tools. Intervention fidelity measures should include (1) fidelity of teaching students the self-regulation strategy, such as completing a self-observation checklist, and (2) implementation fidelity. Implementation fidelity typically involves the teacher or educator completing a checklist to verify that the student self-monitored throughout the entire session and that feedback or reinforcement was delivered according to the predetermined schedule. As a reminder, Chapter 11 presents seven areas of consideration for effective Tier 2 intervention. Many of these considerations are important to consider when designing and implementing self-regulation interventions.

RESOURCES

Table 5.3 provides resources related to self-regulation interventions.

TABLE 5.3. Resources

Estrapala, S., & Grieshaber, J. (2022). Putting the "Self" in self-regulation: Strategies for incorporating student voice in self-regulation interventions for internalizing behaviors. *Teaching Exceptional Children*, 1–9. https://doi.org/10.1177/00400599221097071

This article describes strategies for enhancing goal-setting, self-monitoring, and self-evaluation interventions with student voice.

https://selfdetermination.ku.edu

This website includes interventions, assessments, and research on self-determination, and explicitly focuses on goal-setting and attainment strategies for students and adults.

https://iris.peabody.vanderbilt.edu/module/ss2/cresource/q1/p08

This resource published by the IRIS Center includes sample self-monitoring forms and a table comparing applications of self-regulation strategies associated with study skills.

MoBeGo

Free, research-based self-monitoring application available for iPad.

I-Connect

Free, research-based self-monitoring application available for Apple and Android devices, Chromebooks, and desktop computers.

CASE EXAMPLE

Jordan was a seventh grader in Central Prairie Junior High School, which is part of a rural school district serving a predominantly White farming community in the Midwest. Jordan was friendly and outgoing, earned average grades, and was well-liked by his peers. However, his impulsivity and distractibility had significantly increased since transitioning from elementary to junior high school. Over a 2 month time period, Jordan's teachers became increasingly frustrated with his likeable yet distracting joking around during class, and he had received two ODRs for major classroom disruptions during math. Given Jordan's history of impulsivity, distractibility, and elevated scores on the hyperactivity/inattention subscale of the SDQ, the PST decided that Jordan would benefit from a goal-setting and self-monitoring intervention.

With the help of Mr. Johnson, a trusted adult educator, Jordan decided to write a behavioral goal to be more respectful during math class. He wrote, "During math, I will show respect by raising my hand to participate, staying on topic, and using materials appropriately at least 80% of the time every day." Since Jordan's impulsivity had escalated significantly in recent months, both he and Mr. Johnson agreed that an 80% criterion was appropriately challenging. Due to the limited available technology, Mr. Johnson suggested a traditional paper-and-pencil self-monitoring system using a MotivAider as a cueing method. The two then collaborated to write the self-monitoring question, "Have I been respectful?" along with a three-point rating scale, "0 = no, rarely; 1 = sometimes; 2 = yes, often." Since Jordan engaged in frequent disruptions, at least once every 5 minutes, Mr. Johnson recommended a 5-minute interval. After writing a self-monitoring form, Mr. Johnson and Jordan practiced self-monitoring respectful behavior until Jordan could accurately and independently rate his behavior. The next day, Jordan began self-monitoring during math, and his teacher concurrently completed daily DBRs on Jordan's academic engagement and disruptive behaviors. Mr. Johnson decided to complete daily DBRs instead of concurrent self-monitoring procedures because he felt they would be easier to complete than recording Jordan's behavior every 5 minutes.

After two weeks of daily self-monitoring during math class, Jordan's DBR on academic engagement data had increased dramatically while his DBR on disruptive behavior had declined, and he self-reported high rates of respectful behavior. Due to this sustained improvement, the PST recommended reducing the intensity of the self-monitoring intervention. Mr. Johnson suggested increasing the interval length from 5 to 7 minutes, while keeping the other components the same. The PST will review the DBR and self-monitoring data again in 2 weeks to determine if another adaptation should be made.

CONCLUSION

While inattentive and hyperactive behaviors are typically low intensity and do not create an unsafe classroom environment, they do tend to be frequent and disruptive to learning. These are also academic-related behaviors typically exhibited in the classroom during instruction. This chapter overviewed the signs of student needs in this area followed by detailed descriptions of how to implement goal setting, self-monitoring, and self-graphing as self-regulation strategies aimed at increasing the abilities of students to evaluate and regulate their own attention and activity.

CHAPTER 6

Evidence-Based Interventions for Social Issues

Did you thank your transit driver this morning? Did you hold the door for your colleague carrying an armful of science equipment when you walked in your school building? As humans, when we are around other people, we are constantly using social skills whether we realize it or not. We are also using those skills to prevent and solve social problems. This chapter outlines evidence-based interventions and those with promise that match to the social-problem-solving area of need.

CHAPTER FOCUS

- Understand the signs of social-problem-solving needs.
- Learn how to implement behavior contracts.
- Understand how to implement promising reactive strategies to process social conflict incidents.
- Learn how to implement social skills instruction.

Researching and supporting students' social problem solving has been a persistent challenge in education for decades (Walker et al., 2004). More recently, the field has begun to discuss "social–emotional learning" and the CASEL framework, which positions social skills within self-awareness, self-management, social awareness, relationship skills, and responsible decision making (Collaborative for Academic, Social, and Emotional Learning [CASEL], 2021) and closely ties social learning to emotion regulation. For the purpose of this book and the Tier 2 framework, social and emotional needs are two discrete intervention targets. "Social wellness" refers to how we relate to, and interact, with others, whereas "emotional wellness" refers to how we feel internally. Therefore, this chapter addresses all social needs as "social problem solving." Without fully addressing gaps in social skills and social problem solving, students understandably earn more ODRs, earn more removals from class and academic instruction, feel disengaged with school, and are placed at higher risk for school dropout.

Social-problem-solving skills are sometimes referred to as "soft" skills and are typically learned implicitly as we observe and interact with the people in our surroundings (Gresham et al., 2006). As babies and children practice social interaction, they are negatively or positively reinforced (the reaction of those around them can lead to the behavior occurring more or less often) and they experience the modeling (showing children what to do and not to do) of others around them (Cooper et al., 2020). In a more nuanced view of social skills, though, it is easy to see that social expectations change based on context, culture, and setting, and humans learn to navigate many different social situations across their lifespan. Numerous other variables may also impact social functioning, including personalities, underlying emotional or physical issues, experiences of trauma, or personal communication skills. In educational settings, social skills are often thought of as compliance toward adults and politeness toward adults and peers, but in reality, students use social skills to board the bus, order breakfast from nutrition staff, ask to use the restroom, negotiate disagreements on an academic project, assist a peer who is feeling down, and receive feedback from adults. Many social-problem-solving skills that students and adults use throughout the day go unnoticed and unrecognized. Instead, educators may focus on social-problem-solving skills that are missing, or students who may be interacting socially in a way that we perceive as negative, or against the norm.

You can think of social problem solving in schools as a large umbrella category set of skills having several subsets of skills that microlevel skills fit within, including communication skills, conflict resolution, and cooperation. In one subset are overall communication skills. This group includes basic communication such as saying "please" and "thank you," asking for help, and communicating basic needs. On a more advanced level, communication skills includes recognizing nonverbal cues like body language (e.g., posture, eye contact, smile), talking through rules of a game, and talking to friends about hurt feelings.

In another subset, conflict resolution skills, are basic skills such as respectfully disagreeing with peers or adults, deciding when to speak up and express feelings, and responding to criticism. More advanced skills within this category include acknowledging others' feelings, responding calmly when feelings are big, and knowing when to walk away from conflict.

And in the subset of cooperation skills, we include skills such as sportsmanship, listening to adults and peers, working to understand peers and younger children, and leadership. Getting to know the student will help the PST gain a better understanding of which skills the student needs to work on and under what conditions.

This area of intervention requires careful consideration as to whose social norms we are expecting students to practice, learn, and follow, and whether the "need" is one that points to a student who has not acquired an understanding of social norms in the school setting or whether the student requires supports to demonstrate appropriate social skills in particular settings (e.g., at football practice, in synagogue, at school). For instance, one classroom teacher may require students to make eye contact when they reply verbally to the teacher. Another teacher may require students to say "yes ma'am" or "no sir." Instead of these subjective definitions of "appropriate" social skill demonstration, schools may want to start with revisiting their Tier 1 schoolwide expectations and broadly define what basic social skills should look like when communicating in different contexts and with different people (e.g., teachers, peers, administrators). From there, the PST will have guidance that can help inform Tier 2 interventions in this area.

Most SEB screeners have a distinct category or subscale that reflects risk in social skills. Oftentimes, screeners will ask questions about social-problem-solving issues with younger children, same age peers, and older children or adults. It is important to note that some students may have broad, indiscriminate social-problem-solving needs (e.g., with any age or person) or specific social-problem-solving needs, such as peer conflict or sportsmanship. These nuances regarding whether the social skill need is specific to the school setting or more broad across multiple settings are important for the PST to understand when considering the path forward. These data can inform initial intervention adaptations and ongoing data-based decisions.

In addition to screeners, educators can also consider confirming a specific social-problem-solving need and better understanding the comprehensive social-problem-solving need with additional information. First, ODR data may reflect social-problem-solving needs. Students with minor infractions may have earned these for being disrespectful to teachers, using profanity toward peers, and major infractions for social-problem-solving issues such as fighting, bullying, or threatening students. However, it is also important to note that some social issues do not have obvious externalizing symptoms. Sometimes students with social-problem-solving needs have trouble making new friends (e.g., introducing themselves, communicating clearly), participating in group activities, or communicating clearly to adults and peers. Educators should consider teacher referral information as well as student and family referral to make the most appropriate intervention-matching decision. Families and educators may be able to help the team understand the contexts in which the student displays the skills well and those that they don't, identify areas of social-problem-solving strength, and expand on areas of need.

Taken together, the screening subscales; ODR data; and teacher, family, and student referral information can paint a comprehensive picture of what social-problem-solving skills a student may need. These will drive matching decisions and adaptations to Tier 2 social-problem-solving interventions. To illustrate this concept, consider Jason, a first-grade student at Buckton Elementary School. When the school year started, Jason's teacher observed him trying to make friends with his classmates, but Jason really struggled during unstructured play activities. For example, Jason's teacher saw him try to join ball games with classmates during recess, and instead of asking to join, he pushed his way in and took the ball from a peer. As a result, his classmates rejected his attempts to join and called him a bully. This became an unfortunate pattern of behavior during recess, and classwide sportsmanship lessons did not seem to help Jason. After completing schoolwide screening, Jason's teacher was notified that he was flagged for elevated risk for social skills problems and might benefit from a Tier 2 intervention. Upon receiving this information, Jason's teacher remembered the incident on the playground, reported it to the Tier 2 PST, and suggested that he might benefit from explicit social skills instruction for sportsmanship and making friends.

This chapter focuses on the targeted social-problem-solving needs of students at Tier 2. Specifically, three levels of interventions are described: behavior contracts, problem-solving activities, and explicit social skills instructional groups. These levels are organized by required time, resources, and intensity of intervention. See Table 6.1 for a comparison of various interventions. Resources, fit, core components, and implementation considerations will be described for each level within this category. Finally, we present a case example to highlight intervention in this area.

TABLE 6.1. Comparison across Interventions

	Behavior contract	Reactive problem-solving activities	Social skills instruction
Persons involved	Adult mentor Student	• ABC-GO administrator • Student mediation student leaders • Restorative circle leader and other students	Small-group leader Student
Materials needed	One worksheet individualized to student	• ABC-GO one worksheet • Student mediation—none • Restorative circle—none	Social skills curriculum
Feedback schedule	Regular review discussions and at end of contract period	• ABC-GO after ODR incident • Student mediation—after student incident • Restorative circle—after adult incident	During sessions, ongoing
Data tracked	Met contract criteria or did not meet contract criteria	• All—frequency of requiring the intervention	None, need additional data
Student grade level	3–12	• ABC-GO, K–2, 3–12 • Student mediation, 5–12 • Restorative circle, K–12	K–12, attend to grade level appropriateness of curriculum

For social issues, the least intensive intervention is behavior contracts, followed by problem-solving activities, and finally, social skills instruction. The varying levels of intensity of available social skills interventions highlight one of the reasons we do not use a "one size fits all" approach to Tier 2. If the only intervention educators have available is social skills instruction, while it would address all intervention components found in this category, it is also the most intensive, in terms of teacher time and student time away from academic instruction. Educators may want to start with a simpler strategy, such as behavior contracts to target the student's specific social-problem-solving need, then move to a more intensive intervention within this category if the student does not display adequate progress. We also bring your attention to considerations that are applicable to social problem solving that are discussed in more detail in Chapter 11. First, while students may have a need in one area of social problem solving—such as sportsmanship or authority—students typically also have an area of strength. Perhaps a student gets along well with younger children, or maybe they like to be helpful to a certain teacher. Make sure to celebrate and highlight any social circumstances that the student exceeds in, and note with whom, and under what conditions the student thrives socially. Second, sometimes social withdrawal can be related to a mental health need, so it is important to integrate across data-based problem solving and to team with the mental health supports available in your school. Finally, Chapter 11 also presents information related to adaptations or considerations for students in secondary schools. It is important to remember that peer relations are particularly important in secondary school settings. Peer pressure and peer approval can drive some outbursts, reactions, and poor choices.

BEHAVIOR CONTRACTS

The behavior contract is the least intensive intervention at Tier 2 for social problem solving. Sometimes called a "contingency contract," this simple, flexible intervention is a written agreement between two people (e.g., student, adult) that is used to specify a behavior that needs to occur and the reinforcement that will be delivered for that behavior (Cooper et al., 2020). At its core, the behavior contract addresses an underlying performance issue in which the student knows and understands expected social behaviors, but does not consistently perform them. This performance issue could be specific to one time of day, setting, or context, or it could occur across multiple contexts. Behavior contracts require an adult (or peer, if peer-mediated) to implement the intervention. This includes drafting the contract, checking in on progress toward the contract goal or area of need, and accountability when the contract time period has expired to evaluate whether the student met the contract goal. The mentor adult (or peer) should meet the same general implementer criteria previously discussed: have time and schedule availability to facilitate behavior contracts with at least one student, be skilled at building and maintaining relationships with students, and be willing to sustain the behavior contract intervention with the student for the necessary time that the student requires. In Lane et al.'s book *Managing Challenging Behaviors in Schools: Research-Based Strategies That Work* (2011), there is an entire chapter dedicated to the foundational and varied applications of behavior contracts. Below we describe a few of these. See Table 6.2 for a list of procedural steps for behavior contracts to improve social-problem-solving skills.

Behavior Contract Core Components

Before beginning a contract, it is important to consider if the student is at a developmental level that will enable them to understand the terms of the contract. For younger students or those with disabilities, it may be important to consider icons, graphics, or technology that will help facilitate understanding (Cooper et al., 2020). Figure 6.1 provides an example behavior contract. In the first step to developing a contract, the implementer needs to explicitly define the target social skill with

---

TABLE 6.2. Procedural Steps for Behavior Contract

Before intervention
1. Determine match for student
2. Create fillable template for contract
3. Match student with a mentor

Intervention
1. Student and mentor complete the contract together
2. Mentor checks in regularly to remind of contract
3. At the end of the contract period mentor and student meet to review progress

After intervention
1. Mentor provides contingent reinforcement
2. Administrator does a post-review with family
3. Mentor provides documentation of meeting/not meeting contract to Tier 2 team

---

Date _____

I, April, agree to handle conflicts during Language Arts with my peers in a calm way. I agree to speak kindly to my peers and express my feelings in a way that will help them understand why I am frustrated or feeling angry.

If I am kind to my peers during conflict in Language Arts class for four out of five days this week, February 7th–February 11th, my mentor, Mrs. James and I will spend one lunch period having lunch in her classroom next week rather than the cafeteria. If I am able to speak kindly during conflict for five out of five days, Mrs. James will bring me a sweet treat for our lunch in her classroom.

_____   _____
April Laad   Mrs. James

FIGURE 6.1. Example of a behavior contract.

which the student needs support. Since this category addresses social problem solving, the target skill could fall within any communication, basic interaction, or conflict resolution social skill, and should be focused on supporting the student in the school environment. While there may be numerous skills that the student could use support with, the behavior contract focuses on one skill at a time. The PST should have data that can help define the specific target skill, which should be shared with the behavior contract implementer.

Next, the mentor adult (or peer) needs to discuss this target skill with the student and teach the student what the new skill does and does not look like in their specific educational setting. This initial conversation should be brief but should provide the student with enough foundational understanding to know what is expected of them. At this time, the mentor will also want to provide a rationale to describe why this skill is important to the student (e.g., when we use good sportsmanship we will have more fun on the playground and make more friends). As with all Tier 2 skills, the student needs both to understand why this particular skill is important and to find it personally valuable to them in order to work toward improving in that area. It is also helpful to tie the skill back to the Tier 1 expectations. For instance, how does sportsmanship reflect the Tier 1 expectation of "Be Respectful"?

Third, the student and the mentor should together draft the contract goal or criteria with a mutually agreed upon and achievable skill level (e.g., 4 days out of 5), time line (e.g., 1 week), and contingent reinforcement. This second session may take longer than the first but it is important to truly co-create the behavior contract, rather than try to save time by drafting the contract yourself and present it to the student. Remember, Tier 2 intervention needs to be done "with" the student, rather than "to" the student. If the mentor already surveyed the student for preferences, motivations, and interests, they may already have an idea of what the student would be willing to work toward or for (e.g., extra free time, positive phone call home). The contingent reinforcement (what they receive when they meet their contract) can be tangible (e.g., trinkets, stickers) or intangible (e.g., praise, choice of activity). Some behavior contracts also include a "bonus clause," where the student can earn something extra special if they exceed the terms of the contract.

Fourth, after the mentor and student agree on the final version of the behavior contract and sign the official document, they may choose to have periodic check-ins regarding progress, but the next core component is assessing whether the student met the terms of the contract goal after the contract term has expired. Because the behavior contract is intended to be an efficient, simple strategy, the mentor does not need to track direct observation data to evaluate whether the student met the contract or not. The contract (e.g., time line, behavior, criteria) can be informally evaluated and discussed with the student, and the student can even help to self-evaluate whether the criterion specified in the contract was met. If the mentor and student agree that the contract was met, the student should receive the contingent reinforcement that was written into the contract in a timely manner (e.g., same day). If the student did not meet the contract, they can discuss reasons for this, problem-solve any setbacks, and edit the contract or draft a new contract. It is important to note that with all Tier 2 interventions, the goals are not set as "gotchas" to make it difficult for students to meet expectations. Indeed, the goal criteria should be set to an attainable standard where the student is regularly able to receive contingent reinforcement and build behavioral momentum. If the criteria are too high, it will discourage the student from making efforts to improve and meet their goal, decrease the likelihood they will continue to participate with the mentor, and possibly erode the student–mentor relationship.

There are a few important issues to consider when using behavior contracts. First, it is important to evaluate these four core components for fidelity of implementation, as addressed in Chapter 4. One easy strategy for assessing fidelity of implementation is to review permanent products (i.e., completed documents). The PST could request to review all behavior contracts that have been drafted and completed to determine whether the student has had the opportunity to benefit from the intervention, and that all contracts include the required components (e.g., skill targeted, contract expiration date, contingent reinforcement, signatures). Remember, if a student does not have completed behavior contracts (contract was developed fully, follow-up throughout the contract time was made, accountability at the end of the contract was completed), they have not had the opportunity to benefit from this intervention, and therefore, any changes in the student's social skills cannot be attributed to the behavior contract intervention. Similarly, whether the student met the contract (and even bonus clause) can be used as progress monitoring data for the monthly PST data meetings. The PST can request a record of "yes" or "no" instances where a student met a daily, or weekly behavior contract and the "yes" contracts can be coded as a 1 and "no" coded as a 0, which can be graphed and analyzed visually over time.

PROBLEM-SOLVING ACTIVITIES WITH AN EMERGING EVIDENCE BASE

The next level of Tier 2 social-problem-solving activities is flexible, each with an emerging base of evidence. While none of these strategies have extensive, rigorous, replicated research, they do offer potential promise for application as Tier 2 interventions to improve social-problem-solving skills and respond to a social-problem-solving incident or error. This category is the only one in the entire Tier 2 framework that requires a problem to have happened first, before the student has access to an intervention. All of the other described interventions in this book can be used proactively and preventatively, rather than reactively. The reason these interventions are considered "reactive" is that they occur after a specific event and help students to process and better understand the incident that occurred that had a foundational social skill problem. These interventions match to a skill gap for emerging social problems where the student may not have the skills to handle that problem appropriately. These interventions require students to reflect on the initial situation, behaviors chosen, and consequences of choices, and then develop a plan to repair the social relationship and make a better choice the next time the same situation arises. The interventions are flexible enough to match to peer-to-peer issues or student-to-adult issues. It is also critical to note that these interventions should not be used as a deterrent or punishment, but should be therapeutic, instructional, and restorative.

If your code of conduct also requires a consequence such as suspension or a phone call home, you can pair that consequence with one of the instructional problem-solving activities. This may help the student understand the situation, the choice they made, the potential reasons why, and help to repair the social harm that may have resulted from the incident. These activities can be a more effective, instructional use of time spent in the office for a referral, in-school suspension, or detention; time that may otherwise be spent in nonrelated activities (e.g., drawing or sleeping) or even unwanted activities (e.g., arguing with an administrator, leaving the assigned area). It is also important to note that, like behavior contracts, problem-solving activities should be tied back to schoolwide, Tier 1 expectations (e.g., respectful, solve problems peacefully, assume best intentions) so the student understands the social problem and its solution in the broader context of the school-wide expectations. It may also be helpful to consider how an intervention can be peer-mediated, specifically for adolescent students, who typically respond better to peer feedback and peer suggestions. In some cases, it may be more efficient and effective to develop a peer mediation process for managing the instructional component of social-related incidents, particularly if the incident was a peer-to-peer social incident.

All problem-solving activities must include the same four core components, in which students should:

1. understand the context and environment in which the incident occurred
2. understand the choice that was made and reasons why the choice was made
3. understand the consequences or reactions to the incident
4. repair harm and make a different plan for the same context or situation in the future.

Below, we describe three examples of problem-solving activities using the four core components. The most explicit example of this is the Antecedent-Behavior-Consequence graphic organizer (ABC-GO; McDaniel & Flower, 2015).

ABC-GO

Figure 6.2 provides one example of the ABC-GO. A student who needs to process a negative social incident would fill out one of these independently, in reflection, and discuss this information with an administrator, classroom teacher, or trusted adult. During reflection, the student focuses on what was happening before the incident, naming the reaction or behavior choice they made, and what consequences happened as a result. The student then fills out the reflective, reparative section on what they should do next time given the same antecedent, and makes a plan to apologize to anyone they have harmed. See Table 6.3 for procedural steps to implement the ABC-GO.

For younger children, we would use the same process, but with picture representations that match typical antecedents, behaviors, and consequences for that age group and context. On the back of the form, students could draw a picture of themselves doing the correct behavior as the repair. One powerful aspect of this intervention is being able to look across time at multiple ABC-GO worksheets to help a student see a pattern to their behavior. Consider Maria, for example, who was matched to receive an ABC-GO worksheet if she was sent to the office after not following her

---

ABC Graphic Organizer

Name: _____

What was happening around me:

What I chose to do and why:

What happened as a result of my choices:

Who I need to apologize to:

What I plan to do differently next time in the same situation:

FIGURE 6.2. ABC graphic organizer.

TABLE 6.3. Procedural Steps for ABC-GO

Before intervention
1. Determine match for student
2. Print copies of ABC-GO
3. Notify administrator of intervention need

Ongoing during intervention
1. Student receives ODR and administrator provides ABC-GO
2. After completion, administrator and student meet to review current ABC-GO
3. Administrator and student review any previous ABC-GOs to determine if there is a pattern
4. Administrator and student discuss a repair plan and enact the plan

Ongoing after intervention
1. Administrator does a postreview with teacher who referred
2. Administrator does a postreview with family
3. Administrator provides documentation that ABC-GO was needed

behavior contract. In the spring semester, she had three ABC-GO worksheets in the administrator, Mrs. Garcia's, office. On her fourth visit for a similar issue, yelling at and threatening peers, Mrs. Garcia and Maria reviewed the past three worksheets. Together, they noticed that all of the forms were in the morning right before lunchtime. Maria wondered if she was having "bad" mornings those days. Mrs. Garcia also noted that each of the incidents had the same target behavior, threatening peers. In each of the four incidents, Maria was upset by peer behavior. Instead of staying calm and clearly describing why she was upset, she shouted inappropriate language at the peer in an effort to make them stop doing what was upsetting her. When the peer did not stop their behavior, Maria began making verbal threats. Together, Mrs. Garcia and Maria also noted that each time this happened, Maria was removed from that peer and sent to the office, and Maria described this as a good break from the situation. Maria also noted that she did not like other consequences of her behavior, like having her family called, two in-school suspensions, and being grounded from using her phone at home. Mrs. Garcia described that responding calmly can still allow Maria to get a break from the situation while also avoiding the negative consequences for shouting and cursing at her peers. Together they were able to make a plan and practice calm responses for the next time a peer upset her. They were also able to script a brief apology for the student she most recently threatened.

The ABC-GO matches very well with social-problem-solving issues that often lead to ODRs. If you have other reactive problem-solving strategies and interventions available in your school, you can assign those in this category as other options or in place of the ABC-GO. Other examples include restorative discipline/practice circles and peer mediation panels that facilitate peer-to-peer conflict resolution, described below. It is important to remember these have emerging and promising evidence but are not yet considered evidence-based. Thus, we cautiously include them in this book as promising intervention options to explore.

Student-Led Peer Mediation

Peer mediation should look different based on the ages and grades of the students you serve. This intervention may be best suited for upper elementary through high school and would require differing levels of faculty/staff support depending on the egregiousness of the incident and the ages of the students involved. It is also important to note that peer-mediated interventions could assist with processing difficult peer-related social incidents. However, the peer should not be used as a substitute for working with trained school counselors or administrators to process complex or harmful social incidents such as bullying and fighting. This intervention is matched better to low-intensity incidents such as peer disagreements, students who are teased or don't feel included, and minor academic-related violations such as cheating or not participating in group work. Finally, it is very important to understand that peer mediation panels require adult oversight and training of the peer mediators to handle mediation and conflict in appropriate ways. For example, at Briarwood Middle School, all students learn about the possibility of serving on the Briarwood Student Leadership Panel during their service day. The students who are interested put together an application to submit by November 1. The grade-level teachers choose 10 students from the applicant pool per grade level to form the panel. The student panel is trained and one grade-level teacher leads the monthly meetings. During their student-led panel, any student who has had a peer-involved incident can notify the leader of the panel and request to meet with the panel. Together, they go through the incident and develop possible next steps. The leader follows up with the focus student and reports progress to the Tier 2 team.

The peer mediation panel should be guided by the schoolwide expectations and should be recognized for their contributions and support for other students. A peer mediation panel needs to follow predetermined procedures around four essential components while adapting for the local context for issues such as size of panel and characteristics of students who should serve: (1) choosing students for peer mediation leadership, (2) training peer mediators, (3) scheduling and organizing the peer mediation process, and (4) monitoring peer mediation effectiveness.

Once the aforementioned pre-panel logistics have been determined, the panel is ready to respond when an incident occurs. The student(s) involved in the incident are referred to the peer mediation panel, which follows the same four basic core components in the social-problem-solving category: (1) the student and the panel will discuss the environment of the incident and events leading up to the incident; (2) they will discuss the choice that the student made, reactions from other students, and subsequent additional choices that student made; (3) the panel and the student will discuss what happened as a result of the incident, including harm done to social relationships; and (4) the group will discuss what actions can be taken to repair the harm done and plan for the future. Hopefully the peer mediation panel can make independent judgments, engage in thoughtful discussion, and come to an appropriate conclusion, without much assistance from the faculty oversight advisor. While this description is appropriate for peer-to-peer conflict, it is possible to adapt the peer mediation process to include student–adult conflict and bring in teachers or other adults in the building who were involved in the incident and experienced harm. These conversations would be more delicate and require advanced skill levels and maturity. One exciting benefit of peer mediation as an intervention is that it promotes leadership and communication skills in the students serving on the panel, and is a better contextual and age-appropriate fit for the target student, which more closely resembles conflict resolution in postK–12 life. Educators can explore peer mediation guides to learn more about the process. Table 6.4 provides implementation steps to using peer mediation group as a problem-solving activity for peer-related social issues.

Adult-Led Restorative Justice Conversations

According to the Restorative Justice Exchange (*https://restorativejustice.org/what-is-restorative-justice*), restorative justice has three primary components: encounter, repair, and transform. In this intervention, the negative encounter, or incident, leads to processing the event and repairing

---

TABLE 6.4. Procedural Steps for Student Mediation

Before intervention
1. Determine match for student
2. Create and train student mediation panel
3. Notify student of mediation scheduled session

Intervention
1. Student meets with mediation panel to discuss incident
2. Mediation panel reflects what they heard and offers perspective
3. Student comes to agreement with panel of next steps

After intervention
1. Student enacts plan
2. Administrator is notified of the plan
3. Administrator notifies Tier 2 team of effectiveness

---

the relationship, which can transform the individuals involved, their relationship, and communities. Restorative justice conversations, or circles, are typically facilitated in schools by an adult. These restorative circles, which are reactive in nature, are conducted to process an incident with all individuals involved, whether they are adults or peers, and with the person who has been referred to Tier 2 for supporting social skill development. Restorative circles are a great match for students needing Tier 2 support who have social-problem-solving incidents with adults. The circle addresses the incident as a reflection, allows both the student and the educator to express their perceptions and feelings, and allows them to come to a potential solution and repair the relationship. Without a process like this, teacher–student relationships can be harmed in one incident or over time due to lack of communication, punitive responses only, and failing to repair the relationship. The circle uses the same four components described in this category of intervention: (1) the group discusses the context and environment in which the incident occurred; (2) the target student describes the choice that was made and reasons why the choice was made; (3) the target student describes the consequences or reactions to the incident; and (4) the group discusses repairs for harm done, expresses feelings, and together makes a different plan for the same context or situation in the future. These restorative conversations can happen in addition to regular, frequent proactive community circles in homeroom, other classrooms, or without the proactive community circles as only responsive circles to process social incidents that have occurred. Restorative justice practitioners recommend having a foundation of positive, proactive circles to help build foundational relationships and foster communication, which may decrease the need for additional restorative circles to process negative social incidents.

Whether using the ABC-GO, peer mediation panels, or restorative justice circles, it is important to revisit the idea of using data to evaluate fidelity, monitor student progress, fade intervention, and intensify intervention. In this level of intervention, there are no intervention-included data to use, so we recommend adding something such as the Direct Behavior Rating (DBR; Chafouleas et al., 2009) to gather weekly feedback related to social-problem-solving behaviors. The standard behaviors on the DBR are academically engaged, respectful, and disruptive. However, those behaviors may be customized or adapted depending on the behaviors targeted for change.

TABLE 6.5. Procedural Steps for Restorative Circle

Before intervention
1. Determine match for student
2. Create and train adult to lead restorative circle
3. Notify student of circle scheduled time

Intervention
1. Student meets with restorative circle to describe the event
2. Circle reflects what they heard and offers perspective
3. Adult and student come to agreement of next steps to repair and prevent the incident from occurring in the future

After intervention
1. Student enacts plan
2. Administrator is notified of the plan
3. Administrator or circle leader notifies Tier 2 team of effectiveness

Facilitator's Name: _____ Date of Observation: _____

Circle Participants: _____

Core component	Observation rating score (0= not at all, 1= partially in place, 2= fully in place)
Group discussion of the context and environment in which the incident occurred was held.	
The target student described the choice that was made and reasons why the choice was made.	
The target student described the consequences or reactions to the incident.	
Group discussion to repair harm, express feelings, and to make a different plan for the same context or situation in the future was facilitated.	
Total Score	/8 (Goal of 6)

FIGURE 6.3. Restorative Circle Fidelity Checklist.

It may be difficult to add an assessment to existing intervention procedures, but you will find that these data are critical to making fading, intensifying, and adaptation decisions. You may want to keep a running record of the number of sessions for peer mediation, restorative circles, and examine the permanent products of the ABC-GOs to determine fidelity of implementation quantity. To measure implementation quality, someone would need to observe a student processing an incident with either the ABC-GO, a peer mediation panel, or a restorative circle and assess whether the four core components were used. Table 6.5 provides a list of procedural steps to using restorative circles for social problem solving within Tier 2. A simple observational fidelity checklist may look like the one in Figure 6.3.

SOCIAL SKILLS TRAINING/INSTRUCTION

The most intensive level of intervention within the problem-solving category is social skills training, or social skills instruction. We start with a description of the varying instructional goals of social skills training programs, then describe social skills training procedures, and provide examples and special considerations.

There are two basic types of social skills issues addressed within social skills training programs: skill and performance. Students who do not understand the basic steps to displaying prosocial behavior have acquisition issues, and they will require explicit instruction to learn these skills. Explicit social skills instruction is typically saved for when the team determines that the student needs basic knowledge of the skill, including what it does and does not look like, and structured practice with feedback. In other words, when all the data available for the Tier 2 PST indicate that the student has never—or very rarely—been observed using contextually appropriate social skills, the student should be matched to an explicit social skills instruction intervention. Performance issues occur when the student understands what the correct social behavior is and how to display it, but does not do so in the educational context, or the social skills displayed in the educational context do not match the expectations of that context. In this case, students require more prompting, repetition, feedback, and reinforcement to increase the fluency and accuracy of using the skill, and a way to process the differences in expectation when they navigate across multiple social settings (e.g., after school with their friends, in the mosque, at tennis practice, and during the school day).

Social skills instruction is saved for the most serious social-problem-solving needs, in part because of the time and resources it requires, and because of the nature of filling in acquisition gaps and promoting performance practice. Social skills training requires time from a teacher, counselor, social worker, or other caring adult that is above and beyond the requirement for the less intensive social skills interventions described above. The implementer needs to manage the logistics of determining who should be grouped together (and who should not be in a group together), scheduling groups, and planning the frequency and duration of lessons. If the implementer is teaching social skills to a small group within a classroom they may need to work with the classroom teacher to ensure an alternative activity is available for students not participating in the group. The implementer also needs to know the curriculum or develop their own curriculum (though this is not recommended given the time and energy required). Materials may need to be purchased. And, the team needs to prioritize which social skills each student or group of students needs. Social skills instruction typically does not have to begin with the first lesson and continue linearly through every lesson in the curricula. The implementer can, instead, locate specific lessons that the group or individual student needs, and teach or reteach only those lessons that apply to the specific social need (e.g., McDaniel et al., 2018). This brings us back to the point made in the beginning of this chapter about understanding within which social context or with which person the student has a social-problem-solving need. Remember, some social-problem-solving needs are similar regardless of who is involved, while some are more specific to personal issues related to adult authority or same age peers.

Social skills instruction also requires students to be removed from their peers and other school activities. This may mean time out of the classroom and missed instruction, or time in social skills class rather than in art class, physical education, or recess. We want to limit how much time students miss instruction in any class, so creative solutions like "lunch bunch," where students can meet in small groups over lunch, are helpful. We also want to be sure to limit any labeling or stigma that might come from being pulled out of class. Being sensitive to how this is presented to the focus student and also how it is perceived by their peers is important. In particular, for students already needing social skills supports, we want to be sure to create a supportive classroom environment where they feel safe and included.

To illustrate how to be sensitive and supportive to student needs, we will consider how at Mayweather Elementary School, Mr. Carter, the school counselor, creates topical social skills groups with students in the same grade level. Throughout the week he meets with groups of no more than eight students at a time, sometimes reteaching the students in individual follow-up sessions. His group topics vary from sportsmanship with seventh-grade athletes to solving conflict peacefully with sixth-grade girls. He uses a social skills curriculum that the special education teacher had in her classroom, and he pulls lessons or units that might match the needs of various topical groups. He also surveys individuals to determine what social skills students self-identify as an area of need. Mr. Carter generally holds sessions for 45 minutes, and sometimes he holds 20-minute sessions over lunch with certain groups. On the last day of each month, he pulls session summaries and participation information for the Tier 2 team. In addition, the PST reviews individual checklists completed by the student's homeroom teacher, which are completed daily and specific to the skills each student is working on. Since beginning these social skills groups, the PST has found that the groups reduce reactive procedures that occur during school, particularly when the groups of students have similar challenges during the school day.

Social Skills Curricula and Core Components

You can find many examples of evidence-based, age-appropriate social skills curricula that are already created and include fidelity checklists of their core components. Table 6.6 provides a list of procedural steps to implementing social skills training as a Tier 2 social-problem-solving intervention.

The PST will consider dosage in their intervention plan. Dosage is the number of sessions that will be completed, and/or the length of each session in which the student will participate. If the lesson is a small-group reteaching lesson of a skill covered in a classroomwide social skills lesson, it could be as short as 20 minutes. However, if it is a new, full lesson with a small group, it could take up to an hour. Similarly, if a student has a very specific social skill need, such as improving sportsmanship, they may require as few as four lessons, and if their need is more broad to context, skill, and people, they may require a full curriculum, which can be upward of 25 weekly lessons. As a team, the PST should be making a recommendation about how often (and on what skills) the instruction should be delivered. This will mean deciding minutes per session, sessions per week, and number of expected weeks. It is important to group students by the type of skills they all need to work on, common issues, similar age, and sometimes by gender, similar to the "near-peer" mentoring match.

TABLE 6.6. Procedural Steps for Social Skills

Before intervention
1. Determine match for student
2. Ensure materials and training are available
3. Schedule small groups by similar needs

Intervention
1. Students meet with group leader to review new skills, the rationale, examples, non-examples weekly
2. Together as a group, role-play with feedback from leader
3. Repeat weekly for all necessary skills

After intervention
1. Student is observed using new skills, and generalized to all settings
2. Maintenance of new skills is documented
3. Small-group leader notifies Tier 2 team of progress

If your school already has a social skills curriculum, you can use what you have (assuming there is evidence to support its use in producing positive outcomes). Oftentimes special education classroom teachers or specialists have curriculum that can be loaned out. Some lessons are available for free online, and you can always create your own, as long as you include the core components of effective social skills instruction: (1) make sure the lessons you use are appropriate for the correct developmental level, and (2) make sure that the program follows evidence-based criteria of "teach, model, practice." In a recent book, McDaniel, Scott, and Zaheer (2018) described the eight components of effective social skills instruction that fall within the teach, model, and practice guideposts. First, it is important to explicitly define the new skill. Second, that new skill should be broken down into teachable steps that build up to effectively performing that new skill to mastery. Third, you need to select examples that are a contextual and cultural fit for your school setting and the individual student. Fourth, you should order the skills and examples in a way that when presented, will support the student first in learning the basics and then in being able to demonstrate advanced levels and across multiple settings. Fifth, you should engage students during instruction with plenty of opportunities to respond in a format that meets their preferences. Sixth, it is important to provide explicit and timely feedback and praise during lessons. Seventh, students need support in using these skills throughout the day to encourage mastery and maintenance. Lastly, you should encourage generalization by looking for and encouraging the new skill to be demonstrated by the student across all settings and times of day.

Like other interventions in this category, most social skills training programs do not include an intervention-linked method to evaluate progress toward mastery, though some do provide assessments aligned with the intervention program (e.g., Social Skills Improvement System). While some may ask the classroom teacher to rate the use of social skills on a weekly or daily basis, this is not standard in most curricula. Therefore, like the other social-problem-solving interventions (e.g., restorative practices), you would need to ask the classroom teacher(s) to complete a weekly evaluation of student progress on something such as the DBR scale, which can be easily completed weekly within 1–3 minutes per student requiring this level of support. Or, you could simply mark each time the student displays a target social skill during a 20-min observation period, a few times a week. These data can be used to determine whether the social skills intervention is producing positive results or the student is not responding favorably. If the student is responding in a positive way, the team may decide to slowly fade the number of lessons that will be provided, or the number of minutes per lesson. Similarly, if a student is not demonstrating adequate progress, the team may decide to add lessons, lengthen lessons, or even provide individual, one-on-one lessons rather than lessons in the small group. Figure 6.4 provides an example of a social skills progress monitoring checklist that can be individualized to each student.

Data are also needed to evaluate the fidelity of implementation for social skills lessons. Keeping a record of the number of instructional minutes and the lessons covered will give the team an idea of what level of dosage the student received. However, this will not provide data on the quality of the lessons, or the level of participation and attention from the student. For this, the implementer may complete a self-assessment after each lesson, or an outside observer may watch a lesson periodically and complete a checklist. In Figure 6.5 you will find an example of a lesson log and an example of a fidelity evaluation. This measures dosage. In Figure 6.6 you will find a quality of implementation checklist.

Skill	Frequency count (record a tally mark each time you see this skill)
Appropriate voice volume	
Appropriate taking turns while talking	
Inappropriate communication error	

FIGURE 6.4. Recording Form.

Lesson	Lesson title	Objectives	Date taught	Length of lesson (in minutes)	In place	Partially in place	Not in place
1	Formulating Classroom Rules	To formulate a specific set of classroom rules	9/20	20 minutes	X		
2	PATHS Kid for Today: Complimenting	To explain self-respect and respect for others	10/23	20 minutes	X		
3	Cooperative Learning Skills	To learn to effectively work together cooperatively	11/5	20 minutes	X		
4	The Golden Rule	To learn to treat others with respect at all times	11/12	20 minutes	X		
5	Listening to Others	To learn to remain engaged and be thoughtful of others	11/19	20 minutes	X		
6	Self-Control I: Control Signal powers	Self-assessment Self-control Self-monitoring	12/3	20 minutes	X		
7	Self-Control II: Solving problems in groups	Conflict resolution: Getting in touch with emotions and purpose	12/10	20 minutes	X		
8	Self-Control III: Thinking ahead	Creating a plan Focus on making better choices Best actions	12/17	20 minutes	X		
9	Problem-Solving Meeting	Self-correction Self-awareness	1/7	20 minutes		x	
10	Introduction to feelings	Emotional wellness/positive responses	1/15	20 minutes		x	

FIGURE 6.5. Example of a Lesson Plan Sequence and Checklist.

Skill	Self-rated fidelity score (circle one)		
1. All students in the identified group attended our session.	In place	Partially in place	Not in place
2. I explicitly define the expected social skill.	In place	Partially in place	Not in place
3. I taught the smaller steps.	In place	Partially in place	Not in place
4. I provided a rationale.	In place	Partially in place	Not in place
5. I gave relative examples and non-examples.	In place	Partially in place	Not in place
6. Instruction was engaging and each student had numerous opportunities to respond and participate.	In place	Partially in place	Not in place
7. I provided constructive corrective feedback, praise, and practice opportunities.	In place	Partially in place	Not in place
8. I promoted the use of this new skill throughout the school day by discussing various contexts, time of day, and setting expectations.	In place	Partially in place	Not in place

FIGURE 6.6. Social Skill Fidelity Checklist.

RESOURCES

Table 6.7 provides resources related to interventions for social issues.

TABLE 6.7. Resources

www.pbis.org/video/social-skills-instruction-at-tier-2-sctg-webinar
This 53-minute webinar presents you with information from the National Technical Assistance Center on PBIS regarding implementing social skills instruction within Tier 2.

www.rand.org/pubs/research_reports/RRA1822-1.html
This publication describes CASEL's social–emotional learning initiative and the impacts within participating schools and districts.

www.cde.state.co.us/cdesped/ta_socialskills
This brief fact sheet from the Colorado State Department of Education outlines key information for practitioners wanting to implement social skills instruction.

ies.ed.gov/ncee/wwc/Docs/InterventionReports/wwc_socialskills_020513.pdf
This What Works Clearinghouse document overviews findings from numerous social skills studies and provides excellent summative information regarding various curricula.

CASE EXAMPLE

The Maxwell School of Science and Engineering is a secondary academy in the Pacific Northwest that serves predominantly indigenous students on the native land of the Nez Perce tribe. This moderately sized secondary school is the home school of Nellie, a 15-year-old interested in water and climate issues. Nellie is also a school athlete, who plays basketball and soccer. Recently, Nellie has been referred to the PST for the first time in her school career due to issues with demonstrating kindness to all peers. Nellie has been observed picking on younger students at the multi-age school, saying derogatory things to peers on the bus, and using inappropriate language with classroom teachers when corrected in front of peers. The PST reviewed screening data and teacher incident reports and decided to implement the peer mediation team process available at the Maxwell School for any incidents involving peers that may occur, and their restorative justice consultation discussions for issues that might arise with teachers. In the first month of this plan, Nellie went to the peer mediation team three times. Two of these times Nellie was referred there by a teacher who witnessed incidents of inappropriate language toward peers. One time Nellie brought a peer to the team who reportedly had been leaving mean notes. Each of these three times, the peer mediation team was able to assist Nellie and the other involved students to reach an understanding and resolve the conflict. Nellie had one meeting with the restorative justice team and the algebra teacher, which was also resolved and the two decided to have a weekly check-in to repair their miscommunication and lack of knowing each other well. During the next PST monthly meeting, the team was able to review the records of these sessions to make sure that they took place. They also received DBR scores from the language arts teacher reflecting weekly progress. Because Nellie's behavior had drastically improved, they decided to stick with the interventions they had assigned and review progress the next month. That month, even with exams and stress from basketball, Nellie continued to make progress with zero office discipline referrals in the past month. This progress was communicated back to the home each month and to Nellie's other teachers. The PST decided not to remove any of these supports fully, and to instead shift to weekly check-ins with one peer from the peer mediation team and the algebra teacher as a fading procedure where Nellie could maintain these relationships.

CONCLUSION

Social conflict is unavoidable. Educators who address social-problem-solving areas of need not only address conflict within the school day, but empower the student with skills to use in other settings in the future, and really, for a lifetime. This chapter detailed signs of social-problem-solving areas of need, whether they be with peer conflict, adult or authority conflict, or indiscriminate social-problem-solving signs. Also, this chapter highlighted how to implement behavior contracts. This was followed by a description of promising strategies for responding to social conflict incidents, and teaching students how to process and repair those incidents—peer mediation and restorative justice conversations. Finally, this chapter detailed the well-known social skills instruction interventions for Tier 2 application. Remember to carefully consider the information presented in Chapter 11 regarding critical components to successful and effective intervention at Tier 2.

CHAPTER 7

Evidence-Based Interventions for Emotional Issues

Gerta Bardhoshi

Emotional needs that exist internally, rather than being expressed externally such as conduct needs, tend to go undetected and, thus, are underserved in schools. In this chapter, we discuss how these needs manifest behaviorally, the impact they have on students, and how to effectively intervene based on specific symptoms.

CHAPTER FOCUS

- Understand how emotional symptoms may "look" and affect students.
- Learn about three different interventions for addressing varying emotional needs.
- Understand additional assessment is needed to determine which intervention is likely to be the best fit for addressing the emotional symptoms.

EMOTIONAL SYMPTOMS

When you imagine a student struggling with emotional concerns such as anxiousness or sadness, what are some of the first behaviors that come to mind? Perhaps you have recently encountered such a student and noticed some associated behavioral markers like limited participation in class-

---

Gerta Bardhoshi, PhD, is Professor of School Counseling and Director of Research and Training at the University of Iowa Scanlan Center for School Mental Health. Her work focuses on best practices in school counseling and school counselor burnout.

room activities, few interactions with peers, or frequent trips to the bathroom or school nurse. Perhaps their academic performance was affected, as indicated by poorly completed work or spotty attendance. Or perhaps surprisingly, they were straight A students, as feelings of inadequacy and self-doubt can sometimes be powerful drivers to overperform academically. What do you think is going on with a student struggling with such challenges? How likely would they be to get a referral to a mental health professional in your school or the community? How likely is it that they would receive targeted support, and what would that intervention look like?

Although most educators agree that addressing students' emotional needs is important, many are unsure of the best way to support students whose emotional concerns tend to be less visible or are internal. Students who display what we call externalizing behaviors—aggression, bullying, harassment, or disruption—tend to be identified rather quickly by the adults in the building because these behaviors are not only unmistakable in terms of necessitating intervention, but also interfere with collective school activities and routines. On the other hand, students with emotional needs—anxiousness, fear, sadness, guilt, and social withdrawal—may involve more subtle behaviors that do not trigger the same level of concern from educators, even though such emotional issues can be as harmful for students' mental health and development. Schools should attend to early signals of emotional needs, such as consistent complaints of headaches, stomachaches, or visits to the nurse, social withdrawal or change in social interaction, signs of nervousness during typical daily activities such as extreme test anxiety, fear of using the school elevator, or being called on in class. These early signals can alert the school to targeted levels of emotional needs before they worsen and require a comprehensive mental health assessment and supports. Because educators get to know their students well and students spend so much time in schools, schools are a great fit for noticing these needs and addressing them proactively with school-based interventions that can be delivered feasibly.

A student would be matched by the Tier 2 team to an emotional need intervention first based on screening subscale data. The SDQ and SAEBRS, for example, both have specific subscales to indicate a need in this area. Additionally, the three-part referral system required by the TFI (i.e., family referral, educator referral, and student/self-referral) will be critical to identifying students in need, due to the less visible and less disruptive nature of emotional needs. This procedure requires schools to have easy, accessible, and ongoing ways for the student to refer themselves, the family to refer the student, and any educator to refer the student. Remember that due to the internal nature of this area of need, schools will typically not see emotional need symptoms in ODR data or even classroom logs of incidents. Additional data, or information to consider when confirming and planning for a need in this area, are visits to the nurse and visits to the school counselor or mental health professional. By definition, some emotional symptoms arise as somatic complaints like headaches or stomach aches. Visits to the nurse also may indicate withdrawal from a certain time of day, class period, or group of peers. Especially if visits to the nurse are not due to fevers or actual sicknesses, the team could consider that the student may be emotionally unwell. Similarly, students with emotional symptoms may frequently ask to speak with the counselor, call their families in the middle of the day from the front office, or spend extra time with an administrator or mental health professional in the building. While they may not explicitly say they need additional support, and what kind, notes that document these kinds of visits can help inform the team with regard to confirming a need in this area, and designing an appropriately matched intervention.

Among emotional concerns in childhood and adolescence, feelings of anxiousness is one of the most commonly recognized, with estimates of affected youth ranging from 9 to 15% (Bitsko et al., 2022). *Fear* is the emotional response a student feels to a real or perceived threat; *anxiety* is the associated anticipation of that threat occurring (American Psychiatric Association, 2022). While normative fear and anxiety tend to diminish on their own for many children as they grow and develop, clinical anxiety is more than temporary feelings of worrying and fear. Children with clinical anxiety experience disproportionate fear, anticipation of future threat, and emotional disturbances that often manifest in school in a variety of ways. Students with anxiety may appear on edge and restless, and may present with physical complaints (e.g., nausea, headaches, or feeling out of breath) and academic concerns (e.g., difficulty concentrating, and poor attendance and school performance; APA, 2022; Carpenter et al., 2019). Many anxiety disorders tend to persist if not treated, and can lead to considerable disruptions in personal, academic, and social functioning (Becker et al., 2012; Chiu et al., 2016).

On the other hand, students dealing with sadness and depressive thoughts and emotions may appear outwardly as withdrawn, lethargic, cranky, or irritable. National data indicate that 20% of adolescents ages 12–17 had received a major depression episode diagnosis, with 15.1% having done so in the past year (Substance Abuse and Mental Health Services Administration [SAMHSA], 2020). Students experiencing depression may often complain of bodily aches and pains. In terms of their school performance, they may experience functional impairments in completing their work due to concentration and memory problems, which often results in an abrupt drop in grades. Students may start neglecting extracurricular school activities they once used to enjoy and may have difficulties with peer and family relationships. A sense of worthlessness and blaming oneself for not meeting academic or social expectations is also very common. Perhaps most concerning, clinical depression in children and adolescents is associated with an increased risk of suicidal ideation and behavior, thus requiring careful and timely evaluation and intervention. For these reasons, it is imperative that we attend to the targeted-level emotional needs of students at Tier 2, rather than wait for more serious symptoms to appear.

For some students exposed to a stressful or traumatic event, the distress response is characterized by a negative emotional state that features some of the classic emotional symptoms such as fear and anxiety, but also involves some symptoms we tend to associate with depression, such as guilt, sadness, shame, and negative beliefs about themselves and the world. Usually, these students have been exposed to a traumatic event that provoked intense fear and helplessness, including being exposed to actual or threatened death, serious injury, or sexual violence (American Psychiatric Association, 2022). Learning that these events occurred to a close family member or a friend can also result in this intense posttraumatic response. In addition to these emotional symptoms, students may experience difficulty with memory, problem-solving ability, and confusion. They may appear indifferent or apathetic and may lose interest in school or peer activities. With recent research indicating that most children will be exposed to an extreme stressor by the age of 16 (Copeland et al., 2010), schools are recognizing the importance of trauma-informed, school-based intervention for students (Mendelson et al., 2015). Given that childhood abuse and trauma present as risk factors for suicide, readily available and effective intervention is key (American Psychiatric Association, 2022). Additionally, the world collectively experienced varying levels of trauma recently with the COVID-19 pandemic. Given the prevalence of trauma histories for all students, it is important for schools to consider historical events and experiences like these in getting to know the student and family, and in planning for Tier 2 interventions for emotional symptoms.

What all these emotional concerns have in common is that they interfere with students' ability to engage fully in school and other domains, and if not addressed, can have long lasting mental, physical, social, and economic consequences in adulthood (Cummings et al., 2014). Emotional concerns stemming from anxiousness, sadness, and trauma cause significant distress in students and impact concentration and functioning in and outside of school. Beyond school difficulties such as poor grades, suspension, and dropout, students may also experience family conflicts and interpersonal problems, and engage in risky behaviors, including self-harm. They may experience negative self-evaluation patterns and think poorly of themselves or their abilities. Some students may try to limit social rejection and feelings of inadequacy by withdrawing from academic and social situations, leading to both academic and social problems. Alternatively, some students may overperform academically as competence in schoolwork can become a coping mechanism to manage overwhelming feelings of not being good enough, while their social and personal development suffers. Finally, for some students who have experienced trauma, avoidance of any new and unpredictable situations might lead them to abstain from pursuing normative developmental and social opportunities, leading them to become estranged from others and further convincing them of being seen as socially undesirable.

Another element these emotional symptoms have in common is that they are highly treatable. Evidence is substantial that providing intervention for students facing such challenges can improve academic and social–emotional success (Reback, 2010; Whiston et al., 2011), making schools an ideal setting to deliver such interventions. School-based Tier 2 interventions addressing emotional issues require cross collaboration between educators, school mental health professionals, or counselors, and when necessary, community partners and providers in order to tap into the systemwide resources and expertise needed to provide effective targeted support (Weist et al., 2018). Prior to designing and selecting interventions that can be delivered in the school environment, however, students with emotional concerns should be referred to a school mental health professional, like a school counselor, school social worker, or school psychologist. Ideally, one of these professionals is already part of the Tier 2 PST and, thus, easily positioned to support the design and selection of interventions. Proper evaluation of the type and severity of symptoms is necessary for accurate identification and effective intervention, especially since many of these concerns tend to be co-occurring. While students may receive individual counseling support by mental health professionals inside and outside of the school setting to improve their emotional functioning, it is important that appropriate supports and interventions are also integrated within the classroom to address their academic and social–emotional functioning.

MATCHING AND PLANNING CONSIDERATIONS

School counselors implementing Tier 2 emotional symptom interventions have to first complete essential prescreening procedures for group inclusion to accurately select the students who would most benefit from the intervention. Student selection is based on universal screening practices employed in the school such as those described in Chapter 2, educator or family referrals, and following individual meetings with each student (and preferably family) to assess specific worries and feelings, identify provoking situations, and obtain family consent and student assent. Bardhoshi et al. (2019) recommend that counselors use psychometrically sound instruments to quantify emotional symptoms in students prior to delivering interventions, with best practices recommending obtaining both student and family reports. These types of assessments would occur *after* a student has been identified by the Tier 2 PST as having an emotional, or internalizing, concern through referral or screening (e.g., SDQ, SAEBRS). Students with an existing mental health diagnosis may also be selected for this group, although assessment of severity of symptoms prior to the group beginning is important. It should be noted that inclusion in a group may be limited to students without co-occurring conduct issues. Family commitment to attend two family sessions may be a desirable element for student selection in the intervention. Also, grouping children by age, area of need, and developmental stages is recommended. Finally, Chapter 11 provides general considerations for intervention planning and Tier 2 implementation that relate to emotional symptoms. First, Chapter 11 describes a need to integrate mental health services with Tier 2 communication, planning, and implementation. Additionally, Chapter 11 highlights the need to consider the conditions and context that students are operating in to better understand factors potentially causing disruption or dysregulation. For students with emotional symptoms, we should be on the lookout for online conditions as well, such as online bullying, and inappropriate online interactions.

COGNITIVE-BEHAVIORAL INTERVENTIONS

Some of the most frequently endorsed Tier 2 interventions to address emotional needs are delivered in small groups and are informed by cognitive-behavioral therapy (CBT) principles. CBT is a short-term, goal-oriented treatment for addressing anxiousness and depressive feelings that focuses primarily on changing an individual's thinking patterns (Dobson & Dobson, 2018). In this chapter, we describe three evidence-based cognitive-behavioral school-based interventions focused on building skills to increase student self-awareness, as well as coping and resilience regarding a range of common emotional problems: the Brief Coping Cat for addressing anxiousness; the Penn Resiliency Program for addressing depressive feelings, and the Support for Student Exposed to Trauma for addressing posttraumatic responses. These three programs are simply evidence-based examples of the menu of options your school could have available to address the varying Tier 2 emotional symptoms needs. Schools should determine which program fits best for their local context and available resources. In the resources table (Table 7.5 on p. 113), you will find other examples of similar evidence-based programs that could be substituted for these three. It is important to have more than one program available, or to be able to adapt a single program to address anxiousness and worry, sadness, and trauma exposure.

All these interventions include adaptations that can be delivered by school personnel in academic settings and involve teaching students how to recognize distortions in their thinking, gain a better understanding of a range of behaviors, use problem solving to cope with difficult situations, and gain confidence in their abilities to handle challenges. They are organized from least to most intensive in terms of the severity level of the internalized concern, student time required, complexity, and materials needed.

For the Tier 2 team or PST to match students to one of these potential programs, the team needs to first work collaboratively with the school-based mental health professional (e.g., counselor, social worker, school psychologist) to determine what programs are available, and which programs address the varying emotional needs. Then, the school-based professional can help the team match a specific program and group to the student's specific need. In some schools, there may be an additional assessment measure than can help the team better understand what emotional needs exist and their underlying cause. Additionally, teams may choose to do a crisis evaluation for students with persistent sadness, withdrawal, or depressive thoughts to rule out suicidal ideation or planning. It should be noted that students who are experiencing abuse, are in active crisis, have active suicidal ideation, or exhibit self-harm behaviors are not recommended for Tier 2 intervention. If a second level of emotional symptom assessment is not available in your school, the team will use teacher anecdotal information, collaboration with the family, and even the student to match a specific program to that student's emotional need.

In the following sections on each of the interventions, we describe (1) core intervention components; (2) implementation methods; (3) a brief demonstration of what this might look like in a school setting; and (4) data collection procedures. Key considerations, resources, and a case example are also included. Table 7.1 provides a summary of these interventions.

BRIEF COPING CAT FOR ANXIOUSNESS

There are two forms of the Coping Cat intervention. One is a brief version; the other is a longer version referred to as Coping Cat. A student would be matched to one of these versions based on first, scoring outside the typical range in emotional symptoms, and then either by educator or school-professional anecdotal information, or with the use of an additional assessment measure that can help pinpoint which area of emotional needs exist. Specifically, Coping Cat can be focused to address anxiousness and fears, as is described here.

The Brief Coping Cat (Kendall et al., 2013) is the 8-week condensed version of the full 16-week program, which has been extensively used in schools to support students with anxiousness and worry symptoms that interfere with school performance or are early indicators of concern. A well-established evidence-based cognitive-behavioral intervention, Coping Cat includes many iterations and adaptations that help children to recognize signs and feelings of anxiousness and worry, as well as draw on specific strategies to better cope during high-stress situations. Available in both English and Spanish, it has been validated across several studies and meta-analyses over the past

TABLE 7.1. Comparison of Emotional Need Interventions

	Brief Coping Cat (anxiousness)	Penn Resiliency Program (sadness)	Support for Students Exposed to Trauma (trauma)
Persons involved	Small group with school-based professional	Small group with school-based professional	Small group or individual with school-based professional
Materials needed	Coping Cat Curriculum	Penn Resiliency Program Curriculum	SSET Program Curriculum
Schedule	Weekly, 50-minute sessions (8 weeks or 16 weeks)	Weekly, 90-min sessions (12 weeks) or 60-minute sessions (18–24 weeks)	Weekly 60-minute (10 weeks)
Data tracked	Anxiousness, social validity, and fidelity	Ratings of emotions and thoughts	Ratings of coping strategy use and thoughts and feelings
Student grade levels	1–6	3–8	3–12

two decades (Lenz, 2015; Reynolds et al., 2012) and is endorsed in the National Registry of Evidence Based Programs and Practices by SAMHSA. The brief version was recently developed by distilling it to its core components, presenting a better fit for school settings given concerns over the length of the original program and the research-to-practice gap, while also making it an ideal Tier 2 support (Beidas et al., 2010; Crawley et al., 2013). Its adaptation into a group delivery mode is consistent with recommendations for flexible applications of the Coping Cat program (Kendall & Hedke, 2006; Beidas et al., 2010) and has been reported as effective with diverse populations (Santesteban-Echarri et al., 2018).

This manualized brief intervention is designed for small groups (four to five children) ages 7–13 to help them recognize and understand the emotional and physical manifestations of anxiety, while developing and implementing plans for their effective coping. The eight lessons are delivered weekly by school mental health personnel in 50-minute sessions. School mental health professionals (e.g., school counselors, social workers) are required to use the Brief Coping Cat manualized program (Kendall et al., 2013) to implement this intervention, and to distribute the Coping Cat Workbook to students. The manual describes session-by-session content and goals and is associated with therapeutic homework referred to as a Show-That-I-Can (STIC) task. The manual also includes measures for rating both anxiousness and fidelity to the program. The workbook includes specific STIC tasks, and other helpful tools to facilitate content acquisition and homework completion.

The chapters provide rationale, content, and strategies for each session, focusing on (1) building rapport, treatment orientation, and conducting the first group session; (2) identifying anxious feelings, self-talk, and challenging negative cognitions; (3) problem-solving, self-evaluation, and self-reward strategies; (4) reviewing skills learned and practicing in low-stress situations; (5) practicing in moderately anxiety-provoking situations; and (6–8) practicing in high-stress situations and celebrating successes. Opportunities for implementation flexibility are also identified based on symptom severity and student choice, leading to adaptable customization.

The Coping Cat Workbook includes specific opportunities of varying intensity for students to practice exposure, a feelings barometer, as well as paper cutouts that can be used as achievement certificates. Students also can use the workbook to complete the Subjective Units of Distress Scale (SUDS; Wolpe, 1969) to rate the amount of anxiety they experience each week when completing homework tasks exposing them to stressful situations. Training and supervisory phone consultation for school mental health professionals are also available to help build competence and efficacy with implementation.

In Lessons 1–3, students are first provided with content that combines cognitive strategies (assessing personal abilities, understanding perceived threats, distinguishing anxiousness from other feelings, problem solving) with behavioral skills (modeling, relaxation, exposure). Crucial to the program is teaching the FEAR acronym (F, feeling frightened; E, expecting bad things to happen; A, attitudes and actions that can help; R, results and rewards) so students can learn to recognize and problem solve their specific fears and worries. Lessons 4–8 involve gradual exposure culminating in live high-stress-provoking situations to implement the FEAR acronym. This is combined with out-of-session homework, or STIC tasks, to build and practice coping skills that result in better management of anxiousness, along with ratings, which are reviewed at the beginning of each session. It should be noted that family involvement is highly encouraged in the Brief Coping Cat program to help better practice skills in multiple environments and situations (promoting generalization), as well as provide feedback of students' progress through the program. See Table 7.2 for procedural steps to Brief Coping Cat.

TABLE 7.2. Procedural Steps for Brief Coping Cat

Before intervention
1. School-based professional and team collaborate to create an inventory of available programs
2. Team meets to discuss students with emotional needs
3. Team matches students to emotional need intervention that meets the student's need
4. Small-group facilitator schedules group and coordinates with the student to begin

During intervention
1. Initial group meeting to build rapport and orientation
2. Weekly 50-minute small group meetings:
   a. Review new skill
   b. Identify a coping strategy
   c. Practice new skill in low stress situations
   d. Practice new skill in high stress situations
3. Celebrate success

After intervention
1. Meet with students to follow up and check in
2. Report to Tier 2 team with progress notes

A Brief Demonstration

In *Session 1,* the school counselor (or other school mental health professional) explains the basics of the Brief Coping Cat program, establishes rapport with the students, and encourages getting to know each other. Addressing issues of confidentiality up front helps create a safe space for the adolescents to feel comfortable speaking with the counselor and each other. Expectations and goals for the program may be set. Then, the school counselor starts an activity to define *anxiousness* and *stress,* as well as to teach students to distinguish anxiety and worry from other types of feelings. Using specific examples to illustrate this with each student may help better customize the lesson. The counselor also introduces the concepts of a worry hierarchy and feelings thermometer. In the family version of this first session, the counselor may meet with family to discuss the intervention, gather specific information about the stressful situation, identify their supporting role, and evaluate how they may be unknowingly reinforcing anxious and fearful behavior.

In *Session 2,* the school counselor asks students to share various stressful situations in order to normalize the feeling of worry and teach about the physiology of the fear/stress response and how it is physically experienced by the students. Following solicitation of specific examples from each student, the counselor may then introduce the FEAR acronym. Special focus should be on helping students recognize the anxious self-talk they may use in the specific stressful situations identified, and teaching the use of positive self-talk instead as a cognitive restructuring opportunity. The counselor assigns each student a STIC task, using the workbook. In *Session 3,* the counselor discusses the homework task and provides coaching and encouragement. Then, students are taught specific problem-solving concepts and strategies that can help them better manage their stress, paying attention to how positive thoughts can contribute to reduced anxiety reactions, as well as how relaxation techniques can help them manage physical manifestations of anxiety. Students then create a hierarchy of their stressful situations for their future exposure task and are assigned a STIC task.

Following the first three sessions, the counselor shifts gears by gradually exposing students to hypothetical low-level, and moderate and high-level live stressful situations so they can achieve gradual success. Students are assigned one STIC task per week and are invited to rate their stress levels using the SUDS. In *Session 4*, students apply the FEAR acronym to hypothetical low-stress situations and receive coaching and encouragement by the counselor. The counselor provides feedback and encouragement, pointing out effective strategies and helping problem solve barriers to stress management. Families are also invited to meet with the counselor separately at this point to help facilitate use of coping skills in the exposure tasks to be conducted at home. In *Session 5*, the counselor reviews the student's experience with the home exposure task and invites students to challenge themselves by exposure to a moderately stressful situation. Students should be applying the FEAR plan coping skills practiced up to this point more independently, although the counselor is present for support. Students are invited to further apply those skills in that week's STIC exposure task. *Sessions 6* and *7* repeat this process by preparing and introducing students to increasingly high-stress situations and continually practicing success. Finally, *Session 8* is used to help students practice one final time a feasible stressful task to solidify gains and facilitate a sense of success. This session also includes a summary of the intervention program, the skills learned, and a celebration of the students' success.

Following the eight manualized sessions, the counselor may choose to schedule a program evaluation meeting. This meeting can be used to invite families and students to provide ratings of anxious symptoms, as well as satisfaction with the program and any additional feedback that may be important to record. Family and student instruments that provide ratings of anxiousness and worry prior to and following conclusion of the group sessions are recommended to assess meaningful reduction of symptoms, and essentially monitor progress. School mental health professionals may choose to use a number of recommended free-access instruments for assessing anxiety symptoms with school-age youth, like the Generalized Anxiety Disorder Screener (GAD-7; Spitzer et al., 2006; Bardhoshi et al., 2019), or they can select the free-access Level 2 Child and Parent Anxiety Scales available online as accompaniments to DSM-5-TR. For students with established anxiety diagnoses, the disorder-specific severity measures available on the DSM-5-TR website also include children's versions.

A fidelity checklist is available and can be used to assess the accurate implementation of the content and strategies as described in the manual, either by videotaping sessions and rating them later, rating them live by an external observer, or completing a self-evaluation of fidelity. In addition, treatment satisfaction questionnaires can be used to rate the perceptions of quality of care that students received. The program includes rating eight satisfaction items (e.g. "How would you rate the quality of care you have received?") on a 1 to 4 Likert-type scale, which may be useful for a summative evaluation of the program. It may be advisable to schedule an assessment session at the beginning and end of the program to allow for dissemination and collection of necessary data.

PENN RESILIENCY PROGRAM FOR DEPRESSIVE SYMPTOMS

The Penn Resiliency Program (PRP; Gillham et al., 2006) is a 12-session group intervention designed to prevent and reduce depressive symptoms in late elementary and middle school students. A well-established evidence-based program, the PRP teaches cognitive-behavioral and social problem-solving skills in a group format that helps students understand, relate, and interpret everyday events in an adaptive manner to prevent and combat depressive or sad feelings and thoughts. Available in both brief (12 sessions delivered for 90 minutes each) and extended (18–24 sessions delivered for 60 minutes each) versions, it has been extensively researched across culturally diverse student populations as both a universal and targeted school-based intervention (Brunwasser et al., 2009; Chaplin et al., 2006, Farahmand et al., 2011; Gillham et al., 2006).

When delivered as a targeted intervention, the PRP aims to reduce the depressive emotions of students ages 10–14 who are at increased risk for depression, through the delivery of structured weekly lessons aimed at improving both their cognitive style and behavioral coping skills. Students are identified as higher risk either by having a family with a history of with depression, or experiencing minor depressive symptoms themselves, like persistent sadness and hopelessness. When delivered as an early, targeted Tier 2 intervention, students effectively learn to address the connection between maladaptive thoughts and negative emotional-behavioral outcomes, as well as implement adaptive goal setting, experiencing both a reduction in symptoms and long-lasting benefits (Gillham et al., 2006).

School mental health professionals are required to use the manualized PRP lesson plans to implement this intervention and to use interactive methods (e.g., role plays, skits, stories) to deliver the content, skills, and practices that are the core elements of this intervention. The manual describes session-by-session content and goals, as well as respective activities. Worksheets are frequently used to practice the skills learned in sessions, and scenario-based activities and homework assignments are used to further promote success. School mental health professionals are encouraged to receive direct training through the Penn Positive Psychology Center, as studies support that quality and amount of training of group leaders is an essential element for effective implementation and results in greater symptom reduction (Gillham et al., 2006).

The PRP is based on the principles of cognitive theory (Beck, 1979), and the activating event–belief–consequence (ABC) model (Ellis, 1962). The program has two main components—one focused on an intrapersonal cognitive component, and one focusing on social problem solving. For the cognitive component, lessons focus on the connection between thoughts, feelings, and behaviors associated with depressive thoughts, and teaching students how to think flexibly and accurately. Students also learn about cognitive styles, and how sadness might contribute to a pessimistic explanatory style. Armed with cognitive-restructuring skills they learn in group sessions, students work to challenge negative thinking and replace it with pragmatic alternative interpretations. The problem-solving component targets specific skills, including assertiveness, negotiation, relaxation, procrastination, social skills, decision making, and creative problem solving (Gilham et al., 2006). These skills are essential for coping as students learn to apply them in their lives through weekly group discussions and homework assignments.

A Brief Demonstration

Following selection of 8–10 students, the group leader starts *Session 1* with an introduction to the program and focuses on establishing rapport with students. This session is focused on teaching the ABC model, identifying automatic thoughts that form their own self-talk from recent situations they have faced. *Session 2* discusses explanatory style, and concepts like optimism and pessimism are presented through a series of skits the group can act out, and then alternative interpretations can be generated on the skit scenario. Students are assigned homework to generate alternative explanations for events in their lives. In *Session 3*, the group leader further targets explanatory style by asking students to assume a detective persona in an activity that aims to evaluate automatic thoughts and weigh the evidence, with the purpose of learning how to assess the accuracy of negative beliefs. Students further practice these skills through another detective game, where they receive a portfolio on a fictitious character, and hunt for evidence that either substantiates or refutes the character's automatic thoughts. In *Session 4* the focus shifts toward the future and combating any catastrophizing that might occur after a negative event. Through storytelling of the Chicken Little story, students identify worst case, best case, and most likely scenarios, and practice applying accurate evaluations and perspectives to events from their own lives. *Session 5* focuses primarily on reviewing all the cognitive skills developed in previous lesson, and further applying those to personal negative beliefs. The curriculum shifts in *Session 6* to focus on interpersonal problem solving, with skits used to illustrate interaction styles and role plays used to practice assertiveness and negotiation skills to combat interaction styles rooted in aggression and passivity. In *Session 7,* skills like controlled breathing and relaxation are taught to help cope with negative emotions and stressful situations. Students identify their own positive visual image they can call to mind when feeling angry or anxious, and identify people who they can reach out to for support. *Session 8* addresses avoidance and procrastination by identifying real negative beliefs students hold about specific chores or projects. Applying the cognitive-restructuring skills gained so far, students first challenge negative beliefs, and then problem solve tasks by breaking them into smaller, manageable steps. *Session 9* includes a review of sessions 6–8 and also addresses indecisiveness by learning how to generate pros and cons for different actions, and then realistically evaluating and applying the best course of action with an example from students' own lives. Finally, *Session 10* addresses how to combat the negative interpretation of neutral social cues that tends to be a common experience for children with depression. Students learn to stop and think before reacting, consider alternative explanations, and evaluate their goal in the interaction. Then students generate possible solutions and select a course of action to put into place. Finally, students evaluate the outcome of their action and practice these steps with multiple scenarios offered by the group leader. The remaining *Sessions 11* and *12* provide students with further opportunities to practice social-problem-solving skills with situations in their own lives. The final session is reserved for a review of the program, and a celebration for the accomplishments students achieved through their engagement and participation in the PRP.

Family and student instruments that provide ratings of depression symptoms prior to and following conclusion of the group sessions are recommended to assess meaningful reduction of symptoms for students already experiencing depressive symptoms, and thus, monitor students' response to intervention. School mental health professionals may choose to use a number of recommended free-access or low-cost instruments for assessing the outcome of interventions on depression symptoms of school-age youth, like the Hamilton Rating Scale for Depression (Hamilton, 1960; Bardhoshi et al., 2019) or the Children's Depression Inventory (Kovacs et al., 2011), or they can select the free-access Level 2 Child and Parent Depression Scales available online as accompaniments to the DSM-5-TR. Additional informative measures used in studies evaluating the effectiveness of the PRP include the Hopelessness Scale for Children (Kazdin et al., 1986) and the composite-negative subscale of the Children's Attributional Style Questionnaire (Seligman et al., 1984) to evaluate changes in negative expectations and a pessimistic cognitive style respectively. It may be advisable to schedule an assessment session at the beginning and end of the program, as well as a 6-month follow-up to allow for meaningful collection of necessary data. See Table 7.3 for procedural steps for the PRP for depressive thoughts and feelings.

TABLE 7.3. Procedural Steps for the Penn Resiliency Program

Before intervention

1. School-based professional and team collaborate to create an inventory of available programs
2. Team meets to discuss students with emotional needs and assesses for crisis intervention around depressive thoughts and potential self-harm
3. Team contacts student's family to discuss area of concern
4. Team matches students to depressive thought intervention that meets the student's need
5. Small-group facilitator schedules group and coordinates with the student to begin

During intervention

1. Initial group meeting to build rapport and orientation
2. Weekly 60-minute small-group meetings:
   a. Review new content
   b. Skits, stories, role play
   c. Homework
   d. Practice new skill
3. Review program content and celebrate success

After intervention

1. Meet with students to follow up and check in
2. Report to Tier 2 team with progress notes

SUPPORT FOR STUDENTS EXPOSED TO TRAUMA FOR TRAUMA

Support for Students Exposed to Trauma (SSET; Jacox et al., 2009) is a 10-lesson cognitive-behavioral skills-based support group designed to reduce student symptoms of traumatic stress, as well as the associated feelings, thoughts, and functional impairment that frequently accompanies exposure to traumatic events. Although sadness, fear, and withdrawal may be the primary emotional symptoms, students are selected for this program based on their exposure to either community, family, or school violence, or after having experienced a traumatic event such as a natural disaster, accident, abuse, or neglect. Developed as an adaptation of the Cognitive-Behavioral Intervention for Trauma in Schools program (Jaycox et al., 2010; Kataoka et al., 2003; Stein et al., 2003), this version is designed specifically with teachers and school counselors in mind, with the assistance of a backup clinician of record who can provide services for students at high risk or those in crisis. Several studies evaluating SSET's implementation in schools as a trauma-focused intervention have included diverse students, with results supporting its effectiveness in reducing PTSD symptoms, as well as in improving school performance (Allison & Ferreira, 2017; Hoover et al., 2018; Kataoka et al., 2011).

This intervention is designed to be delivered weekly in support groups consisting of 8–10 late elementary through early high school students, in meetings lasting 60 minutes each. The group leader (e.g., teacher, school counselor) is required to utilize the 10 structured lessons included in the free-access SSET manualized program (Jacox et al., 2009). The manual describes lesson-by-lesson content, activities, and scripts, along with respective goals, objectives, and materials. In order to best prepare group leaders to engage with students and families, the manual also includes a program handout for students and family letters and handouts. Although no specific rating scales are included in the manual, it is recommended that students are selected based on assessments that identify their exposure to traumatic events, as well as feelings of anxiety and fear associated with that exposure. Given the complexity of addressing trauma in a school environment, group leaders are required to receive in-person training and use consultation from a clinician of record to ensure potential clinical needs or complications that arise are adequately addressed.

Along with delivering instruction about common reactions to trauma, the SSET program also engages students in practicing specific cognitive, mindfulness, and trauma-processing skills, including relaxation, identifying maladaptive thinking, learning cognitive techniques to challenge and restructure negative thoughts, problem solving, securing social support, and developing a trauma narrative. Although families are not involved in the group, families are kept abreast of the activities students complete and are instructed on how to best help students practice the skills they have learned.

A Brief Demonstration

Following selection of a small group of students, the group leader starts *Session 1* with an introduction of group members, the topic, expectations, as well as a worksheet on writing down a small portion of the trauma story. *Session 2* includes instruction on the common reactions to trauma, such as nightmares, avoidance of reminders, and feeling scared, as well as systematic relaxation practices for combating the anxiousness, worry, and negative emotions associated with the trauma. *Session 3* aims to connect thoughts and feelings by teaching students how to observe their own thoughts and actively challenge thoughts that are getting in the way, as well as how to decrease unrealistic thoughts and increase helpful thinking. Worksheets such as the fear thermometer help students gauge the intensity of their emotions, and opportunities to apply these skills with real-life examples from their lives enhances success. In *Session 4*, the group leader further explores the topic of helpful thinking, using a hot seat activity to identify a list of helpful thoughts they can pull from when feeling like they are "in the hot seat." The group can suggest hot seat scenarios, and students are assigned homework to practice the hot seat thinking at home. *Session 5* engages students in a fear hierarchy activity, where they can choose a fear to actively work on by actively breaking it down into smaller steps and working backward from the easiest to the middle steps, while applying anxiety-stopping strategies, such as thought stopping, distraction, and positive imagery. Students identify a fear step they are going to face that week as a homework assignment. Following acquisition of both knowledge and skills to apply to traumatic responses, the group leader shifts gears in *Session 6* by starting work on the trauma narrative. Students learn to objectively approach the trauma and begin safe sharing of the story with others by writing a short, factual newspaper story regarding their trauma and reading it to the group. As a homework assignment, students draw a picture to accompany their story. In continuing to develop the trauma narrative in *Session 7*, the group leader engages the students in writing a personal story about their traumatic events that they later read to the group. This is facilitated by a discussion of the many elements that go into writing a trauma story, including time and place, key events, feelings, thoughts, and sensations, and important points they want to communicate about what happened to them. As this tends to be an emotionally fraught session, students are encouraged to use all the skills practiced in previous sessions to turn down the temperature of their fears and anxiety. The homework assignment for this session includes drawing a personal picture

TABLE 7.4. Procedural Steps for Support for Students Exposed to Trauma

Before intervention
1. School-based professional and team collaborate to create an inventory of available programs
2. Team meets to discuss students with emotional needs and assesses for crisis intervention around depressive thoughts and potential self-harm
3. Team evaluates whether the student is in crisis, is in a currently abusive situation, or is otherwise not a good fit for this intervention
4. Team matches students to trauma exposure intervention that meets the student's need
5. Small-group facilitator schedules group and coordinates with the student to begin

During intervention
1. Initial group meeting to build rapport and orientation
2. Weekly 60-minute small-group meetings:
   a. Review new content
   b. Set and review goals
   c. Activities to practice coping strategies
   d. Communication with family
   e. Practice new skill
3. Review program content and celebrate success

After intervention
1. Meet with students to follow up and check in
2. Report to Tier 2 team with progress notes

to accompany their story. *Session 8* shifts into social problem solving, with the group leader helping brainstorm solutions to common social problems with friends or family members. Students learn to generate several thoughts and respective actions pertaining to each problem, and then select favorite actions based on pros and cons of each action. For a homework assignment, students choose a current interpersonal problem to solve by applying the skills learned in session. *Session 9* allows students to further practice social problem solving and getting out of the hot seat by reviewing key skills covered in previous sessions. Selecting real-life interpersonal problems enhances applicability in the students' lives. Finally, *Session 10* engages students in reflecting on their challenges and progress achieved and anticipating future challenges and identifying skills to address them, as well as providing time and space for a group celebration for program completion. Following completion of SSET with students, group leaders connect with families to highlight progress and identify areas that may require additional work, referral, or follow-up. See Table 7.4 for procedural steps for the SSET intervention.

KEY CONSIDERATIONS

Although each of the small-group interventions covered in this chapter includes recommended student age ranges, it is important to apply developmental considerations in the selection of students for these interventions, as well as in the delivery of the content. For example, not all students age 12 will have identical cognitive and maturity levels, and the engagement in group activities where confidentiality cannot be guaranteed, and self and social perceptions can be affected, necessitates careful consideration. When possible, student selection needs to take into consideration both their cognitive and their behavioral development. Evaluating student insight regarding their emotional concerns, as well as their motivation for addressing them, should be weighed along with their behavioral repertoire in stressful situations prior to inclusion in a group setting, given the propensity for some stress-based reactions (e.g. shutting down, aggression, name-calling, self-harm) to be disruptive to the overall climate and progress of the group. For students who have difficulty with abstract thinking and verbal expression, individualized attention when utilizing complex cognitive techniques like "cognitive challenging" and "generating alternative solutions" may be needed, with examples adapted to situations and events the students themselves recognize. Furthermore, wholistic information gathering and observation may provide more comprehensive data points for both identifying and assessing desired student outcomes. Family and teacher reports, as well as observation, can be incorporated to thoroughly measure student symptoms prior, during, and following the intervention, and account for measurement limitations pertaining to self-report.

Multicultural considerations are also essential when providing programming on skills aimed to address internalizing emotional concerns. Emotional expression is culturally based, and working to establish rapport and trust is important for addressing internalizing symptoms that may not be easily observable. Allowing room for students to discuss their own coping and cognitive style, their view of themselves and the world, as well as their goals are culturally responsive ways to engage with students on a personal level and minimize erroneous assumptions. All successful interventions are rooted in establishing genuine connections, so relationship building with students should be not an afterthought but a first priority. Students who feel seen and appreciated are more likely to engage in the vulnerable and difficult task of sharing and overcoming their emotional concerns. Students who opt to participate in such group interventions show remarkable resilience and should be provided the warmth and encouragement they deserve.

Working with students with emotional needs can be depleting for educators and school mental health professionals, so keeping yourself grounded, healthy, and supported is key. Educators should not work in isolation. Involving colleagues, administrators, or mental health professionals in your school, and reaching out for consultation will ensure a thoughtful and measured approach.

Even though these Tier 2 interventions are evidence-based, there are many student, group-leader, or school factors that can interfere with optimal results, and keeping expectations realistic is also important to help guard against potential emotional fatigue in delivering such interventions. Caring about students' emotional concerns, selecting evidence-based programs, and putting in the time and effort needed to deliver multiple-session interventions like the three covered in this chapter is truly commendable. Not all change can be neatly captured, but feeling like you matter as a student, and knowing that adults in your school believe in your ability to overcome difficulties can sometimes make all the difference.

RESOURCES

Table 7.5 lists resources related to interventions for emotional issues.

TABLE 7.5. Resources

www.psychiatry.org/psychiatrists/practice/dsm/educational-resources

This website of the American Psychiatric Association provides free-access online assessment measures that school mental health professionals can use to assess severity of internalizing symptoms pre- and postintervention, as well as a parent/guardian version to assess a range of internalizing symptoms. Please note that these tools are used to enhance clinical decision making and for progress monitoring, and not for diagnosis.

www.schoolmentalhealth.org/Resources/Early-Intervention-and-Treatment-Tiers-2—3

The National Center for School Mental Health provides a quality guide for early intervention and treatment services that can be delivered as Tier 2 interventions, with specific guidance to help school mental health professionals advance the quality of their services and supports.

www.nasponline.org/resources-and-publications/resources-and-podcasts/covid-19-resource-center/return-to-school/tier-2-social—emotional-learning/mental-and-behavioral-health-interventions-post-covid-19

The National Association of School Psychologists provides resources and guidance on a number of Tier 2 interventions that are culturally responsive and appropriate for post-COVID-19 recovery, including programs covered in this chapter, such as the Coping Cat workbook and cognitive-behavioral interventions for trauma in schools. This resource includes key re-entry considerations for educators, school counselors, and school psychologists for adapting these programs to the emerging postpandemic realities in the schools, as well as guidance on equity considerations after school closures.

Depressive symptom programs to consider

- ACTION Program: Patel, P. G., Stark, K. D., Metz, K. L., & Banneyer, K. N. (2014). School-based interventions for depression. In M. D. Weist, N. A. Lever, C. P. Bradshaw, & J. Sarno Owens (Eds.), *Handbook of school mental health: Research, training, practice, and policy* (pp. 369–383). Springer Science + Business Media.
- Interpersonal psychotherapy—adolescent skills training (IPT-AST): Young, J. F., Kranzler, A., Gallop, R., & Mufson, L. (2012). Interpersonal psychotherapy-adolescent skills training: Effects on school and social functioning. *School Mental Health, 4*(4), 254–264.

Anxiousness and worry programs to consider

- Cool Kids: *www.cebc4cw.org/program/cool-kids/detailed*
- Baltimore Child Anxiety Treatment Study in the Schools (BCATSS): Ginsburg, G. S., & Drake, K. L. (2002). School-based treatment for anxious African-American adolescents: A controlled pilot study. *Journal of the American Academy of Child and Adolescent Psychiatry, 41*, 768–775.

Trauma exposure programs to consider

- Cognitive-behavioral intervention for trauma in schools: *https://traumaawareschools.org/index.php/learn-more-cbits*
- Chafouleas, S. M., Koriakin, T. A., Roundfield, K. D., & Overstreet, S. (2019). Addressing childhood trauma in school settings: A framework for evidence-based practice. *School Mental Health, 11*, 40–53.

CASE EXAMPLE

James, a 13-year-old White student attending eighth grade at a suburban public high school, is referred to the school counselor by his math teacher, Mrs. M, due to recent academic and classroom behavioral performance difficulties. Mrs. M reports that James is displaying attentional and organizational difficulties in the classroom, including often appearing forgetful, having difficulty paying attention to instruction, and appearing antsy. Mrs. M is particularly concerned with James's recent math performance and his inability to follow directions in the classroom and complete multistep equations consistently. Mrs. M notes that James does not engage with other students during group work, and never asks questions about problems he doesn't understand. The teacher communicates that James's scores from the seventh-grade statewide achievement test indicated that James was proficient in math prior to starting eighth grade. However, missing points in math assignments and receiving an F on a recent math test prompted the teacher to request a remediation meeting to assist James in math. What concerns Mrs. M the most is that James skipped class the day of the next math test. Mrs. M notes that while she is thankful James is not disruptive in the classroom, she also wonders whether this may have contributed to these issues going unnoticed before. Given the academic rigor and expectations for eighth-grade math, Mrs. M hopes the school counselor can figure out how to best help James quickly, before he falls too far behind.

A brief meeting with James substantiates some of the concerns Mrs. M reports, as James lists math as his most difficult subject and gives a dismal report of his performance in the class. When asked what has changed in math since seventh grade, James says that he can't seem to get his stuff together and is convinced he will no longer be able to attend a good college based on his current grades. He also reports that he frequently feels out of breath and nauseous in class. Although bright and polite, James appears rather embarrassed by this first encounter with the school counselor and reluctant to engage in extensive discussion. The school counselor is aware that anxiety frequently manifests in physical and academic concerns, and wonders what James's parents' perceptions are regarding his performance in school, and whether they have also noted some of these reported behaviors at home. She makes a phone call to James's mom to discuss the case and secure consent to gather additional information that might inform the scope and focus of a potential intervention. The mother reports that James has been very stressed out about school lately and worries about his performance in school and his future prospects. He also seems to have curbed some of his social activities. Fortunately, the school had just conducted universal screening using the Strengths and Difficulties Questionnaire. After consulting with the Tier 2 PST, Mrs. M notes that James is scoring high on almost all items of the emotional symptoms subscale of the SDQ, and two items of the hyperactivity subscale. Using formal assessment to gather information from both parents and James regarding some of the reported symptoms seems like a logical next step. The mother agrees to complete a brief scale evaluating James' symptoms, and the counselor administers the DSM-5-TR Level 2-Anxiety-Parent Measure, to assess the general domain of anxiety. According to the scoring instructions, James's score of 30 results in a T-score of 65.8, indicating moderate anxiety.

A brief follow-up with James confirms that he often feels on edge and worried. And although James does not endorse any specific symptoms of depression, he says he often feels like something really bad is about to happen. He admits that math is a class he is extremely worried about, but that he also worries about his other classes and his ability to be successful in general, which feels overwhelming. He reports not feeling relaxed even around his peers, and worries that others think less of him because of his school performance. The school counselor decides to administer the GAD-7 to James to determine the severity of his anxiety symptoms. After 5 minutes of James indicating how bothered he has been feeling over the past 2 weeks by seven core anxiety symptoms, the school counselor quickly scores the GAD-7. James's score of 11 exceeds the cutoff, indicating clinical importance. Consulting the scoring instructions, the school counselor concludes that James is experiencing symptoms consistent with moderate anxiety. She discusses these results with James, being careful to normalize some of his experiences, and works to obtain commitment and instill hope for improvement. After some consultation with James's family and teachers, and after ruling out exposure to trauma or suicidal ideation, the Tier 2 PST decides to invite James to join a small counseling group focusing on teaching students coping skills to address their anxiety symptoms in school.

The 8-week group intervention is based on the Brief Coping Cat program and is divided into two main parts, with the first focusing on psychoeducation and skill training, and the second devoted to practice of these skills through exposure tasks. A total of five students with moderate anxiety have been selected to participate, and the counselor has reserved a private room for the 50-minute meetings. Through each successive session and homework assignment, James learns to recognize feelings and physical signs of his anxiety, identify problematic thinking and apply coping thoughts instead, engage in relaxation, and apply problem solving to a number of hypothetical and actual anxiety provoking situations. With the assistance of his counselor, he makes a plan for entering anxiety-provoking situations, and practices learned skills with gradually increasing anxiety-provoking situations, like asking a clarifying question in class, participating in group discussion, starting his homework, taking a test, and reaching out to a peer. By starting easy, and being exposed to hypothetical anxiety situations first in the group, James feels more confident to slowly experiencing high-level anxiety situations alone. Meanwhile, the counselor encourages James to repeat the techniques he acquired and celebrate wins. Through his participation in the group, James seems to be developing a friendship with one of the other male students in the group and seems more comfortable talking about his experiences.

Given the extensive literature supporting the effectiveness of school counselor-led interventions in addressing symptoms of anxiety in students, James's positive record of past academic functioning, and his openness to seeking support, the school counselor is hopeful that James will experience a measurable improvement in both emotional and academic functioning following completion of all eight sessions. Scores from the posttreatment assessment will offer crucial comparative data and inform the need for additional follow-up, intervention, and referral. Feedback on the satisfaction James and his parents have experienced with the intervention will be important data for evaluating the success of this intervention, identifying further adjustments, and for sharing with school administration.

CONCLUSION

Whereas students who demonstrate disruptive behaviors in class rarely go unnoticed, students who are experiencing anxiety, depression, or a response to trauma may display more subtle behaviors. Still, intervention for these behaviors is critical to support the mental health and, in turn, academic and social success of students with significant emotional needs. In this chapter, we described how these symptoms manifest, additional assessments for Tier 2 teams to help pinpoint specific needs, and effective interventions for addressing these needs.

CHAPTER 8

Integrating Academic and Social–Emotional–Behavioral Interventions at Tier 2

Stephen Kilgus

David Klingbeil

Julia Porter

The focus of this chapter is on the integration of SEB and academic interventions for students who need Tier 2 supports in both domains, or have co-occurring academic and SEB needs.

CHAPTER FOCUS

- Understand what co-occurring needs are across academics and SEB.
- Develop a working knowledge of an integrated MTSS.
- Understand the six steps to integrating academic and SEB interventions for students with co-occurring needs.

Academic and SEB needs frequently occur together, and sometimes one might trigger the other. Have you ever worked with a student who does not feel confident in an academic subject, and who then goes on to display disruptive or aggressive behaviors? How about the opposite? Have you ever worked with a student who has experienced so much exclusionary discipline for behavioral infractions that they fall behind in an academic skill or subject? We can find students with co-occurring needs by inspecting integrated sources of data and information. First, if you have a

Stephen Kilgus, PhD, is Professor of School Psychology at the University of Wisconsin. His work focuses on school mental health, primarily in areas related to assessment.

David Klingbeil, PhD, is Assistant Professor of School Psychology at the University of Wisconsin. His work focuses on academic and social–behavioral development within multi-tiered systems of support.

Julia Porter, MS, is a doctoral student in School Psychology at the University of Wisconsin.

universal SEB screener, you will easily be able to determine who has a need in an SEB area. Those data can be triangulated with integrated sources mentioned in Chapters 2–7 such as ODRs, visits to the nurse, and classroom-managed social conflict notes. Similarly, academic needs can be measured with academic screeners, or regular academic assessments. Teachers may also use grades, end-of-year performance testing, or academic progress monitoring to detect an academic area of need. It is important to explore which teachers, times of day, or class periods students have both an SEB need and an academic need. In order to match interventions to academic co-occurring needs, it is best to have an integrated multi-tiered systems of support (MTSS) team that is capable of discussing both academic needs and SEB needs. With this comprehensive team, students with co-occurring needs can be discussed and planned for during the same meeting, with all of the contributing information available, rather than in two separate meetings with separate teams. This will help with layering interventions or even braiding together SEB intervention with academic supports. It is also important to note that Tier 2 teams that meet separately for academics and SEB needs may miss the presence of issues in one area or the other. For example, a student who is not a skilled, on-grade-level reader may try to escape reading instruction and demonstrate off-task or disruptive behavior in the classroom. This would look like a self-regulation need to the team that only meets about SEB needs. However, if the team was integrated, both academic and SEB needs would be considered together, and the team would likely start with reading tutoring (and perhaps with some behavioral supports like goal-setting and reinforcement) while encouraging on-task behavior as reading progresses. Guidelines for making these decisions will be provided throughout this chapter.

Chapter 11 dedicates a section to intervening for students with multiple areas of need, which is pertinent to co-occurring academic and SEB needs. The co-occurrence of academic and SEB needs in students is common, as is the negative impact these needs have on school functioning (Darney et al., 2013). Students with SEB challenges are often below grade level in one or more academic areas (e.g., reading, math; Algozzine et al., 2011; Darney et al., 2013). Long-term negative outcomes are also more likely to occur for students with co-occurring academic and SEB needs compared to students with needs in just one domain. Such outcomes can include a higher likelihood of mental health needs, low academic achievement, special education placement, suspensions, and school dropout (Darney et al., 2013; Reinke et al., 2008).

The co-occurrence of academic and SEB needs can begin as soon as a student starts school, although how those behaviors present, and the consequences of those behaviors, differs across developmental level (Darney et al., 2013). Table 8.1 provides some examples of how behavior needs present in schools and under academic challenges.

Research on the development of co-occurring academic and SEB needs has been inconclusive. Hinshaw (1992) completed the first major review of the literature and described four pathways that could explain the relationship between academic and SEB needs. The first two proposed pathways are unidirectional (think of a one-way street). It could be that a student's academic challenges lead to SEB challenges, such as when a student's reading challenges lead them to engage in disruptive behavior to avoid or escape reading instruction. Alternatively, it could be that SEB challenges lead to academic challenges, such as when a student who is frequently off-task misses key instructional content, thus limiting their academic skill growth. A third pathway is bidirectional (think of a two-way street), meaning academic and SEB needs influence each other in an interactive manner. This could be when a student's off-task behavior leads to limited skill growth, which leads to them further disengaging from instruction, thereby further worsening academic performance. Accord-

TABLE 8.1. Co-Occurring Academic and Social, Emotional, Behavioral Challenges across Grade Levels

	Elementary school	Middle/high school
Escape behaviors	Talking out of turn or disrupting class to get out of a nonpreferred activity (e.g., a challenging academic task)	Putting one's head down or walking out of the classroom during challenges activities or tasks
Low engagement	A persistent pattern of passive off-task behavior, such as staring off or flipping through books unrelated to instruction	Disinterest in academics and limited feelings of school belongingness
School refusal	Children refusing to come to school or having difficulty staying in the classroom due to academic anxiety	Skipping class or entire school days due to nonpreferred academic tasks or academic anxiety
School dropout		Persistent challenges in attendance and academic performance, coupled with low school engagement, increases the likelihood of school dropout

ing to Hinshaw (1992), there could be some other factor that explains why students experience both academic and SEB needs, such as language impairment, intellectual ability, inattention, and/or environmental variables (e.g., low socioeconomic status).

It is clear that it is important to provide both academic and SEB interventions when supporting students with co-occurring challenges, as an intervention in only one area is unlikely to drive improvement in both (Algozzine et al., 2011). These interventions can be provided concurrently (i.e., at the same time), either as two stand-alone strategies or in an integrated manner when a single intervention includes elements of academic and SEB supports. Academic and SEB interventions can also be delivered sequentially (i.e., in a staggered fashion), with an intervention beginning in one area followed by an intervention in the other area.

MTSS AS A FRAMEWORK FOR INTEGRATED ACADEMICS AND SEB

At Levi Elementary School, there is one Tier 2 MTSS team or PST that meets about grade-level academic and SEB concerns. With six grade levels, the grade-level team is comprised of all classroom teachers in that grade plus the counselor and an administrator. Often the math and reading coaches are available and also attend meetings. During the grade-level monthly meetings, the PST starts with students who are currently receiving an SEB or an academic Tier 2 intervention. They then discuss any students of concern and highlight both academic and SEB strengths and needs. Their reading and math coaches are trained in self-regulation interventions, and they often serve as the adult in charge of goal setting and behavior contracts.

Although MTSS is a relatively new framework, its origins are rooted in combining long-standing three-tiered frameworks of positive behavioral interventions and supports (PBIS) for SEB needs and response to intervention (RTI) for academic needs (McIntosh & Goodman, 2016). The goal of MTSS is to structure and interweave supports that will prevent and respond to academic and SEB needs in a single system. Given the interconnectedness of academics and behavior, MTSS provides teachers, administrators, instructional and behavior coaches, and other school personnel with efficient structures and systems to prevent and treat co-occurring issues, rather than addressing them separately, which can create redundant and often ineffective data collection, decision making, and instructional delivery.

RTI is a preventative and response framework to address universal academic instruction and respond to academic needs. RTI is based on a three-tier model in which students advance through progressively more intensive treatment phases if their learning difficulties do not diminish with the evidence-based treatments offered at the less intensive tiers of intervention. At Tier 1, students are exposed to high-quality, research-based curricula and instructional methods that are intended to support the majority of students in building academic skills. At Tier 2, students who are nonresponsive to Tier 1 supports receive additional support in a small-group setting that is matched to their needs in terms of their performance level and rate of progress. This support can represent additional exposure to Tier 1 content or the delivery of a supplemental program. At Tier 3, students with the most significant needs receive the most intensive support that is individualized and provided with greater dosage.

RTI logic implies that if a student does not make academic gains using procedures that are evidence-based and shown to be effective with the majority of students, then the student who is struggling could benefit from additional, layered academic support that is tailored to areas of need and presented in smaller groups, in addition to the curricula and instructional methods applied at Tier 1. Students identified as requiring advanced tier support in addition to universal academic instruction are monitored by the Tier 2 or Tier 3 team, who also determines initial and ongoing interventions.

In an MTSS, the RTI system described above interconnects with the PBIS system for SEB needs that is described throughout the book thus far. To do this, the academic and SEB systems are designed to link together; the single team is unified in addressing academic and SEB needs, the data are managed and collected in as much of an integrated process as possible, and the data-based decision-making process across and within academic and SEB needs is consistent. This process is seen as crucial given the interconnected nature of academic and SEB needs. To address a student's academic needs (e.g., below-grade-level reading performance) requires consideration of their SEB needs (e.g., engagement with instruction that will support reading growth), and vice versa. Co-location of academic and SEB decision making is intended to increase the likelihood of coordinated decision making that considers the whole child.

AN INTEGRATED MTSS PROCESS FOR CO-OCCURRING NEEDS

An MTSS model designed to address co-occurring academic and SEB concerns requires certain elements if it is to be successful. First, it must include assessments that can detect students exhibiting concerns in each of these areas. Though schools employ many identification methods, research suggests the most defensible approach involves the administration of universal screening tools (Miller, Cohen, et al., 2015). Second, the MTSS model must also include assessments that provide information regarding the nature of student concerns, thereby informing the selection of interventions aligned with each student's unique needs. Multiple frameworks have provided guidance regarding how needs might be conceptualized and thus the best approaches for assessing student concerns. Harbour and colleagues (2022) proposed six steps to responding to co-occurring academic (RTI) and SEB (PBIS) needs in an integrated MTSS system.

Step 1: Screening and Needs Assessment

Within any given school, there are several students that will experience concerns in academics or SEB functioning. There will also be a notable proportion of students exhibiting concerns in both areas (Kilgus et al., 2019). Research suggests the most defensible means to identify students exhibiting concerns in one or both areas is universal screening, defined as the collection of data across every individual (e.g., student) within a population (e.g., district, school, or grade) to identify those possessing some condition of interest (e.g., co-occurring concerns; Jenkins et al., 2007). At Pleasant Grove Middle School, one team meets on October 1 to discuss and review both academic and SEB screening data. They have a data guru who helps them pull lists of students who are in need of Tier 2 for academics only (and which areas), those in need of SEB only (and which areas), and those with needs in both areas. The team then meets to discuss academic needs only and then academic and SEB needs while the math and reading coaches are present. Next, they meet about students with only SEB needs and invite in their district mental health specialist and social worker.

SEB Screening

As described in Chapter 2, there are several SEB screening tools that have been developed to date, including the BASC-3 Behavioral and Emotional Screening System (BESS; Kamphaus & Reynolds, 2015), Social, Academic, and Emotional Behavior Risk Screener (SAEBRS; Kilgus & von der Embse, 2014), and the Strengths and Difficulties Questionnaire (SDQ; Goodman, 2001). Some screeners provide information related to SEB concerns (e.g., internalizing or externalizing behaviors), others provide information regarding SEB strengths (e.g., social–emotional competencies), and some provide information about both.

Academic Screening

Numerous academic universal screening tools have also been developed to date, including those specific to reading, writing, and mathematics. Two broader categories of academic screening tools have emerged. The first category includes curriculum-based measurement (CBM) tools, which are defined by the use of brief probes of skills (e.g., oral reading fluency) predictive of broad and general outcomes (e.g., overall reading proficiency). The second category includes computer adaptive tests (CATs), which are automated tests that adapt on a student-by-student basis to provide information about each student's unique abilities relative to academic skills. Several vendors have developed CBM or CAT-based universal screening tools, including Acadience Learning, DIBELS, easyCBM, FastBridge, and Renaissance Learning.

Integrated Academic/SEB Screening

Notably, some screening tools also afford information regarding the presence of SEB needs that are proximal to academic performance. For instance, the SAEBRS Academic Behavior subscale is an indicator of the extent to which students are prepared to access and benefit from academic instruction (Kilgus et al., 2013). Research suggests the subscale predicts several outcomes, including academic enabling skills (e.g., motivation, organization, academic engagement), academic achievement, and attentional challenges that interfere with academic performance (Ezell, 2018; Kilgus et al., 2013, 2016). In addition, the BASC-3 BESS Adaptive Skills risk index affords information regarding skills associated with success at home and school (Dowdy et al., 2019), including related to adaptability, organization, motivation, and ability to work within a group. Lower scores on the SAEBRS and BASC-3 BESS subscales could indicate which students need additional support given SEB needs that are related to academic performance. See the "Step 2: Assign and Implement Matched Intervention(s)" section below for more information on supports that are aligned with such needs.

Academic and SEB screening tools typically yield categorical information that can be used in determining a student's risk for difficulty. This information can then be cross-referenced in determining whether a student is exhibiting risk in one or both areas. Some students might require academic and SEB support within the same tier, while others might require supports across multiple tiers. For instance, a student might require Tier 2 supports for their SEB concerns and Tier 3 supports for their academic concerns. This example reflects the reality that students are not "tiers," but rather are dynamic individuals that necessitate differing forms and levels of support across their various domains of functioning.

Specific Needs Assessment

Needs in SEB and academic domains can be defined as the difference between what is expected of the student and their current performance (Kratochwill & Bergan, 1990). For instance, literacy screening benchmarks might suggest a student should be able to correctly read 100 words per minute in the winter of third grade, yet they are currently reading only 65. Similarly, state-level standards for social–emotional skills might indicate that a late elementary student should be capable of describing a range of emotions and their causes. However, teachers and parents report a student struggles to communicate their feelings and inconsistently uses appropriate coping strategies.

Once a student has been identified as exhibiting some need(s), the next step is to analyze the factors that contribute to the identified need(s) to inform intervention selection. This step can be complicated for students with co-occurring needs, reminding us of the universal "chicken and the egg" question which has yet to be settled. This step has historically been referred to as "problem analysis." A behavioral approach to assessment is well suited for conducting problem analysis for students with co-occurring needs (Tilly, 2008). Adopting a behavioral approach to assessment means that we ensure our assessment addresses the environmental conditions that contribute to the behavior(s), we use assessment data to design the intervention, and we continue assessment throughout the intervention process to inform further modifications to the intervention as necessary. Figure 8.1 illustrates how assessments and interventions interact within this process to support student needs.

A critical question for students with academic, SEB, or co-occurring concerns is whether the needs are occurring due to skill issues, performance issues, or both (see Chapter 2). When students do not have the underlying skills necessary to exhibit the expected performance, then intervention would likely include skill instruction (e.g., academic, social skills). When students have the skills necessary but do not deploy them routinely, intervention may need to target skill fluency or generalization. When needs are performance issues, intervention may address aspects of the environ-

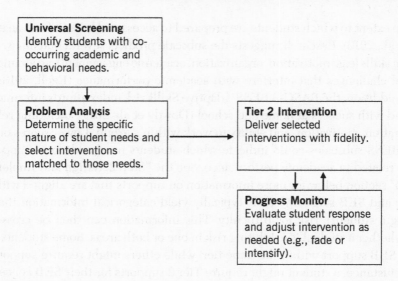

FIGURE 8.1. Data-based decision-making approach to supporting student needs.

ment to increase reinforcement for the expected behavior and reduce reinforcement provided for competing unwanted or "problem" behavior.

For students with co-occurring SEB and academic needs, it is critical to determine the interplay between the observed behaviors in both areas (Berry Kuchle et al., 2015). For example, could a student's challenging behaviors be caused by their attempt to escape academic tasks that they find too difficult (e.g., student who lacks oral reading confidence disrupts the lesson before their turn to read)? Are their perceptions of a task's difficulty related to lagging academic skills that are necessary to complete grade-level tasks? When assessment data indicate the concerns in SEB and academic concerns are related, integrated interventions targeting both domains may be warranted (Gettinger et al., 2021). Although the processes for conducting problem analysis for SEB and academic concerns may seem unalike, there is support for using a functional analytic approach to analyze needs across both areas (Bruhn et al., 2020; Daly et al., 1997). In the following sections, we describe this approach and a general framework for aligning analyses across SEB and academic skill areas.

Step 2: Assign and Implement Matched Intervention(s)

Once educators have reviewed the relevant assessment data, developed a hypothesis for why the co-occurring SEB and academic needs are occurring and whether the two areas of need are related, and selected an intervention to address each need or a single intervention that addresses both areas of need (e.g., goal setting during math calculation instructional time), two additional questions may require answers. First, what is the most optimal or preferred order of intervention implementation? Statewide achievement test data suggests that the percentage of students (in grades 3 through 8) who need more than Tier 1 support exceeds typical conceptualizations of MTSS in the literature (15% of students receiving supplemental support, 5% receiving intensive support; Tilly, 2008) in many schools (Klingbeil et al., 2023). When choosing interventions for students with co-occurring SEB and academic concerns, educators should consider if a student's needs in either domain would prevent them from benefiting from an intervention in the other domain. In that case, it may be prudent to prioritize intervention targeting the domain that may interfere with the intervention efforts in the other area first. When it is unclear which area may interfere with the other, implementing intervention(s) targeting areas of concern in both domains may be warranted. As we describe below, integrated interventions that concurrently target academic and SEB domains (e.g., Gettinger et al., 2021) may be more feasible to implement.

Second, for some students, would the needs in one domain warrant intensive support, rather than Tier 2 support? The question whether the concerns in one area may interfere with intervention efforts in the other is still relevant. Yet, it is important to note that it may be necessary to combine intensive support in one area with Tier 2 support in another. In such situations, it may be feasible to start the Tier 2 support first (which by nature should be readily available) while continued problem analysis occurs to target the intensive supports (e.g., a comprehensive functional behavior assessment) and determine the necessary individualized supports.

At Pleasant Grove, the integrated PST discusses each initial Tier 2 case using the framework of first identifying whether the student has an academic only, SEB only, or SEB and academic area of need, and second, pinpointing subscale areas of need identified in those domains. They have a matrix of available academic and SEB interventions and work to match students to the least intensive intervention necessary. They are always cognizant to avoid layering on too many interventions for one student. As previously described, they leverage math and reading coaches when possible to help implement SEB interventions for students with co-occurring academic and SEB needs. This helps the team divide the work and keep an eye on both areas of need.

Order of Intervention for Co-Occurring Needs

As noted at the outset of this chapter, research is inconclusive regarding the causal relationship between academic and SEB functioning. Thus, one cannot assume that support in one of these areas will lead to improvement in both areas for students exhibiting co-occurring concerns. Accordingly, it is likely a combined intervention approach that integrates academic and SEB supports is the best course of action. Yet, it is likely that many schools will not have the time, resources, and personnel to provide all students support across both areas. Students might then begin with intervention in one of these areas, followed by support in the other if the initial course of intervention is not sufficiently effective. Below we provide information regarding three different approaches to intervention, including (1) initial academic support, (2) initial SEB support, and, finally (3) combined academic and SEB support. Resources that might be utilized to support each of these approaches are outlined in Table 8.2.

ACADEMIC INTERVENTION FIRST

Once students are identified as needing additional intervention, and an appropriate target for intervention is identified via problem analysis, the next step is to select an academic intervention. Tier 2 interventions are typically delivered in small groups, for 20 to 40 minutes, three to five times per week. The goal of Tier 2 intervention is to help students quickly build the necessary skills so that they can succeed in Tier 1 instruction once the intervention supports are removed (Fuchs et al., 2017). Providing additional opportunities to practice the skills identified in the problem analysis is critical to accomplishing this goal.

TABLE 8.2. Resources for Assessment and Intervention of Academic and SEB Skills

Resource	Skill areas	Processes addressed
Books		
Shapiro, E. S., & Clemens, N. H. (2023). *Academic skills problems* (5th ed.). Guilford Press.	Reading, math, writing	• Problem analysis • Intervention targeting • Intervention strategies with step-by-step directions
Codding, R. S., Volpe, R. J., & Poncy, B. C. (2017). *Effective math interventions*. Guilford Press.	Math	• Problem analysis • Intervention targeting • Intervention strategies with step-by-step directions
Burns, M. K., Riley-Tillman, T. C., & VanDerHeyden, A. M. (2012). *RTI applications* (Vol. 1). Guilford Press.	Reading, math, writing	• Problem analysis • Intervention targeting • Intervention strategies with step-by-step directions
von der Embse, N. P., Eklund, K., & Kilgus, S. P. (2022). *Conducting behavioral and mental health assessments in MTSS*. Taylor & Francis.	SEB	• Problem analysis • Intervention targeting • Intervention strategies with step-by-step directions
Chafouleas, S. M., Johnson, A. H., Riley-Tillman, T. C., & Iovino, E. A. (2021). *School-based behavioral assessment: Informing prevention and intervention*. Guilford Press.	SEB	• Problem analysis • Intervention targeting
Intervention websites		
Intervention Central *www.interventioncentral.org*	Reading, math, writing, SEB	• Intervention strategies with step-by-step directions • Also has strategies for studying/organization
Missouri Evidence-Based Intervention Network *https://education.missouri.edu/ebi*	Reading, math, SEB	• Intervention strategies with step-by-step directions • Interventions are categorized by the instructional hierarchy
Pirate Math Equation Quest *www.piratemathequationquest.com*	Math problem solving	• Intervention strategies with step-by-step directions
Resilience Education Program (REP) *https://smhcollaborative.org/rep*	SEB	• Intervention strategies with step-by-step directions
Review websites		
Evidence for ESSA *www.evidenceforessa.org*	Reading, math, SEB	• Review evidence for Tier 1 (universal) strategies • Review evidence for Tier 2/3 interventions

(continued)

TABLE 8.2. *(continued)*

Resource	Skill areas	Processes addressed
National Center on Intensive Intervention—Tools Charts *https://intensiveintervention.org/tools-charts/overview*	Reading, math, SEB	• Reviews evidence for a number of screening and progress monitoring tools • Reviews evidence for academic intervention tools
What Works Clearinghouse—Practice Guides *https://ies.ed.gov/ncee/wwc/practiceguides*	Reading, math, writing, SEB	• Published practice guides that rate evidence for recommendations when delivering intervention in various skills areas • These guides highlight key components to look for in free or published intervention strategies.
CBM assessment tools (free)		
Acadience Learning *https://acadiencelearning.org*	Reading, math	• Free, downloadable curriculum-based measures • Useful for screening and progress monitoring in grades K–8 (reading) or grades K–6 (math) • May also be useful for survey level assessments
DIBELS 8th edition *https://dibels.uoregon.edu/materials/dibels*	Reading	• Free, downloadable curriculum-based measures • Useful for screening and progress monitoring in grades K–8 • May also be useful for survey level assessments
EasyCBM *www.easycbm.com*	Reading, math	• Free, downloadable curriculum-based measures • Useful for progress monitoring assessments • Free version has limited number of assessments and grades in comparison to the purchased version. • May also be useful for survey level assessments
SuperKids Math Worksheet Generator *www.superkids.com/aweb/tools/math/index.shtml*	Math	• Makes single-skill CBM probes for survey level assessment in math computation
SEB progress monitoring tools (free)		
Direct Behavior Rating (DBR) *https://dbr.education.uconn.edu*	SEB	• Free, downloadable DBR tools • Useful for progress monitoring • May also be useful for universal screening
Behavior and Feelings Survey (BFS) *https://weiszlab.fas.harvard.edu/measures*	SEB	• Free, downloadable BFS tools • Useful for progress monitoring

Note. A number of other assessment tools exist that may be used for screening and progress monitoring. We only included measures that were free to download (as of February 2023) in the table.

There is no shortage of academic interventions, across reading, math, and writing, available to educators. These interventions range from free intervention scripts available online to intervention programs that must be purchased. Intervention scripts with step-by-step directions for the interventions we describe below (as well as a number of other supports) can be found in the sources listed in Table 8.2.

Selecting an appropriate intervention may be daunting. However, the instructional hierarchy described in the problem analysis section above is also suitable for categorizing intervention components that are aligned with student skill levels. Regardless of the specific intervention chosen, maximizing student engagement during intervention sessions is critical for students with co-occurring academic and SEB concerns. Ensuring that practice opportunities are at the appropriate instructional level, providing students with choices regarding intervention tasks or content, and reinforcing positive behaviors using extrinsic reinforcement are helpful methods to maximize student engagement during academic intervention (Kruger et al., 2016).

Researchers have reliably demonstrated that intervention components can be matched to the student's level of performance to optimize intervention effects (Daly et al., 1997). When student performance is inaccurate and slow (i.e., in the acquisition stage), interventions should emphasize explicit instruction and immediate corrective feedback to facilitate accurate responding. When reviewing available programs and interventions to determine if instruction is explicit, practitioners should look for interventions that (1) segment complex skills into manageable units, (2) precisely explain how to perform the skill via clear descriptions and modeling of the skill being used, (3) use faded prompts to promote accurate practice, and (4) provide practice opportunities to facilitate accurate performance (Hughes et al., 2017). Examples of free interventions that are well-suited for students in the acquisition stage of learning include incremental rehearsal, listening passage preview, and cover-copy-compare.

Once students are accurate in performing the targeted skill, the next step is to facilitate the appropriate rate of responding (i.e., the proficiency stage). Interventions at this stage should emphasize repeated opportunities to practice, perhaps with a timing component, with delayed corrective feedback. Some explicit instruction may be helpful, but since students should be able to perform the skill accurately, most of the intervention session should be focused on facilitating repeated practice of the skill. Example interventions that facilitate repeated opportunities to respond in this manner include repeated reading, word sorts, and explicit timing.

Knowing the intervention components to look for, based on the student's current level of responding, will allow educators and practitioners to review interventions (either those on hand or those in the literature) to select an evidence-based intervention that is aligned with the student's needs. Selecting an intervention that matches the student's current level of performance is likely to facilitate larger improvements in academic achievement than choosing interventions based on some other modality will (Burns et al., 2012). For readers more familiar with SEB intervention, this is similar to choosing an intervention based on behavior function rather than behavior topography.

SEB-RELATED INTERVENTIONS FIRST

An approach involving an initial SEB intervention could employ various Tier 2 interventions specifically designed for students experiencing difficulties within the academic context (e.g., hyperactivity/inattention). Some interventions are designed to teach students key academic enabling skills (e.g., staying on task, completing assignments), which will enhance their ability to be prepared for and benefit from academic instruction. As noted above, the SAEBRS Academic Behavior and BASC-3 BESS Adaptive Skills subscales would be particularly appropriate indicators for which students would benefit from these interventions. One example of this intervention type is the Homework, Organization, and Planning Skills (HOPS) curriculum, through which students are taught a variety of skills crucial to academic performance. Research suggests HOPS implementation is associated with improvements in organized action, time and materials management, homework completion, and planning (Langberg et al., 2012).

Other Tier 2 SEB interventions are designed to prompt and reinforce students for engaging in positive behaviors that promote their academic engagement, work completion, and academic performance. One such intervention is Breaks are Better (BrB; Boyd & Anderson, 2013), which was designed for students exhibiting problem behavior for the purpose of escaping academic instruction. BrB is founded upon Check-In/Check-Out (CICO) procedures, which are described in greater detail in Chapter 4. Like CICO, students in BrB check in and out with a mentor each morning and afternoon, respectively. Students also receive performance feedback from their teacher(s) at multiple points throughout each school day. A daily progress report (DPR) form facilitates this process. Teachers use the DPR to rate students relative to personalized behavioral targets aligned with schoolwide expectations (e.g., "Asked for help the right way, if I needed it" as an indicator of "Responsibility"). Students can then earn a reward contingent upon meeting a daily goal for percentage of points earned.

Students enrolled in BrB can take a predetermined number of breaks each day. Students are taught the times during which breaks may be taken (e.g., large-group instruction), when breaks should not be taken (e.g., while taking an exam), the activities they can engage in during breaks (e.g., reading a book, drawing a picture, using a computer tablet), and how to respond to a break request denial (e.g., say "That's ok" and return to the task at hand). Students are further taught that requesting a break involves (1) determining if it is an appropriate time to take a break, (2) delivering a predetermined signal to their teacher that they would like to take a break, and (3) taking a break appropriately if granted. Finally, students are taught they can earn DPR points or rewards for each break they do not use when they meet their daily goal. This component of the intervention is intended to support students in increasing their tolerance for academic activities while promoting their positive behavior.

Combined Academic and SEB Intervention for Co-Occurring Needs

An alternative approach to Tier 2 intervention could include combined interventions, which blend academic and SEB supports into a single integrated strategy. Rather than implementing academic and SEB strategies in parallel and isolated fashion, combined approaches deliver components that are intended to complement and build upon one another. One example of a combined strategy is the Academic and Behavior Combined (ABC) Support intervention. ABC Support was designed to simultaneously address reading fluency and academic engagement, incorporating elements of repeated reading and CICO (Gettinger et al., 2021). Specifically, the intervention was designed to teach key academic and SEB skills, while also including elements to prompt and reinforce the display of these skills.

ABC Support includes multiple "evidence-based kernels" from other academic and SEB interventions, which are integrated into individual elements. Such elements include, but are not limited to, (1) an integrated set of reading and behavior expectations, which are taught to students via the acronym READ (*R*ead carefully; *E*nthusiasm and excitement in voice; *A*ttention and positive attitude; *D*o best reading and behavior); (2) goal setting specific to both oral reading fluency (i.e., words correct per minute) and behavior (i.e., percent of points earned on a DPR), (3) feedback and praise relative to both reading and behavior expectations, and (4) generalization of skills to other settings via the use of visual aids that allow students to self-evaluate their performance relative to expectations. Research supports the efficacy of ABC Support in improving oral reading fluency and academic engagement, as well as the educator perceptions of ABC Support feasibility and acceptability (Gettinger et al., 2021). It should be noted that other integrated interventions are emerging in the literature, including those that target social–emotional concerns. One example is a reading intervention with anxiety management instruction (RANX), which has demonstrated the capacity to promote reading outcomes while simultaneously mitigating reading-related anxiety in elementary students (Vaughn et al., 2022).

Step 3: Ensure Interventions Are Feasible and Implemented with Fidelity

It is important for teams to evaluate the fidelity with which interventions are delivered. Support for students with co-occurring concerns can be potentially complex, involving the delivery of multiple interventions and/or the evaluation of student performance across multiple domains. When evaluating whether a student has responded to interventions (e.g., via progress monitoring), it is important to know whether the interventions have been delivered as intended. Fidelity data might help to explain patterns in progress monitoring data. For instance, consider a student whose is receiving ABC Support, and whose monitoring data suggest improvement in behavior but a lack of progress in academics. Fidelity data might suggest that while the SEB portions of the intervention are being consistently delivered, academic intervention sessions are not occurring in accordance with the prescribed schedule. These findings would suggest that the best course of action is not to change the intervention, but rather to implement strategies that will lead to more consistent intervention implementation. Researchers have generated guidance for the evaluation of fidelity assessment, suggesting that it (1) can be founded upon direct observation, interventionist self-report, or permanent product review; and (2) should take a multidimensional approach, involving the evaluation of adherence, quality, and exposure (Sanetti & Fallon, 2011).

Which approach to fidelity assessment will be most appropriate will depend on the intervention. For instance, in evaluating the fidelity of HOPS or other academic interventions (including the academic component of ABC Support), practitioners can examine to what extent students have received the intended intervention dosage. This can be tracked by attendance logs of which students attended each session and how long each session lasted. An interventionist could also self-report whether they delivered various key components of each intervention, such as verbal overviews and modeling of instructed skills along with opportunities to practice. In evaluating the fidelity of BrB (or the CICO component of ABC Support), it is appropriate to examine the completed DPRs as a permanent product of intervention implementation. DPRs should indicate whether (1) students attended morning Check-In (DPR was received) and afternoon Check-Out (DPR was returned), (2) teachers provided feedback following target activities throughout the day (indicated by completed ratings), (3) reward was delivered contingent upon goal attainment, and (4) DPR results were communicated to the student's caregiver (as indicated by signed and returned DPR).

At Pleasant Grove, after forming the integrated academic and SEB Tier 2 team, they decided that the number of students who required an SEB intervention warranted hiring a behavior coach to make their Tier 2 plan feasible and sustainable. This new position would allow for better SEB support on the Tier 2 team and fill the full-time behavior coach position required for CCE.

Step 4: Progress Monitor across Domains

Next, progress monitoring data should be collected on an ongoing basis (e.g., monthly) to evaluate student response to intervention. Research strongly supports the use of CBM tools for academic progress monitoring (Van Norman et al., 2018). The SEB progress monitoring literature is far less robust, but there is evidence to support the use of various direct behavior rating (DBR) tools (e.g., DBR single-item scales; Chafouleas, 2011) and brief behavior rating scales (e.g., Behavior and Feelings Survey; Weisz et al., 2020). Though research has yielded guidance regarding multiple decision rules that can be applied to CBM data in determining intervention effectiveness, there is a lack of clear support for such rules with SEB tools (Bruhn et al., 2020). Thus, it is recommended that decision making be founded upon visual analysis and the evaluation of effect sizes (see von der Embse et al. [2022] for more information on the evaluation of progress monitoring data).

Step 5: Ongoing Data-Based Decision Making

With regular (e.g., monthly) progress monitoring data, data should be used to inform intervention-related decisions, such as whether interventions should be faded or intensified. It is important to note that making these instructional decisions does not necessarily mean changing the intervention to a new intervention. Conversely, many academic interventions can be intensified (e.g., 30 minutes per week rather than 15) and faded (e.g., once a week rather than daily small group) without changing the intervention. The same holds true for SEB interventions. These interventions can be intensified (e.g., adding a midday check-in) or faded (e.g., shift to self-evaluation) without changing the intervention. In this way, the system remains more efficient and the effort load on educators stays low. The integrated Tier 2 team should make these decisions on a regular basis and communicate the decisions and progress to the family and other educators involved in the student's learning. The data guru, Mr. Myorka, was the Pleasant Grove specialist who created easy-to-use Google Sheets for all of the classroom teachers and interventionists to enter progress monitoring data across all SEB and academic domains. Given his talents for organizing and analyzing data, he also created visual representations of student progress and goal attainment. During their Tier 2 meetings, Mr. Myorka displayed graphs and charts representing student outcome data across academic and SEB domains, as well as implementation fidelity, for the Tier 2 team members to view. From these data, the team was able to make sound, data-based decisions for maintaining, fading, or intensifying interventions based on rates of progress.

Step 6: Fidelity to the Process

The final step in an integrated MTSS for co-occurring academic and SEB needs is ongoing evaluation of the system and process. For this, several considerations are critical. First, educators should ensure that the integrated teaming process is cohesive and efficient. Particularly at the advanced tiers (i.e., Tiers 2 and 3), it is important for academics and SEB not to be addressed in separate silos, but for individual student cases to be discussed and conversations to take place regarding co-occurring needs, which to respond to first, and causes of these co-occurring needs. Teams will need both the content knowledge/expertise and time to have these important case-by-case discussions. Second, the system must monitor and respond to rates of tier movement. As mentioned earlier, a student may respond to Tier 2 SEB intervention and return to receiving only Tier 1 supports, while also moving to Tier 3 supports for reading. Integrating these two domains can be complex when it comes to tier movement and monitoring tier movement but these decisions should be flexible and person-centered.

Third, it is critical that the team and administration consider the training required for educators engaged in Tier 2 teams and intervention implementation. When considering students with co-occurring academic and SEB concerns, it may be helpful to ensure that Tier 2 problem-solving teams include educators with expertise in academic skill development and instruction along with individuals with an understanding of behavior function and intervention. Teams should also consider the expertise and resources required to implement the interventions, as designed, in a standardized fashion. Many of the evidence-based interventions suitable for use at Tier 2 can be implemented using peers (or computers/tablets in the case of academic interventions), which can reduce the resource demands. Regardless of who delivers the intervention, teams should ensure that interventionists are trained to implement the intervention and provided with feedback on implementation with regard to the social acceptability and feasibility of the intervention.

CASE EXAMPLE

Mrs. Rivera reported that Monica, one of her third-grade students, was exhibiting both academic and SEB struggles. Mrs. Rivera's school uses the FastBridge assessment system for administering universal screening tools. Screening results corroborated her concerns, as Monica's scores fell in the Some Risk range on the SAEBRS Academic Behavior subscale and High Risk range on the aReading computer adaptive screening tool. A closer examination of the screening data suggested that Monica struggled with reading fluency, as well as being prepared for instruction (e.g., through organization of her materials) and maintaining academic engagement.

The school's problem-solving team elected to enroll Monica in the ABC Support intervention so that she could receive integrated academic and behavioral intervention. The team also chose to monitor Monica's response to intervention using (1) DBR single-item scales, which afforded an estimate of any change in Monica's academic engagement during math and literacy blocks each day of the week, and (2) FastBridge CBM-Reading probes, which would be an indicator of any change in Monica's oral reading fluency. Data collection began prior to intervention to establish a baseline, and then continued throughout intervention to determine the extent of academic and behavioral change in accordance with ABC Support implementation. The team also elected to evaluate ABC Support implementation in two ways. First, interventionists self-reported whether they delivered key components of reading instruction during each section. Second, the team conducted permanent product reviews to determine whether the major components of CICO were implemented each day.

Monica completed an initial 10-week course of intervention. A review of DBR data indicated her behavior improved. During baseline, she was academically engaged during instruction 65% of the time on average. During intervention, this improved to an average of 92%. Unfortunately, Monica's reading fluency did not improve as expected, with her growth not aligning with a goal line for her performance if she was to catch up to her peers by the end of the year. The problem-solving team was therefore considering more intensive academic interventions for Monica to ensure she received the level of support needed to promote her academic growth.

CONCLUSION

Student needs don't always fit into a neat box of "academic" or "SEB." Oftentimes, students have needs in both areas, and sometimes they are causational. In response, educators should not operate in separate boxes of "academic" intervention and "SEB" intervention. Instead, an integrated MTSS allows advanced tier support to be addressed by one unified PST collaborating to address both academic and SEB needs. The simple six-step process described in this chapter promotes integration and efficiency and decreases the likelihood of educators working separately in silos or addressing only one area of need for students with co-occurring needs. Finally, carefully read Chapter 11 and the considerations for implementation that relate to co-occurring academic and SEB needs. Of importance is the discussion regarding examining conditions. It is possible with co-occurring needs that exist only in one class period or with one classroom teacher that the classroom context, peers, routines, instructional procedures, or personal relationship with the teacher are contributing to or causing poor functioning and learning in that one class period. Similarly, it is important to note that when students do not have a co-occurring academic and SEB need, they then have a strength in one or the other area. Highlight and celebrate areas of strength, even if it is one academic subject that they are interested in and perform well in, while the others need improvement.

CHAPTER 9

Data-Based Decision Making and Ongoing Adaptations at Tier 2

In this chapter, we highlight an approach to ongoing, monthly data-based decision making and designing adaptations based on these data for fading and intensifying.

CHAPTER FOCUS

- Understand various progress monitoring options.
- Learn how to make data-based decisions about intensifying or fading interventions.

DATA-BASED DECISION MAKING

A key element to all three tiers is data-based decision making, but, historically, Tier 2 has been a bit neglected (Bruhn & McDaniel, 2021) across training and publication, at least when it comes to progress monitoring and determining if students are responding to intervention. This decision-making process happens after the intervention has been in place and is based on progress monitoring data collected and reviewed monthly. In this next section, we hope to fill this gap by providing concrete recommendations that are easily applicable within a Tier 2 system during intervention. Our recommendations are adapted from an original article called "A Step-by-Step Guide to Tier 2 Behavioral Progress Monitoring" (Bruhn et al., 2018). In that article, authors described a tried-and-true process that is both systematic and effective. The key, however, is for the Tier 2 team to be planful as the process may feel cumbersome at times. But keep in mind that it is a systematic approach designed to maximize both efficiency and effectiveness, with the ultimate goal of helping students achieve their best and transition back to Tier 1 successfully. Further, using data in the Tier 2 process has several benefits beyond determining the effects of intervention—data can help promote communication among stakeholders and the Tier 2 team, as well as guide decisions about the allocation of resources (Alberto & Troutman, 2012). Thus, the importance of collecting, analyzing, and using data in the Tier 2 problem-solving process cannot be understated. So, once initial adaptations have been agreed upon by the team, it is time to begin planning the data-based decision-making process. This process is used to determine how students are responding to intervention, while considering implementation fidelity. In addition to describing how to collect and use data to determine student response, we also offer recommendations for making intervention adaptations for students who are making adequate progress and for those who are not.

Step 1: Selecting a Measurement Method for Progress Monitoring

The first step in the data-based decision-making process is to select an appropriate method of measurement. This step is dependent on the answer to three questions:

1. What is the behavior targeted for progress monitoring?
2. What is the intervention being implemented?
3. What method can we do consistently and accurately over time with the resources available?

It is likely that time and personnel (implementers) available will dictate what is feasible. In terms of behaviors, some behaviors lend themselves to systematic direct observation (SDO), whereas others might be more conducive to a Direct Behavior Rating (DBR; Chafouleas, 2011) or intervention-based measures (IBMs; Bruhn et al., 2018). We briefly describe each of these measurement tools. Then, we encourage readers to use Table 9.1 as a guide for determining which method or tool is best. These tools are best for measuring observable behaviors. For students with emotional needs, these measures may be appropriate if their symptoms include observable manifestations. However, in Chapter 7, we offer additional measures that are more appropriate for assessing improvements in anxiety and depression. These measures can be used to determine response to the recommended cognitive-behavioral interventions, but are generally administered before and after intervention (not necessarily during intervention like other progress monitoring tools). Table 9.1 provides a comparison of various screeners.

Systematic Direct Observation

SDO is exactly what it sounds like. An observer who is not teaching or implementing sits (generally in a classroom) and directly watches the student while using a systematic method for recording the student's behavior in real time—that is, as it is occurring. As a classroom teacher, this can be a bit tricky to do while teaching at the same time (think talking, walking, chewing gum, and multiplying three-digit numbers all at the same time kind of tricky). Therefore, if the PST wants to collect SDO data, we encourage the team to designate one or two observers who have the schedule flexibility to conduct observations (e.g., behavior specialist, reading coach).

When using SDO, it is important to define what the behavior is and how an observer would know it was occurring by noting specific examples and non-examples. For instance, if you wanted to conduct SDO on disruptive behavior, you might define it as any behavior that causes a distraction to other students, the teacher, or the student themself. Examples include talking out of turn,

TABLE 9.1. Methods of Measurement

Measure	Variable measured and used for progress monitoring	Rating of quality of data (0 = low on sensitivity or objectivity, 1 = moderately sensitive or objective, 2 = very sensitive and objective)	Rating of difficulty (0 = easiest, 1 = moderately difficult, 2 = very difficult)
Systematic direct observation			
Event recording	Number of behaviors that occurred (i.e., frequency)	2	2
Time sampling	Number of intervals the behavior occurred	2	1
Direct Behavior Rating	0–10 rating on Academic engagement, Respectful, Disruptive. Can be daily or weekly	1	1
Intervention-based measures			
CICO DPR	Daily Progress Report scores	0	0
Goal-setting form	Whether the goal was met or not	0	0
Behavior contract	Whether the behavior contract was met or not	0	0
Self-monitoring form	Report of self-regulation variable such as on-task behavior	0	0
Self-graphing	Graph made by student of self-regulation variable	0	0
ABC-GO form	How many ABC-GOs (and therefore major social issues) have occurred in a given amount of time	0	0

Note. Adapted from Bruhn et al. (2018).

making inappropriate noises with body or materials, throwing materials, and talking to peers about nonacademic topics during group work time. Non-examples include raising hand to talk, using materials appropriately, and talking to peers about the task or providing ideas during group time.

After defining the behavior, the team should select a recording system. Although multiple recording systems exist (e.g., duration, latency, whole interval, partial interval), for teams who are not formally trained in SDO, we recommend two that are the most practical and feasible—event recording (frequency count) or time sampling. We also recommend for ease of use to only collect data on one behavior, rather than two more at the same time. With event recording, observers simply count the number of times they see the behavior. That is, every single instance of the behavior should be recorded. This can be done on a simple sheet of paper with tally marks, with a counting device (e.g., *https://tallycounterstore.com/collections/hand-clickers*), or electronically (e.g., smartphone app). One important tip—when counting behaviors, the session length needs to be the same each time so you can compare apples to apples. Four instances of disruptive behavior in a 20-minute session is much different than four instances in a 60-minute session. When session lengths vary, which they are likely to do, then it is best to convert the count to a rate by taking the count divided by the session length (4/20 minutes = 0.20 per minute; 4/60 minutes = 0.07 per minute). Event recording is best used for discrete behaviors with a distinct beginning and ending. These data are also very easily graphed for visual analysis.

Unlike event recording, in time sampling, the behavior is only recorded at a certain time interval. For instance, the team might decide the observer should record whether or not the behavior is occurring every minute (60-second mark). In this case, the team would create a form divided into intervals. Then, the observer would use some type of timing mechanism (e.g., smartphone app, kitchen timer) to prompt the observer to look at the student and record (e.g., yes/no, +/–) whether the behavior is occurring at that exact instance in time. Time sampling is best for behaviors that are more continuous in nature such on-task or off-task behavior. Back to the example, if the observer recorded off-task every minute for 20 minutes (i.e., 20 intervals), then to obtain the percentage of off-task behavior, simply take the number of intervals in which off-task behavior was marked as occurring, divide that by the number of intervals in the session, and multiply by 100. So, if the student was marked off-task in 5 of 20 intervals, the student was off-task for approximately 25% of the session. While these percentages may be a bit more complicated to record and calculate, these data are also very easy to graph.

Remember that although event recording and time sampling require some training and practice, they allow observers to capture what is going in the classroom immediately. SDO is generally the most accurate and sensitive way to measure behavior, which makes it the preferred and recommended method of experts in behavior who are interested in demonstrating behavioral change. However, we know that the resource-intensive nature of SDO makes it difficult to conduct on a regular basis, which is important for fair and accurate progress monitoring. When SDO is not possible, teams may want to consider Direct Behavior Ratings (DBR; Chafouleas, 2011). Figures 9.1, 9.2, and 9.3 provide example data collection forms for SDO.

Student Name: _____   Observer Name: _____

Target Behavior: _____

Examples: _____

Non-Examples: _____

Date	Start time	End time	Total time	Frequency (tally marks)	Total occurrences	Rate (total/time)

FIGURE 9.1. Event data recording sheet.

Student Name: _____   Observer Name: _____

Target Behavior: _____

    Examples: _____

    Non-Examples: _____

Length of Observation: _____   Length of Intervals: _____

Interval	Behavior			Interval	Behavior	
	Yes	No			Yes	No
1				11		
2				12		
3				13		
4				14		
5				15		
6				16		
7				17		
8				18		
9				19		
10				20		

Total Occurrences of Behavior: _____

Percentage of Intervals ($\frac{\text{Total Occurrences}}{\text{20 Intervals}} \times 100$): _____

FIGURE 9.2. Momentary time sampling data recording sheet.

Direct Behavior Ratings

Like SDO, DBR is exactly what it sounds like. A teacher, rather than outside observer, directly observes the student's behavior over a predetermined, sustained amount of time and then provides a rating of that behavior on a scale of 0–10 (Chafouleas et al., 2010). The scale also includes anchor words (e.g., 0 = never, 10 = always) to aid the teacher in scoring. In practice, if the student is struggling with respectful behavior in math class, the team may decide the math teacher should provide the DBR. At the end of math class, the teacher would complete the rating. The original DBR consisted of three predefined behaviors: (1) academic engagement, (2) respectful, and (3) disruptive behavior. However, teams can deviate from this standard form and elect to rate behaviors that are targeted for change with the Tier 2 intervention. In addition to having evidence of reliability and validity (*www.intensiveintervention.org*), the major benefit of using DBR is that it is quick, easy, and requires relatively little training (Riley-Tillman et al., 2008), so it can be used in a variety of contexts and interventions.

Intervention-Based Measures

A third option for measuring progress is what we refer to as "intervention-based measures" (IBMs). These are measures that are built into the intervention or data that are already collected as part of the intervention. For example, some commercially available, manualized curricula (e.g., Social Skills Intervention Guide; Elliott & Gresham, 2009) may include assessments that can be used to track progress. These assessments are designed to track the skills targeted in the intervention. Similarly, CICO also includes an IBM in the daily progress report. On this report, teachers rate the student's behavior throughout the day and the score on the report is used to determine if the student met the daily goal. It is important to remember that if these built-in assessments are being used, they cannot just be used during intervention. They need to be completed pre-intervention, or baseline, as well to provide a comparison over time (see Figure 9.4).

Another example of an IBM is the teacher recording in self-monitoring interventions. Although self-monitoring interventions do not have to have the teacher completing parallel procedures, in the case that they are, these data can be used to track student progress. In the MoBeGo self-monitoring app mentioned in Chapter 5, for example, the teacher records 5 days of baseline data. Then, after an initial goal is set, the student begins to self-monitor with the teacher also completing monitoring at the same time. Both data are graphed within the app. An innovative feature of MoBeGo is the data-based algorithm that uses the teacher's data to determine if the student is making adequate progress and then makes recommendations on how to adjust the intervention as needed (e.g., raise the goal from 50% to 60%).

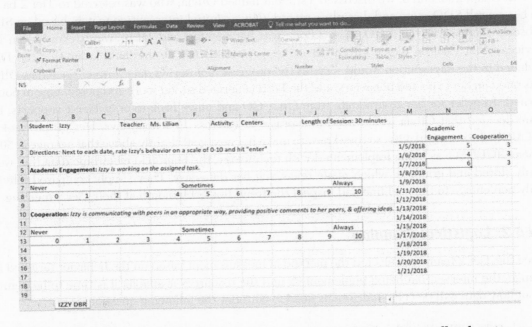

FIGURE 9.3. Izzy's Direct Behavior Rating form in Excel. Adapted from *https://dbr.education.uconn.edu/library/information-for-parents-and-professionals*.

Student Name: _____   Observer Name: _____

Target Behavior: _____

    Examples: _____

    Non-Examples: _____

Length of Observation: _____   Length of Intervals: _____

Directions: When prompted, at each interval mark whether the student was performing the positive behavior ("Y" for yes) or was not performing the positive behavior ("N" for no) at that moment. Both the student and teacher should record at the same time, but this may be done on different forms. Both data may be graphed, but the teacher data will be used to determine responsiveness. Graph the number or percent of "Y."

	1	2	3	4	5	6	7	8	9	10	Total "Y"
Student											
Teacher											

FIGURE 9.4. Intervention-based measure for self-monitoring intervention.

In Chapters 2 and 3, we discussed a student named Olivia, who was referred to Tier 2 based on her overall SDQ score and discipline record. Olivia's initial intervention match, based on SDQ subscale scores, was CICUCO. Mrs. Lopez was her mentor, and DPRs were recorded on her device, rather than on paper. Given her assignment to CICUCO, the team knew that the DPR included in the intervention would serve as the progress monitoring data source. Each day, Olivia was rated on her expected behaviors, and the DPR generated a total score and percentage of points earned. In order for her to graduate from CICUCO and move back to only Tier 1 supports, the team decided that Olivia would need to average 80% across 10 school days. Her initial week of CICUCO she averaged 42%, so they knew to make her next goal slightly above that average at 50%. Since CICUCO was being implemented with technology, the team had electronic data that were easily stored and graphed, which made reviewing her data easy. They simply compared Olivia's daily percentage to the goal line and inspect the trend line each month at their Tier 2 meeting.

Step 2: Logistical Planning

Once the Tier 2 team has selected the method of measurement based on the behavior targeted for change, the intervention being implemented, and the resources available, it is time to be planful about how data will be collected. Teams need to consider the following questions:

1. Who will collect the data?
2. Does the data collector need additional training, and if so, how, when, and by whom will training be delivered?

3. How often will data be collected? Will the baseline data collection schedule differ from the intervention data collection schedule?
4. When/where will data be collected (e.g., during math class)?
5. What materials are needed for data collection (e.g., paper, timer, app, mobile device) and who will be in charge of ensuring access to materials?
6. Will data be graphed, and if so, who will graph the data and how?

Answering these questions prior to data collection will alleviate potential headaches down the road that could derail data collection, make the data collected unreliable, or create an inefficient system. Planning ahead is critical to a smooth, effective, and efficient process (Bruhn et al., 2018).

Step 3: *Collecting Data and Establishing Criteria*

The other component of planning is a bit more complex as it involves setting criteria for adequate progress. Unfortunately, unlike in academics, there are no established growth rates for behavior, nor are there validated decision rules for indicating when a change to intervention is necessary (Bruhn et al., 2020). Further, most teachers are not trained in data-based decision making for behavior, as it is often not a requirement of their undergraduate training program. However, criteria for determining adequate progress cannot happen until baseline data have been collected. These data should be used to establish evaluative criteria and decisions.

Baseline data are data collected prior to intervention implementation. These data indicate the student's present level of performance and, ideally, baseline data would be collected for 3–5 days to get a consistent perspective of the current level of need. After these data have been collected using the method selected in Step 1, the team should analyze the data to determine if the student's behavior is relatively stable, getting worse, or at an acceptable level. If the data indicate the behavior is stable or worsening, then it is likely time to begin intervention once criteria have been established. The team needs to decide what level of behavior indicates responsiveness to intervention and how long that behavior needs to be maintained before fully transitioning back to Tier 1. Let's say, for example, that teachers were rating a student on the CICO daily progress report (without the student knowing) and the 5-day baseline average was 50%. The initial CICO intervention goal may be set just slightly above baseline (50%) at 60%. And the team may decide the goal to reach mastery is for the student to earn 90% of possible points on average for at least 2 weeks before fading intervention. They agree to look at a weekly average of the DPR on Fridays and evaluate whether the student is making adequate progress toward the end goal. They may set criterion like, "the student will improve 10% each week" until they reach 90% or higher for 2 consecutive weeks. The decision rule might be, "If the student improves 10% each week, intervention will continue as is. If the student does not improve at this level each week, intervention will be adapted according to response." This weekly evaluative decision will determine if and how an adaptation is necessary.

Step 4: *Considering Implementation Fidelity*

After the team has set the data collection schedule and collected baseline data, they begin implementing the assigned Tier 2 intervention while continuing to collect data on the student's behavior and following a systematic evaluation process. During the evaluation process in which teams determine if a student is making adequate progress, a key component in this process is implementation fidelity. That is, is the intervention being implemented consistently and accurately? Knowing the answer to this question will influence how student responsiveness is perceived and what next steps should be. Although this is discussed in much more detail in Chapter 10, we briefly discuss it here to reinforce just how important implementation fidelity is.

Specifically, data may indicate that the student is not making adequate progress and thus appears nonresponsive to intervention. Here is where implementation fidelity comes in. If the intervention was not implemented reliably, the student did not have a fair chance to improve their behavior. The team may have to make decisions about how to ensure accurate intervention implementation prior to discarding the intervention, adapting the intervention, or referring the student for further assessment. Similar decisions must be made when the student appears to be responding positively. If Tier 2 intervention fidelity data indicate that interventionists are adhering to the planned protocol, adaptations to either intensify or fade intervention may be in order depending on the student's response.

Step 5: Making Adaptations

The final "step" in the process—and it seems like a bit of a misnomer because it is really a task that may occur multiple times—is making ongoing adaptations based on the student's response. This is different than initial adaptations that are driven by a student's traits or contextual factors. These adaptations, on the other hand, are driven by the ongoing progress monitoring data collected by the Tier 2 team and are made on a regular basis during implementation. We refer to these as "vertical," or ongoing, adaptations. The reason ongoing adaptations are important is because the intervention should not be stagnant, but rather, it should be designed to (1) increase the likelihood of improved behavior and (2) ensure that behavior sustains over time. Classic behavioral science tells us students should never stay in CICO for months on end with an 80% goal with no attention to progress, or lack thereof. This is a recipe for unwanted behavior to reemerge or even get worse, yet some educators and districts advocate for a standard treatment, rigid protocol such as this. In the following section, we dive more deeply into ongoing data-based intervention adaptations to make during implementation. We discuss the types of ongoing adaptations and how they can be used with the various interventions included in the Tier 2 identification and intervention framework.

ONGOING ADAPTATIONS

As the last, but continuous (think ongoing loop rather than straight line with a destination), step in the data-based decision-making process, the team is charged with making ongoing adaptations. That is, they can decide to intensify interventions for students who do not respond, or they can begin to reduce (or fade) interventions for students who have been responsive to intervention and are meeting established criteria. Remembering Olivia's case above, her initial average was 42% with her first goal set at 50% and the plan that ultimately she would reach 80% for 10 school days. After setting her 50% goal, the team met and noticed that her overall average increased to 56% in 1 week. The team celebrated this progress and reported it to both Olivia and her family but decided not to change anything in the intervention. In the second monthly meeting, Olivia's average increased to 67%. Again, the team celebrated and decided not to change anything about the intervention. At the third monthly meeting they noticed a new average of 77%, almost reaching her overall goal. Given this tremendous progress, they decided to fade the midday check-up with Mrs. Lopez, shifting her to CICO only. The team decided to check in on progress the next month to see if that change impacted her progress. At the fourth monthly Tier 2 meeting the team discussed Olivia's new average of 82%. While she had one daily score of 65%, Olivia had reached her overall goal. At this meeting the team decided that Mrs. Lopez would meet with Olivia to celebrate this success and discuss strategies for them decreasing their meetings (e.g., mornings only) with a contingency plan where Olivia knew if she needed to talk to Mrs. Lopez throughout the day, she could have a "Band Pass" to have access to Mrs. Lopez, or just a break in the band room. This fading procedure worked excellently and stayed in place for one more month until Olivia was eventually faded off of CICO as well.

Planning for Nonresponse

For students who have not demonstrated response, this is an especially important step that is sometimes missed, inadvertently or intentionally. Just because a student is not making adequate progress in an intervention according to the data (assuming it is implemented with fidelity), it does not mean it is a mismatched intervention, it is an ineffective intervention, or the student should be referred for further assessment. Before concluding any of those things, the team should consider intensifying or changing elements of the intervention such as goals, feedback, reinforcement, dosage, and other relevant components. For example, a student may be in CICO and not reaching their daily 70% goal. To increase the likelihood of success, the goal could be lowered to something more attainable. It is important to remember that lowering the goal does not mean you are lowering the expectations for students. Rather, you are making it possible for the student to achieve success. Remember, success breeds success. So, once the lower goal is reached, the goal can then be raised!

Feedback is an important component of many interventions, as it can be used to help students become more self-aware while also providing an opportunity for a positive adult–student interaction. A vertical adaptation for students who do not respond is to simply increase the opportunities for feedback. This may involve adding a midday check-up with a mentor to CICO (i.e., CICUCO) or the teacher providing feedback to a student at the end of each self-monitoring interval rather than just at the end of a session. Changing the reinforcement process follows similar logic. If reinforcement (e.g., homework pass, extra recess, special lunch, prize from prize box) is not part of the initial intervention design, it can be added as a contingency. That is, the student has to meet a goal or follow intervention procedures to earn a reinforcer. Prior to designating what the reinforcer is, the team or interventionist should meet with the student to determine what is reinforcing, as that will vary from student to student. Providing choices to students will certainly help improve the reinforcing value.

Dosage is an oft-recognized way to increase the intensity for intervention. Dosage simply refers to the amount of intervention the student receives, and it can be modified in different ways for different interventions. For example, small-group interventions in which students are pulled out for specific skills instruction (e.g., problem solving, social skills) may increase in frequency or duration. If they are meeting once per week, perhaps they meet twice per week. Or, if they are meeting for 15-minute sessions, they could meet for 30-minute sessions.

Planning for Students Who Respond

Similar to when students do not respond, when a student is responding positively they should not remain in a static intervention forever, nor should intervention just be stopped "cold turkey" (Estrapala et al., 2018). A better approach is to slowly fade or change the same intervention components mentioned above—goals, feedback, reinforcement, dosage, and so forth. Research has shown that this gradual approach can result in students' behavioral improvements maintaining over time (e.g., Bruhn et al., 2018; Bruhn et al., 2022; Lane et al., 2012; Miller et al., 2015). The fading adaptations are similar to those done for students not demonstrating response (intensifying), just in the opposite direction. That is, goals are slowly increased; feedback and reinforcement are reduced or made more intermittent; and dosage can be decreased. In Table 9.2, we provide specific examples for how this can be done across a variety of Tier 2 interventions.

CONCLUSION

Educators have a variety of options for collecting data, but the most important thing is to select a method that will actually get used and used effectively. Collecting inaccurate data, or collecting data but never using it, is frustrating for everyone involved in the intervention process. But when the data help paint a picture about how the student is doing and the team uses those data to make successful decisions, the process can be very empowering for educators and students alike. Of course, student response cannot be determined without understanding implementation fidelity. In the next chapter, we dig deeper into fidelity and its critical role across Tier 2 systems, practices, and data.

TABLE 9.2. Fading Tier 2 Interventions by Category

	Relationship with facilitator	Goal focus and structure	Ongoing feedback	Contingent reinforcement	Frequency/dosage
CICO	Fade contact to morning or afternoon, fade to every other day	Increase DPR goals by 10% with goal met	Shift to self-rating and teacher verification	Stretch contingent reinforcement to weekly or increase criteria, eventually praise only	Create a weekly check-in/check-out
Social problem solving	Fade contact with session leader	Increase expectations of prosocial skill use to fewer errors, use across entire school day, use in other locations	Shift to student self-evaluation, session leader feedback intermittent	Contingent reinforcement shifts to intrinsic, having more friends, getting along better	Weekly sessions move to monthly or twice a month or reduce number of minutes per week in session
Self-regulation	Fade to student self-monitors only, less contact with classroom teacher	Increase self-monitoring goal rate, increase student independence with self-monitoring procedures	Ask student for self-evaluative feedback first, then fill in with praise and any other corrective feedback not noted	Decrease contingent reinforcement, promote self-reinforcement	Decrease frequency from daily to every other day, to general weekly monitoring form
Emotional symptoms	Set proactive, brief check-ins with student while decreasing therapeutic or instructional time with student	Have the student self-evaluate feelings, emotions, work toward addressing those independently	Decrease feedback to every other day or weekly during check-ins	Fade contingent reinforcement to intrinsic reinforcement for improved emotional or internal feelings and well-being	Fade frequency of sessions per week, fade from 1:1 to small group, fade number of minutes per session

Note. Adapted from Estrapala et al. (2018).

CHAPTER 10

Technical Assistance to Facilitate Fidelity and Effectiveness at Tier 2

Are you *actually* implementing what you planned? How do you know? These questions are common across all educational initiatives and are particularly important regarding intervention practices implemented with students. We call this issue of adherence to core components "implementation fidelity," also known as "treatment integrity." This includes fidelity across system, procedures, and interventions. In this chapter we discuss these issues, along with the importance of social validity and feasibility.

CHAPTER FOCUS

- Understand the importance of implementation fidelity, social validity, and feasibility.
- Understand how to measure implementation fidelity, social validity, and feasibility.
- Learn how to create effective action plans to improve implementation fidelity.

OVERVIEW OF FIDELITY

Implementation, or treatment, fidelity is a component of intervention planning and delivery that is typically tied to implementation science, or issues surrounding the uptake or translation of evidence-based interventions to real-world practice. This field and area of focus should be paired with developing evidence-based educational interventions. In general, when referring to an intervention or treatment, fidelity means that the components of the intervention were implemented consistently, accurately, and as designed (Yeaton & Sechrest, 1981). Often, researchers are concerned with ensuring treatment fidelity so they can accurately interpret outcomes, and they may break fidelity down into its constituent parts—*adherence* (delivery of specified components), *exposure* (dosage), *quality of delivery* (implementer attitude, enthusiasm, and preparedness), *participant responsiveness* (participants' engagement and enthusiasm), and *program differentiation* (different from other treatments; Dane & Schneider, 1998). For ease of understanding and application, we focus mostly on adherence and exposure aspects of treatment fidelity. We also acknowledge that treatment fidelity can be influenced by a number of factors, including intervention complexity, training and coaching, experience and expertise of the interventionist, and the interventionists' and participants' attitudes toward the intervention.

Other components of implementation science, which we will explore later in this chapter, include social validity and feasibility. While these implementation science components are important in most fields, including medicine, they are critical to the translation of educational research to educational practice. Oftentimes, researchers develop and study interventions in controlled, scientific studies with large resources (e.g., time, funding, expertise). Even when researchers reveal statistically significant outcomes for interventions studied in these tightly controlled experiments, the work has just begun. The next step to improving outcomes for students, educators, and families is to disseminate the newly deemed "evidence-based intervention" to be portable, useful, and acceptable across varying school settings and individuals under typical school conditions—not experimentally controlled ones.

Typically, education researchers closely monitor and ensure implementation fidelity, which helps to define the study's independent variable (i.e., the intervention being tested). However, when a new intervention reaches the dissemination phase and educators are trained to implement, the importance of evaluating and maintaining appropriate levels of implementation fidelity may get lost. Educators are accustomed to adapting interventions and practices to fit their context, resources, and needs. Some may say fidelity is even an "f word." Some might say focusing on implementation fidelity takes more (seemingly nonexistent) time to collect fidelity data, makes practices and interventions too rigid, and adds an unnecessary level of accountability. However, measuring implementation fidelity and initiating action plans to improve implementation fidelity makes training, implementing educational initiatives, and purchasing resources worth the time, personnel, and cost invested. Let's look at an example.

Suppose a school district decides to purchase a new reading curriculum with grade-level kits for K–5 and sends their classroom teachers and reading specialists to a 3-day training. However, the teachers return to their classroom and independently pick out anywhere from 3 to 15 lessons or materials that they liked the best to use in their classroom. Would you expect oral reading fluency, comprehension, or phonemic awareness scores to increase? We would only expect positive outcomes, similar to those produced in research studies, when the intervention is implemented with adherence to the core components of what makes that practice or intervention evidence-based. Similarly, if a school team attends a training on Tier 2, receives materials for five new evidence-based Tier 2 interventions, then goes back to the school and implements only a few components from two interventions, they should not expect to positively address the needs of all students requiring Tier 2 intervention. Nor should they expect improved outcomes.

Not only does focusing on implementation fidelity increase the likelihood of an intervention producing positive outcomes, it is also a strategy to evaluate why interventions seem to be "not working" for a school, classroom, or individual student. Within the Tier 2 context in PST meetings, monthly progress updates are provided. If a student is deemed to not be responding to intervention, the team should first stop to consider if the Tier 2 system, the procedures for that student, and the specific Tier 2 intervention have been put in place with fidelity, rather than assuming the student themself requires a more intensive or different intervention. That is, how can we determine whether an intervention is working if the student never received critical intervention components (e.g., consistent feedback, reinforcement)? For these two primary reasons, we will focus first on overall Tier 2 system fidelity, measured by the Tiered Fidelity Inventory (TFI; Algozzine et al., 2014), followed by fidelity to the Tier 2 procedures for each individual student, and then specific intervention fidelity.

Tier 2 System Fidelity: The TFI

In 2005, partners with the national PBIS Technical Assistance Center published the School-wide Evaluation Tool (SET; Horner et al., 2004) to evaluate Tier 1 PBIS fidelity. At the time, Tier 3 fidelity tools had already been developed (e.g., Prevent–Teach–Reinforce; Dunlap et al., 2010), but no tool was available to evaluate Tier 2 fidelity. In 2019, the same group published the TFI that is used to evaluate fidelity at each of the three tiers. For the first time, schools were able to assess whether they were implementing broad Tier 2 system components with fidelity. The subscales include: teams, interventions, and evaluation. Each of the 13 items across the three subscales is scored on a 3-point Likert scale (i.e., 0, 1, or 2) and requires evidence for each score. The TFI can be used to evaluate the tiers of support that a school is currently implementing, or across all three tiers, even when training and implementation may not have started yet on a specific tier. Each of the tier subscale scores is expected to reach 70% or higher to be considered "implementing with fidelity" and therefore should result in expected positive outcomes. While the Tier 1 subscale requires a school walkthrough and individual interviews of students and educators, the Tier 2 subscale relies only on archival materials (e.g., permanent product meeting notes, data, or annual reports). The TFI should be conducted at least once per year and lead to an updated action plan. The percentage of implementation (e.g., 65%) can indicate an overall level of implementation fidelity, but the critical next step is to assess which items out of the 13 were scored at a 0 or 1. For each of these lower-scored items, the team decides on actions they will take to improve the score prior to the next administration of the TFI. For this reason, the overall score or percentage is important, but addressing the individual items that have low scores is a critical step to ensuring improved implementation. This will make the time and resources invested in Tier 2 worthwhile. As an example, Morris Middle School decided that they would evaluate overall PBIS fidelity each May, across all three tiers. At each tier, and specific to Tier 2, they would analyze the TFI results for the Tier 2 subscale to determine: areas of success, areas requiring a slight improvement, and areas that need significant improvement. For each of the items that were scored a 0 or 1, the team would act to improve those items. In some cases, this meant changing simple procedures such as meeting times. For other items, it meant more significant changes such as introducing the screener procedures to be universal, rather than targeted and based on teacher nomination.

The Tier 2 Procedural Fidelity Checklist

Beyond overall systems fidelity, which evaluates how well the team, broad interventions (e.g., how many you have available, whether they are matched to student need), and evaluation process are working, the individual procedural fidelity checklist is used to evaluate how well individual interventions are executed for each student receiving Tier 2 intervention. For this, the Tier 2 Identification and Intervention (T2I2) Procedural Fidelity Checklist in Figure 10.1 is used. The same team at Morris decided to use a procedural fidelity checklist on 20% of the students receiving Tier 2 intervention each year. For every 10 students on Tier 2, two of them had full procedural checklists completed to monitor whether the procedures being used were put in place with adherence to the initial plan. The data collected helped the team identify common areas that were implemented as intended and those that were not implemented as intended across the eight procedural checklists they had the first year.

This tool includes 25 individual items across seven subscales. The subscales are presented in order of the step-by-step process that should be implemented with each student Tier 2 case: resources, identification, matching, decision rules and initial adaptation, progress monitoring, data-based decision making, and communication with stakeholders. Like the TFI, each item is scored on a 3-point Likert scale (0, 1, or 2). Unlike the TFI, this tool can be completed either during Tier 2 case management (e.g., while the student is receiving Tier 2 supports), or after Tier 2 supports have concluded. During intervention, first, educators may assess the level to which each intervention task is completed, which may help to identify steps that were omitted, not completed, or scored with a 2. This process can be used to formatively evaluate whether a student is not responding to Tier 2 due to a lack of procedural fidelity. For instance, the team may discover that no initial or ongoing adaptations were actually made to intervention procedures, despite data indicating they were necessary. In the second application, the team might complete this tool after a student has concluded Tier 2 services. This would allow the team to summatively evaluate the extent to which procedures were completed as intended. With either approach, the overall percentage of fidelity should lead educators to identify individual items that can lead to an action plan to improve procedural fidelity and increase the likelihood that the Tier 2 process is both consistent and effective.

Tier 2 Intervention Fidelity

Within the Tier 2 system, multiple and varied evidence-based interventions should be available. In Chapters 5–9, we describe several interventions and their core components. We also highlight strategies to evaluate the adherence to implementing these core components for each intervention. This level of fidelity assessment offers the most proximal, nuanced, and direct view of implementation fidelity, and should be evaluated regularly (e.g., weekly, monthly) for each student receiving Tier 2 intervention prior to the monthly PST data meeting. By assessing individual intervention fidelity (not just the overall Tier 2 system using the TFI), Tier 2 teams can provide the implementer with ongoing feedback regarding their implementation practices, check to see the student actually has an opportunity to benefit from the intervention, and ensure that core components have not been changed or omitted in the adaptation process. At Morris, the individual implementation was monitored at 6-week intervals. Every 6 weeks, the administrative team would observe Tier 2 interventions and review permanent products (e.g., goal-setting sheets, CICO DPRs). The week-long data collection period would ensure at least 20% of students were observed and multiple permanent products were reviewed.

Each Tier 2 intervention will have a different form for evaluating fidelity that includes explicit descriptions of core components, and an evaluation method to determine if that component was in place fully, partially, or not at all. Intervention fidelity is most accurately evaluated using an observer who records observed intervention components. This observer could be someone from

Student Name: _____

Item	Criteria for Scoring	Rating (0, 1, 2) or N/A
Resources Subscale 1		**6 Total**
1.1 Referral to Tier 2 received and responded to within 72 hours	0 = Referral not responded to 1 = Referral responded to after 72 hours 2 = Referral responded within 72 hours	
1.2 Team allocated time to meet and review student case	0 = Team did not have time to meet 1 = Some team members were given time to meet 2 = All team members were allocated time to meet	
1.3 Team had the correct forms, resources, materials needed to complete the case administration	0 = Team did not have any forms or materials needed 1 = Team had some forms or materials needed 2 = Team had all forms or materials needed	
Identification Subscale 2		**10 Total**
2.1 Universal screener completed by appropriate staff	0 = Screener informant has not known student for requisite time (e.g., 1 month). 1 = Screener informant has known student for a portion of the requisite time. 2 = Screener informant has known student for the entirety of the requisite time.	
2.2 Completed all items on screener	0 = Screener not complete 2 = Screener complete	
2.3 Screener data were scored for total and subscales	0 = Screener data left as raw and not scored for total and subscales 1 = Total or subscales were scored but not both 2 = Total and subscales were all scored	
2.4 Screener analysis report developed	0 = Screener analysis data not summarized in a report 1 = Screener analysis data summarized in anecdotal report 2 = Screener data summarized in formal report	

(continued)

FIGURE 10.1. Tier 2 Identification and Intervention (T2I2) Procedural Fidelity Checklist.

Item	Criteria for Scoring	Rating (0, 1, 2) or N/A
Domain Identification and Matching Subscale 3		**4 Total**
2.5 (a) Referring teacher, (b) administrator, and (c) team are made aware of the new Tier 2 case	0 = Confirmation of Tier 2 case not communicated 1 = Confirmation of Tier 2 case communicated to at least one group or person 2 = Communication of Tier 2 case confirm communicated to all three groups	
3.1 Specific, prioritized domain(s) identified by the team using screening data	0 = Intervention assignment does not match screener domain 1 = partial match such as assignment to the correct strategy but not to level of intensity 2 = Intervention assignment matches screener domain	
3.2 Evidence-based Tier 2 interventions within identified domain(s) are matched to intensity of (a) need, (b) contextual fit, (c) student characteristics, (d) available resources	0 = Intervention is not matched 1 = Intervention is matched to at least two of the components 2 = Intervention is matched to all four components	
Decision Rules and Initial Adaptation 4		**6 Total**
4.1 Team identifies and records decision rules for (a) expected mastery criteria, (b) pace of expected improvement, (c) level of improvement per monthly data analysis	0 = Team does not identify or record decision rules 1 = Team identifies and records at least one rule 2 = Team identifies and records all three rules	
4.2 Decision rules have been applied to ongoing data-based intervention decisions	0 = Team does not revisit or adhere to decision rules documented 1 = Team discusses decision rules but does not apply them in making decisions 2 = Team adheres to decision rules, updates decision rules, and applies them in making intervention decisions	
4.3 Team identifies and records potential intervention adaptations to improve effectiveness if student does not respond	0 = Team does not identify or record adaptations for nonresponse 2 = Team identifies and records potential adaptations for nonresponse	

(continued)

FIGURE 10.1. *(continued)*

Item	Criteria for Scoring	Rating (0, 1, 2) or N/A
Progress Monitoring 5		**8 Total**
5.1 Team identifies and records progress monitoring schedule for student case (e.g., daily, weekly)	0 = Team does not identify or record progress monitoring schedule to be used 2 = Clear progress monitoring schedule is identified and recorded	
5.2 Team identifies and records progress monitoring tool that matches intervention and SEB domain	0 = Team does not identify or record appropriate progress monitoring tool that matches intervention and SEB domain 2 = Progress monitoring tool identified is matched and appropriate	
5.3 Team identifies and notifies who will collect progress monitoring data	0 = Team does not identify who is responsible for monitoring progress 1 = Team does not report notifying the person responsible for monitoring progress 2 = Team identifies and notifies the person responsible for monitoring progress	
5.4 Team identifies and notifies who will bring progress monitoring data to case review meeting monthly	0 = Team does not identify or notify the person responsible for providing progress monitoring data to the case review meeting 1 = Team identifies but does not notify the person responsible for providing progress monitoring data to the case review meeting 2 = Team identifies and notifies the person responsible for providing progress monitoring data to the case review meeting	
Data-Based Decision Making 6		**8 Total**
6.1 Team meets at least monthly to review student case	0 = Team does not meet at least monthly to review student case 1 = Team meets informally at least monthly to review student case 2 = Team meets formally at least monthly to review student case	
6.2 Team presents progress monitoring data for discussion	0 = Student case meetings do not have progress monitoring data presented 1 = Student case meetings have some progress monitoring data presented informally 2 = Student case meetings have formal progress monitoring data presented including a visual graph	

(continued)

FIGURE 10.1. *(continued)*

Item	Criteria for Scoring	Rating (0, 1, 2) or N/A
6.3 Data are used to identify next steps (e.g., fading, intensifying, tailoring)	0 = Data not available to make data-based decisions 1 = Some data are used to identify next steps informally, or steps may not match data provided 2 = Data are used to identify matched next steps in a formal process	
6.4 Fading, intensifying, tailoring and adaptations are put into action	0 = Next steps are not followed up on 1 = Next steps are discussed but not put into action 2 = Next steps are acted upon in a measurable, observable way	
Communication with Stakeholders 7		**8 Total**
7.1 Team communicates confirmation of Tier 2 student case upon referral or screening analysis to (a) caregivers, (b) student, (c) staff	0 = Team does not communicate confirmation of Tier 2 case 1 = Team communicates to at least one included group 2 = Team communicates confirmation of Tier 2 case to all three stakeholder groups	
7.2 Team communicates progress updates monthly to (a) caregivers, (b) student, (c) staff	0 = Team does not communicate progress updates monthly 1 = Team communicates progress updates monthly to at least one group 2 = Team communicates progress updates monthly to all three stakeholder groups	
7.3 Team communicates tier movement decisions to (a) caregivers, (b) student, (c) staff	0 = Team does not communicate Tier movement decisions 1 = Team communicates Tier 2 decisions to at least one stakeholder group 2 = Team communicates Tier movement to all three stakeholder groups	
7.4 Team requests caregiver input regarding motivation, home circumstances, collaboration, and coordination	0 = Team does not include caregiver input throughout the handling of the Tier 2 student case 1 = Team includes caregiver input at least once throughout the handling of the Tier 2 student case 2 = Team includes caregiver input at least twice throughout the handling of the Tier 2 student case	
TOTAL		____/50 = ____%

FIGURE 10.1. (*continued*)

the Tier 2 team, an administrator, behavior specialist, instructional coach, paraprofessional, or anyone with sufficient understanding of how the intervention should be carried out. However, implementation fidelity can be implemented using self-report or self-evaluation methods with the proper forms and full, comprehensive trainings to understand the intervention. With self-report, intervention fidelity can be assessed during intervention implementation or directly after intervention implementation. Some interventions can be evaluated for implementation fidelity using a permanent product review (e.g., goal-setting sheets completed, self-monitoring app sessions completed). Regardless of whether the evaluation is completed (1) by an outside observer or self-report by the interventionist, and (2) in real-time during the intervention process or shortly after, results of the evaluation should be used to ensure the core components of the intervention are intact and implemented consistently. This is the only way the student has the potential to benefit from the intervention they were assigned and entitled to receive. It is also the only way teams can make accurate decisions about student responsiveness.

Similar to the annual evaluation of overall, procedural, and intervention fidelity, PSTs should annually and more regularly assess system and intervention social validity, feasibility, and usability. This becomes particularly important when implementation fidelity is low and can point PSTs to the underlying causes of low fidelity.

Beyond Fidelity: Social Validity

At Morris Middle School, the Tier 2 team was satisfied with overall progress but wondered how the students and faculty felt about the interventions, procedures, and mentors. They decided to gather information from the students directly at the end of each semester and also asked for full faculty feedback at the December and April faculty meetings. Social validity, often called social acceptability, is another implementation science component that is important to consider in the translation of research-based science to real-world practice. Generally, social validity refers to the acceptability of the goals, procedures, and outcomes of an intervention (Baer et al., 1968). Acceptability of goals refers to the idea that the behaviors targeted for change are important, and thus, a worthy goal. Acceptability of procedures is pretty straightforward—are the procedures practical, useful, and feasible? Finally, acceptability of outcomes refers to the extent to which the targeted behavior changed for the better and to a socially acceptable level.

With educators being pulled in multiple directions, asked to serve on multiple committees, and implement numerous initiatives and interventions, it is important to consider the perceptions of educators within the Tier 2 system and those of PST members. Importantly, to encourage person-centered, culturally responsive planning and intervention, individual students who receive and participate in interventions, and their caregivers should also be able to provide ongoing social validity feedback and be asked to participate in annual evaluation. We discuss social validity in the context of system, procedures, and interventions, similar to the fidelity discussion above. Within these discussions, we consider educator, student, and caregiver voices as equally important social validity informants.

System Social Validity

Sometimes Tier 2 initiatives come from the district-level as obligations handed down to schools. Conversely, there are times when a single building-level administrator attends Tier 2 training for their school or initiates Tier 2 without it being a district requirement. In these cases, we recommend assessing buy-in prior to implementation, as top-down initiatives may face some resistance. In both cases, we also recommend evaluating social validity of the overall Tier 2 system annually, which can be done easily at the time in which the TFI is completed at the end of the year. End-of-year, system-level social validity surveys could include the important items in Figure 10.2.

Tier 2 Procedural Social Validity

Similar to procedural fidelity, PSTs should regularly evaluate whether the procedures required for each Tier 2 student case are equitable, consistently used, acceptable, and sustainable. Procedural social validity can be evaluated quarterly, and by the PST who implements the identification, matching, planning, and evaluation procedures. A building-level administrator should ask open-ended, perhaps anonymous questions of the PST about the procedures used for individual cases of Tier 2 students (e.g., "How do you think the interventions are working for seventh graders this year?"; "Do you see our Tier 2 setup as feasible?"). An administrator may find that one grade level or another finds their procedures more difficult, too time consuming, or ineffective. These are important data that can be used to inform more nuanced changes to the PST's procedures and expectations. Similarly, an administrator may find that procedural fidelity is consistently low, which may be due to a lack of buy-in by the PST or implementing teachers in the building. In this case, it would be futile to continue implementing or invest in resources for additional training until greater understanding of buy-in issues is achieved. Finally, evaluating procedural social validity will also assist in being able to spot-check issues as they arise and provide an opportunity to prevent morale or perception issues to sabotage long-term, sustained Tier 2 implementation, or inconsistent applications of Tier 2 procedures across students.

Item	Scoring/Open Feedback (e.g., yes, mostly, not at all)
Do you think our Tier 2 plan is working for all students?	
Is the current Tier 2 plan cost-effective?	
Is there a positive time benefit to implementing our current Tier 2 plan?	
Is our Tier 2 plan culturally responsive and appropriately adapted to the needs, resources, and contextual factors in our school?	
If you serve on the Tier 2 PST, is the PST time used in an efficient manner?	
If you serve on the Tier 2 PST, does your team have adequate resources to effectively implement Tier 2 procedures and interventions?	
If you serve on the Tier 2 PST, does the current plan meet the needs of all students at Tier 2 and reduce overreliance on Tier 3 supports?	

FIGURE 10.2. Social Validity Checklist.

Tier 2 Intervention Social Validity

Perhaps most importantly, the PST and/or building administrator should assess the perceptions of implementing educators, students, and their caregivers related to the interventions that are implemented. Person-centered planning requires that we move away from "implementing to" (e.g., delivering interventions to students and their caregivers) and move toward "implementing with" (e.g., delivering interventions with students and their caregivers). This work is done not only on the front end in the planning phases, but should be ongoing with feedback opportunities throughout the time in which the student is receiving intervention. Let's examine implementer/educator and student perceptions each separately.

First, the Tier 2 implementer will most likely be an educator in the building. Sometimes we may use a volunteer or staff member (e.g., custodian, paraprofessional, school nurse) if they are available, so we present this evaluation more broadly for whomever is implementing the intervention. As discussed in previous chapters, we hope to identify implementers not only who have time within their schedule to support a student with an intervention, but also who are skilled at building relationships with students and can genuinely highlight positive aspects and growth in that student. Planfully identifying implementers with these variables in mind on the front end will help avoid some implementer social validity pitfalls later but does not prevent them altogether. An implementer may have personal or professional issues that come up and interfere with their ability to effectively serve in their role; they may lack proper training to effectively implement the intervention and feel confident about their practice; and they may not perceive interventions or their applications in your school as effective or acceptable. Rather than overlooking these critical concerns from implementers, it is important to provide open and ongoing opportunities for implementers to provide the PST and/or building administrator with feedback to prevent pitfalls and improve intervention effectiveness. The implementers of Tier 2 interventions have a valuable perspective and are typically willing to share it if given the opportunity. Providing opportunities to share perceptions will support ongoing buy-in and sustainability.

The most important perception data to gather regularly is student perception data. It is important to remember that all of the Tier 2 interventions described in this book require the student to participate with the implementer. If a student wads up their point sheet, refuses to come to small group, or leaves social skills instruction, you have no intervention from which they can benefit. This is really no different than a doctor prescribing you an exercise program. If you hate the exercise, what is the likelihood you will do it, let alone improve your health? With this in mind, it is critically important to both know your student in the planning side of the process, and open channels for feedback regarding the intervention they are receiving on an ongoing basis. Students can help identify adaptations and improvements that may not occur to the PST or implementers. Within the time built in for intervention, implementers can probe students about their perceptions of the intervention (e.g., "How did you all like the social skills lesson we did today?" "How can I make it better?") but it is important to provide formal, formative probes of student social validity. This can be done in brief, monthly probes such as the 5-item questionnaire in Figure 10.3, adapted from the Children's Intervention Rating Profile (Witt & Elliott, 1985).

Assessing student perceptions of intervention acceptability will not only help identify necessary adaptations and improve intervention effectiveness, but will also promote buy-in for the intervention. This is critical to the sustainability and strength of the implementer–student relationship and intervention, should it need to be implemented long-term (e.g., more than 4 months).

	Rating Scale (0 = not at all, 1 = sometimes, 2 = yes)
I like spending time with my Tier 2 coach.	
I am glad I get to participate in Tier 2 intervention.	
I think my Tier 2 intervention is helping me do better in school.	
I think my Tier 2 intervention was designed with my strengths, interests, and preferences in mind.	
I would choose to continue to participate in this Tier 2 intervention.	

FIGURE 10.3. Student Social Validity Checklist.

System, Procedural, and Intervention Feasibility and Usability

At Morris, the team worked very hard the first year and saw positive results. They wondered, though, if the new process was sustainable. They questioned, "If we had a different team or administrators, would they be able to implement the system?" and "How difficult was it to implement our procedures?" To answer these questions, they gathered information about the feasibility of the system they implemented that year.

The final level of implementation variables to consider across systems, procedures, and individual interventions is feasibility. This is a component of implementation science that is often driven by underlying social validity issues and impacts implementation fidelity. Feasibility is the degree to which a stakeholder (e.g., educator, student) finds the procedure or practice easy, doable, or practical. Feasibility is also related to perceived usefulness. For example, educators can perceive an intervention as easy to implement, but if they don't think that the intervention is helpful, they most likely will discontinue implementing, or change the intervention in a way they perceive to be more helpful. In the same vein, when implementers observe positive changes in students' behavior, they are likely to view the intervention as useful and feasible (Bruhn et al., 2020). Self-efficacy may also factor into perceptions, with implementers feeling better about their implementation ability when they see improved outcomes, and in turn, viewing the intervention as feasible (Bruhn et al., 2020). All stakeholders involved with implementing the system, PST procedures, and individual interventions should be asked to describe the feasibility and usability. This evaluation can take place during annual evaluations, regular social validity probes, or in separate interview or focus-group sessions with educators or PST members.

We hope that we have highlighted the importance of evaluating fidelity, social validity, and feasibility along with regular outcome measures (e.g., ODR, attendance, grades). These three variables impact outcomes and are often interconnected, so understanding them is key to strong implementation and accurate decision making. Use the Figure 10.4 decision tree to assist with questions about outcomes related to fidelity, social validity, and feasibility.

TIER 2 TECHNICAL ASSISTANCE

In the second portion of this chapter, we overview broad initial training to support fidelity, social validity, and feasibility during initial implementation, follow-up coaching to provide ongoing support across initial implementation, and annual evaluation to identify areas of strength and weakness, with the idea that training and coaching are imperative to sound implementation and stakeholder buy-in.

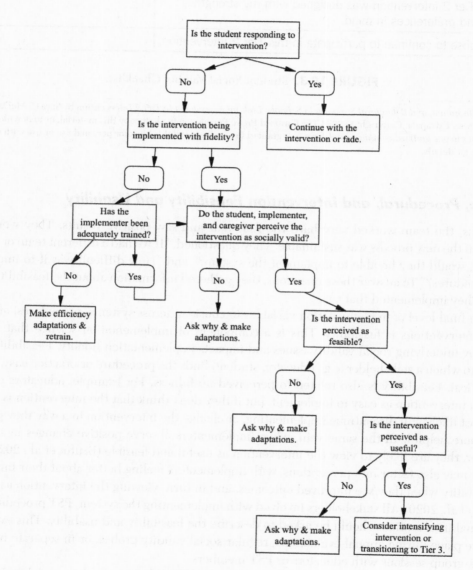

FIGURE 10.4. Decision-making guide.

Initial Training to Support Fidelity

We start by outlining Tier 2 training. At Sunnyset Elementary School, the principal received state funding to send a team to Tier 2 training. The principal expected the team to learn about Tier 2, develop a systematic process, and implement fully the next year and beyond. For this, the school reached out to the state's technical assistance provider. The new Tier 2 team attended 2 days of training in July and planned to roll out implementation when teachers returned in August. This required the team to meet three times for 2-hour planning sessions in July and early August. As part of the initial training process, the principal hired the technical assistance provider to meet with the Tier 2 team monthly for the next school year as ongoing support. The principal never preferred "spray and pray" (i.e., sitting for training once and hoping the team can implement on their own afterward) methods and knew his team would respond well with ongoing supports.

Initial training is the first time a school team has gone through training. Subsequent retrainings or booster sessions are for a school who has previously received training but has had turnover or declining fidelity and requires retraining. Retraining decisions are typically made using fidelity and outcome data. If the Tier 2 system is not producing positive outcomes, or if fidelity scores fall consistently below 70% on the TFI, your school may need to be retrained. All training, initial and booster, should be aligned with the Tier 2 TFI to help support fidelity during training. The TFI includes components such as who needs to be on the team, attendance rates, and how many referral systems, and, therefore, these should be explicitly provided during initial training. Whether the training is initial or a booster or repetition of a previous training, the procedures are the same. Training can be conducted in person or virtually through synchronous platforms such as Zoom or asynchronous recorded modules with an in-person or synchronous component. It is not recommended to receive only asynchronous training. Additionally, what is typically a 2-day training workshop can be delivered in two back-to-back days, or the initial training content can be spread across monthly 1-hour, or quarterly 3-hour training sessions. Some schools or districts prefer to receive training on an individual step of Tier 2, then allow educators the opportunity to put that step into practice, then receive training on the next step, and so on. Similarly, some building administrators cannot find 2 full days to allow PST members to attend in-person training and these flexible hybrid or step-by-step training approaches may be needed.

Regardless of the format, a small team from each school should attend training. This should always include an administrator, the related service providers (e.g., social worker, school counselor, school psychologists, mental health therapists), and the other PST members who will implement the Tier 2 system. It is important to note that every educator who implements a Tier 2 intervention does not need to attend initial Tier 2 training. Implementers should receive intervention training in a turnaround, as-needed basis after the team attends PST training. The reason behind this is that initial training content primarily describes Tier 2 system issues and procedural requirements, and also highlights individual Tier 2 interventions. Training on specific interventions comes later.

The 2 days of training are broken down into (1) PBIS or MTSS review, (2) Tier 2 logic, (3) Tier 2 readiness, (4) teaming and communication, (5) resource mapping and identifying implementers, (6) identification, (7) matching, (8) planning intervention, (9) progress monitoring, and (10) meetings and evaluation. It is important to provide exemplars, "look fors," and common issues across all 10 of these content areas. It is also important to differentiate training content and activities based on local contextual factors such as grade level, availability of resources, and district or school needs (including school improvement plans). In traditional training opportunities, this information is used to develop a school-level Tier 2 Blueprint during the second half of the second training day. Use Figure 10.5 as a template for a Tier 2 Blueprint.

School-level, individual plans should include specific planning decisions made by the team, and should be seen as a "living, breathing" document that is changed annually based on evaluation data, outcomes, and any school- or district-level changes that occur. Training should *not* be didactic in nature where the team simply "sits and gets" (Chappuis et al., 2009). Instead, effective training should focus on developing skills through engagement with training activities that support learning such as problem-solving examples, opportunities to practice completing a screener, role playing Tier 2 intervention implementation, and participating in question and answer discussion time. To build understanding, skills, and self-efficacy, trainees need ample opportunities for practice, feedback, discussion, and reflection (Bruce et al., 2010).

Follow-Up Ongoing Coaching

The Sunnyset Elementary team left their 2-day training with a great initial plan. They built their plan using 2-hour sessions across the summer to develop and finalize materials and run the new Tier 2 plan by the principal. However, once they began the process, they developed questions and required some modeling from their coach, Ms. Teresa. Each month, Ms. Teresa from the state met with the Tier 2 team during their regularly scheduled Tier 2 meeting. At first, Ms. Teresa ran the meetings and modeled how to follow the agenda and stay on topic. Starting in November, she began turning over portions of the meeting to the team, and by March, the team independently led meetings while she was only present to help problem solve when an issue arose. For example, in March, the team had to figure out how to work with students who demonstrated SEB needs related to changes in routines and procedures due to spring break and upcoming testing. And in April, the team was stuck on several students who still had not responded to Tier 2 intervention and the decision of whether to refer to Tier 3 or not. In May, the team needed help doing their initial TFI Tier 2 and analyzing all of the procedural fidelity, social validity, and feasibility data. They also wanted to draft a report for the full faculty and needed help analyzing year-over-year data.

Following initial Tier 2 training and subsequent implementation whether in a stepwise approach or all at once, follow-up and ongoing coaching for the PST will be necessary. Follow-up coaching to support implementation to fidelity should also be aligned with the TFI and procedural checklists. Follow-up coaching may occur in person or virtually and should be provided during monthly PST meetings throughout an academic year. In line with typical professional learning series, follow-up coaching should be scaffolded by the coach to promote independence across all Tier 2 system components, procedures, and interventions at the conclusion of coaching. It is possible later coaching boosters may be necessary after a school has reached independence in an effort to encourage sustainability. An example meeting agenda facilitated by a Tier 2 coaching agenda is located in Figure 10.6.

In concluding the discussion regarding initial training and follow-up coaching, we think it necessary to discuss locating effective training providers and the "train the trainer" model of professional learning. Because the structures and resources available in each state, district, and school vary drastically, initial training should be conducted by a provider who has been appropriately and thoroughly trained and has had direct observation of their training with evaluative performance feedback. In some cases, a state provider may receive training and is able to turn around that training to regional providers, districts, or schools. In other cases, districts may decide to use

Tier 2 Identification and Intervention Blueprint

School Name: _____

School Year: _____

1. TIER 2 TEAMING

Who is on the team?
- ☐ Administrator: _____
- ☐ Grade-level/student knowledge: _____
- ☐ Behavioral expertise: _____
- ☐ Other: _____

Team roles:
- ☐ Leader: _____
- ☐ Notetaker: _____
- ☐ Timekeeper: _____
- ☐ Data Expert: _____

When will the team meet (monthly day/time)?: _____

How will the team report back to teachers?

How will the team report back to caregiver/parent?

2. IDENTIFICATION/SCREENING

What universal social, emotional, behavioral screener will we use?
- ☐ Strengths and Difficulties Questionnaire (SDQ)
- ☐ Social, Academic, Emotional, Behavior Screener (SAEBRS)
- ☐ Other: _____

How will we implement this screener?
- ☐ Universal, teacher completed
- ☐ Targeted, teacher nomination then teacher completed
- ☐ Other: _____

When will the universal screener be completed?:
- ☐ 4–6 weeks into the new year (Date: _____)
- ☐ More than once per year (Dates: _____, _____, _____)
- ☐ Other: _____

(continued)

FIGURE 10.5. Tier 2 Identification and Intervention Blueprint.

Who will complete the screener (what period teacher)?: _____

Where do scores/score reports get submitted?: _____

Date for planning meeting to conduct initial data meetings: _____

Secondary data to consider in identification and planning:
☐ Office discipline referrals and suspensions
☐ Attendance
☐ Academic

How will students receive support throughout the year?:
☐ Teacher Request for Referral Form is complete and available
☐ Student Self-Referral Form is complete and available
☐ Caregiver/Parent Referral Form is complete and available

Other notes:

3. TIER 2 INTERVENTIONS

Conduct:
☐ Check-in/Check-out
☐ Check-in/Check-up/Check-out
☐ Check, Connect, Expect
☐ Other: _____
Match/Adaptation/Align with Tier 1 notes:

Hyperactivity/Inattention:
☐ Goal setting
☐ Self-monitoring
☐ Self-monitoring with self-graphing
☐ Other: _____
Match/Adaptation/Align with Tier 1 notes:

Peer Problems/Prosocial:
☐ Behavior contracts
☐ Problem-solving activities (ABC-GO, restorative chat, peer mediation)
☐ Social skills lessons (small group, individual)
☐ Other: _____
Match/Adaptation/Align with Tier 1 notes:

(continued)

FIGURE 10.5. *(continued)*

Emotional Symptoms (for school counselor):
- ☐ Emotion regulation strategies (emotion identification, calming, mindfulness, trauma informed practices)
- ☐ Small group (brief CBT, SEL group)
- ☐ Individual sessions (full CBT, SEL)
- ☐ Other: _____

Match/Adaptation/Align with Tier 1 notes:

4. PLANNING AND PREPARATION

Educator professional development:
- ☐ ALL teachers will receive training on the screening and teaming process
- ☐ ALL teachers will receive training on interventions they will interact with
- ☐ ALL teachers will receive training on progress monitoring procedures
- ☐ Other: _____

How will we track enrollment/proportions?
- ☐ Number/proportions of students identified for Tier 2 (quarterly) _____
- ☐ Number/proportions of students staying at Tier 2 (quarterly) _____
- ☐ Number/proportions of students moving to Tier 3 (quarterly) _____

Plan for monitoring intervention fidelity:

Plan for monitoring annual Tier 2 fidelity:

5. DATA-BASED PROGRESS MONITORING

What data will we have available?:
- ☐ DPR (from check-in/check-out variations)
- ☐ Self-monitoring scores
- ☐ Goal setting (instances when goal was met)
- ☐ Behavior contracts (instances when contract was met)
- ☐ Direct behavior rating
- ☐ Other: _____

Who will be responsible for collecting these data?

Who will be responsible for bringing these data to the monthly meeting?

Who will be responsible for graphing/storing these data (data expert)?

How will these data be shared/communicated out?:
- ☐ Email caregiver monthly by team lead
- ☐ Share data and intervention decisions with grade-level team in meeting
- ☐ Share data updates with student
- ☐ Other: _____

FIGURE 10.5. *(continued)*

Tier 2 Meeting Agenda

1. **Introductions and Expectations**
   a) Roles and responsibilities
   b) Are team members correct/representative?
2. **Tier 2 Fidelity (Blueprint, Intervention, Procedural Fidelity)**
   a) Missing interventions/components
   b) Questions
3. **Student Outcome Data**
   a) SDQ overall and subscale scores
   b) Interventions needed/put in place, adaptations with fidelity
   c) What goals are we setting for the target behavior?
   d) How are we monitoring progress?
   e) How are we communicating with other teachers and family?
   f) How many students are:
      i. Staying at Tier 2
      ii. Moved back to Tier 1 only
      iii. Moved on to Tier 3
4. **Next Steps (items to do, homework, next meeting)**
5. **Meeting Evaluation**
   a) Are our meetings having the desired effects on students?
   b) Were our meetings effective in improving implementation?

FIGURE 10.6. Example of a monthly meeting agenda.

an external training partner such as an educational consultant or professor with expertise in this area. Regardless, the same training provider should conduct both initial training and follow-up coaching in order to maintain consistency. Like most educational initiatives, the "train the trainer" model is frequently preferred. In this model, the team is trained by a trainer. Once fluent, the team becomes the "trainer" who passes along what they learned to the rest of the school. We have found that if training providers are able to attend a minimum of five school-level trainings, and either implement in those schools or serve as co-trainers for those schools, they should have sufficient background knowledge and problem-solving skills to adequately turn around training as a training provider.

ANNUAL EVALUATION

Above we highlighted the several evaluation requirements that will promote system and individual outcomes. There are three final, important notes about evaluation to consider. Evaluation assists us with making data-based decisions and keeps us from continuing to implement ineffective or inefficient systems and practices.

First, it is important to take an annual glance at Tier 2 outcomes, similar to what is commonly done with Tier 1 at the end of each year. In addition to assessing year-to-year changes that are common with Tier 1 evaluation, such as decreases in office discipline referrals, suspensions, and alternative school placement, Tier 2 outcome evaluation should also include an analysis of proportions across tiers. Tier 1 is sufficient to serve approximately 80% of all students, Tier 2 should be sufficient to serve 15–20% of students, and Tier 3 should be saved for 1–5% of students. The administrator and/or PST should analyze overall proportions of students receiving the three tiers of intervention annually. This will require schools to track numbers of students who (1) are referred to Tier 2; (2) remain at Tier 2 levels of support and for how long; (3) transition back to Tier 1 supports only; and (4) receive Tier 3 supports and/or are referred to special education for SEB needs. Once an effective Tier 2 system is in place, these numbers should remain steady across years. If results indicate disproportionate numbers of students across tiers, the team should inspect further issues of resources, contextual changes, perceptions, and need for further training or retraining. For example, if there is an uptick in the number of students needing Tier 2 support, a closer examination of Tier 1 implementation may be warranted.

Second, above we highlighted the importance of evaluating system, procedure, and intervention perceptions from all stakeholders involved. Annual evaluation should include an analysis and subsequent discussion and action planning that includes findings from implementers/educators and students. Perception data is important to keeping your Tier 2 system effective and efficient, promoting or maintaining stakeholder buy-in, and making critical culturally and contextually responsive adjustments to your system, procedures, and interventions. Schools and districts do not remain static, nor should Tier 2 implementation efforts. The PST should ensure the Tier 2 Blueprint is updated annually to reflect data-based, necessary changes.

Finally, the third area for annual evaluation, which is included in the Tier 2 TFI as a subscale, is an evaluation of professional learning needs. On an annual basis, the PST and administrative team should evaluate what booster or retraining is needed, as well as if ongoing coaching should be discontinued or prolonged, and should identify implementers who may need new training on interventions they will put in place. School personnel change year to year, as may the composition of the PST. Therefore, there may be individual members of the PST who need to attend a booster Tier 2 training, and educators who join the school may require an overview of the Tier 2 system or implementation training for a specific intervention for which they will be involved. After evaluating and planning for changes to improve outcomes and perceptions, the administrative team should consider what training or retraining is available, and who requires initial training, booster, retraining, or overview content. Figure 10.7 provides an example assessment schedule across the various variables.

For Sunnyset Elementary School, the Tier 2 team who attended the initial 2-day training and worked with their Tier 2 coach, Ms. Teresa, completed their first full annual evaluation. They submitted a report of the initial process, the resulting impact, and the fidelity, social validity, and feasibility data to the principal. Together, the team and principal needed to make a few changes for the next year for continuous improvement. First, they decided that several issues were not feasible long term. They replaced the principal as a mentor because he was not available enough in the mornings. They also stopped using grandparent volunteers because they were not at the school every day. Additionally, they received funding to hire a full-time behavior coach so they could offer Check, Connect, and Expect. Procedurally, the team decided to keep their meeting dates and times, but moved to a process where they quickly reviewed students who were progressing and focused the remaining 50 minutes on students who were not progressing. They also decided to provide a whole-school Tier 2 overview training in the first week and add the outside mental health provider to the Tier 2 team.

ASSESSMENT	FALL	WINTER	SPRING	MONTHLY	ANNUALLY	OTHER
TRAINING						
Tier 2 readiness (PST)						
SYSTEM FIDELITY						
Tier 2 TFI (PST)						
Tier 2 procedural fidelity (PST)						
SOCIAL VALIDITY						
Student						
Interventionist						
Caregiver						
INTERVENTIONS						
Conduct						
Social						
Emotional						
Inattention						
Academic						
SCREENING						
Initial						
Outgoing						
PROGRESS MONITORING						
Data Collection						
Data Analysis						

FIGURE 10.7. Tier 2 Assessment Schedule Form.

CONCLUSION

The saying goes "you can't benefit from an intervention you didn't receive." This applies to everything from taking medication as directed, to completing physical therapy homework assignments, to addressing SEB needs in schools. This chapter described the rationale for measuring fidelity and how to use those fidelity data to improve implementation effectiveness. These descriptions apply to overall system fidelity, fidelity to the process for each student receiving Tier 2 intervention, and to intervention fidelity or adherence for all interventions that students receive.

CHAPTER 11

But Wait, There's More

Final Thoughts on Important Topics to Ensure Tier 2 Success

As we conclude, we would like to leave you with a few important final considerations when adopting a systematic Tier 2 process for your school or district. Throughout this book we have provided the foundations to a systematic process, as well as a step-by-step approach to identifying and meeting the targeted, or Tier 2, social, emotional, and behavioral needs of students. However, it is important to note that every school and district have varying needs and resources, and thus the Tier 2 approach presented in this book may need to be adapted based on the local context. Regardless of any contextual adaptations, we leave you with seven final considerations and a resource, Figure 11.1, for reflecting on the extent to which you and your team are following each of the final considerations. We recommend teams complete this tool at the end of the school year alongside the TFI, as your responses to these items can help guide improvements to your Tier 2 plan the following school year.

AVOIDING DEFICIT IDEOLOGY, APPLYING HIGH EXPECTATIONS

At their root, Tier 2 interventions, whether in an academic area or an SEB area, are addressing an area of "need." In the past, we labeled these as "deficits" or "problems," and we would like to illustrate why we advocate for a simple change in language to avoid discussion of deficits. All educators should examine structures and systems that may be leading to what are seen as areas of need. Equity educator, researcher, and consultant Paul Gorski (2010) has said, "Deficit ideology is an institutionalized worldview, in an ideology woven into the fabric of U.S. society and its coalizing institutions, including schools." Learning about deficit ideology, and arguing against making decisions based in deficit ideology, requires developing solutions that address inequitable systems. That is, we must first identify dominant majority expectations, structures, and systems, rather than

Critical Implementation Item	Score (0 = not started, 1 = somewhat in place, 2 = fully in place)	Action Planning Steps for Items with a 1 or 0: What task needs to be completed, by whom, and when
Are we consistently inspecting our own part (e.g., not implementing with fidelity, expectations not contextually relevant) in Tier 2?		
Are we examining strengths as well as needs?		
Are we discussing students in positive rather than negative terms (e.g., "Tier 2 student," "frequent flyer," "deficits")?		
Are we holding high expectations for all students?		
Are students experiencing fewer punitive disciplinary actions?		
Are we providing positive feedback for student effort?		
Are we sharing progress with students?		
Are we considering context, conditions, and structures in power insted of blaming individual students?		
Are we working with students directly to be able to demonstrate new skills across all settings?		
Do we have the right partners at the table with an equal voice during planning (e.g., family, mental health)?		
Do we have an explicit plan at Tier 2 for students with multiple areas of need within SEB?		

FIGURE 11.1. Tier 2 Implementation Self-Assessment.

focusing on "fixing" individual students who fall victim to oppressive and inequitable systems and structures in our schools. When we study and learn about deficit ideology, the next step is working to identify it when we see it and hear it. Within PST meetings it may be easy for deficit ideology to creep in, especially if the team is using subjective or vague criteria to enter into Tier 2 and while assigning intervention. For example, a Tier 2 team may unintentionally place all students of color into social skills groups, while all White students receive a goal-setting intervention. Next, when we are actively pushing back against deficit ideology, we examine structures, systems, and underlying causes of problems, rather than responding by focusing on individual deficits within students and ignoring systemic and structural contexts. This book repeatedly asks you to center person-appropriate and contextually appropriate adaptations. We emphasize the importance of getting to know each individual student—their strengths and areas of need. We should get to know their culture, preferences, family, goals, and priorities. This will help us to better understand the underlying systemic or structural issues, rather than focusing on what we perceive as individual deficits.

Another strategy for disrupting deficit ideology in order to promote equitable and supportive schools for all students and families is to stress establishing and maintaining high expectations for all students. Within a deficit ideology, educators may lower their expectations for students demonstrating Tier 2 needs, when in fact they should do the opposite. Educators should believe that with equitable and accessible systems, and supports, all students can reach their potential. Expectations and discussions around that achievement level should be consistently communicated to all students.

TIER 2 AS THERAPEUTIC, INSTRUCTIONAL

When Tier 2 systematic work began over 15 years ago, it was common to hear educators refer to students requiring Tier 2 supports as "frequent flyers" or "Tier 2 students." The term "frequent flyer" referred to students who frequently were referred to the office for discipline issues. This term may have originated in the commonly shared belief that Tier 2 supports were for students who had earned two or more office referrals. We know now that this process is not only reactive and requires several major incidents to have occurred before a student is eligible for intervention, but is also flawed because it would typically only identify students with externalizing behaviors, yielding a singular, subjective method for identifying students with social, emotional, or attention needs. Similarly, labeling students as "Tier 2 students" is not only stigmatizing, it is also inaccurate. Students who receive Tier 2 SEB supports commonly do not receive Tier 2 supports in other areas, and labeling them "Tier 2 students" paints them with too broad a brush. Additionally, using this label presumes that students with Tier 2 SEB needs don't also receive Tier 1 supports, which they should, or receive Tier 3 supports in another area. Throughout this book, we intentionally use the phrase "students who require Tier 2 supports" or "students with Tier 2 SEB needs." This also centers the student as an individual with needs, rather than centering needs that are assigned to a student.

It is also important to point out that throughout this book, we have referred to the systematic process for Tier 2 and all Tier 2 interventions as opportunities to provide therapeutic, instructional supports and *not* punishment. Though disciplinary incidents may still occur while a student is receiving Tier 2 supports, it is imperative to pair Tier 2 intervention with disciplinary consequences outlined in your school's code of conduct. Additionally, no Tier 2 intervention should be viewed as a "gotcha" where students are given goals, contracts, or expectations that cannot be reasonably met. Nor should the student receive some form of punishment (e.g., additional harsh feedback, shaming, withholding rewards, removing rewards previously earned) when they cannot reach their Tier 2 criteria. Instead, Tier 2 interventions must be set up in a way that a student can be successful, receive positive feedback, meet goals, and earn contingent reinforcement. This approach will often enable "behavioral momentum" that educators can build on. Meaning, when progress moves in the right direction, the student will become more motivated to participate in Tier 2 interventions, and actively use their newly learned skills throughout the day.

LEVERAGING STRENGTHS

Another important consideration to integrate into your Tier 2 process is identifying and leveraging student strengths to improve student success rates. While this book focuses primarily on systematically identifying areas of need and matching evidence-based intervention to those areas, it is also important to objectively and systematically identify areas of strength and leverage those strengths to build behavioral momentum and relationships with students. Oftentimes the PST will quickly identify areas of need when examining screening scores, and these are areas that fall outside of the "average" range. While efficient use of reliable and valid screeners is important, sometimes teams overlook areas where the student does not score in an elevated range. In other words, areas of strengths to build on. For example, a student may score in a highly elevated range for conduct and peer problems, but within the average range for emotional and attention areas. These two areas should be discussed as areas of strength, as the student is able to regulate their emotions and attend to academic tasks. Teams should plan to build on those two areas of strength when designing intervention for conduct or peer problem areas of need. They could praise a student for their emotional awareness and self-regulation, while also regularly highlighting completed schoolwork and focused time during instruction. And since the area of need is specific to peer problems, the team could point out prosocial skills being used with younger children and adults. Secondly, the SDQ also identifies an area of strength: prosocial behavior. On the SDQ, students can be identified as having an area of strength in the prosocial domain if they are helpful and kind to younger children, get along well with adults, and are generally generous and socially thoughtful. If the screener you decide to use does not have an area of strength built in, you may consider identifying a second brief strengths screener, or add a prompt in your meeting agenda to identify and discuss student strengths as a team.

EXAMINING CONDITIONS

Tier 2 supports should not be discussed and provided in a vacuum. Schools and teams should take an honest appraisal of the conditions that the student is experiencing as well as individual student needs. It is important for school teams to consider school, classroom, social, and home/community conditions the student interacts with, and how condition changes may be required prior to implementing intervention with a student. Below we review potential conditions within each system that can affect a student's SEB needs, reminding us that students are not individually to blame for their SEB needs.

Schoolwide

In Chapter 1, we discussed the importance of evaluating the fidelity of Tier 1 implementation prior to implementing Tier 2 practices and procedures. We also want to evaluate the degree to which Tier 1 is effective. If Tier 1 fidelity looks sufficient, yet the culture or climate of the building is still punitive, or not inclusive or safe, schools should aim to address those issues prior to determining students require Tier 2 supports. This is especially important for those students who may be marginalized or experience a lack of belonging and inclusivity. It would be natural for a student to be socially and/or emotionally withdrawn, inattentive, or even impulsive if they feel unsafe at school, or not included. One potential solution is to provide a refresher of Tier 1 for the educators and students. Additionally, schools could assess school climate and culture directly.

Classroom

Similarly, schools and school teams should consider whether the classroom context is a condition contributing to what looks like a Tier 2 student need. That is, does the teacher's use of evidence-based classroom management strategies support SEB success? Although this is often a touchy subject for teachers, it is important to consider whether the teacher themselves or the classroom setup is contributing to students needing additional SEB supports. Specifically, teachers who lack positive, equitable, structured classroom practices that promote belonging and inclusion may need additional classroom practice (e.g., classroom management) supports prior to intervening for students. This may be particularly true with two identifiable data points.

First, if a single teacher or set of teachers have significantly higher numbers of students who qualify for Tier 2 supports, or if those same teachers have higher rates of classroom-based office discipline referrals, the root cause may be that the classroom, teacher, or instructional strategies require intervention, rather than the student(s). In this case, a group contingency intervention is recommended. In a group contingency, reinforcement is provided to the group (or class) when one student or group member (i.e., dependent), each individual group member (i.e., independent), or all group members (i.e., interdependent) meet(s) a predetermined goal (Hirsch et al., 2016). Hirsch and colleagues (2016) wrote a step-by-step process to setting up group contingencies in the classroom. Or, you could use more formalized group contingencies like the Good Behavior Game, which has been around for over 50 years (Barrish et al., 1969), or the CW-FIT program (Wills et al., 2018), as both interventions have demonstrated evidence of improved classroom behaviors (e.g., less disruption).

Second, for students who change teachers frequently throughout the day, it may become apparent that a student only displays SEB needs in one classroom, not indiscriminately across all periods. While this may indicate an area of academic frustration, it may also indicate that one teacher's classroom culture, instructional strategies, or teaching style may be contributing to what appears as a Tier 2 area of need.

Social Context

Across all SEB areas of need, it is important for schools and school teams to consider the social context that each student is experiencing and whether social conditions may be contributing to what appears to be a Tier 2 area of need. Specifically, students with these areas of need may be experiencing bullying (online or in person), social isolation, or temporary social peer group conflict. The school team should discuss each student's social context: who their friends are, if have their friendships changed, if the student demonstrates signs of bullying or being bullied, or if the student has reported bullying or teasing. Peer social changes and disruptions can negatively impact any student, making them appear as though they require intervention. Rather than immediately assigning intervention, it is important to rule out deleterious social conditions that the student is experiencing as the root cause of the identified area of need. For example, if a student is experiencing online bullying, they may appear disengaged and withdrawn, and absences may increase. On the surface, this may look like an emotional area of need, and while the student may need emotional coping strategies, the online bullying must be identified and addressed for the student to be able to demonstrate improved emotional functioning at school. Myriad curricula and supports are available to address bullying prevention and response to bullying:

- *www.stopbullying.gov*
- *www.pbis.org/topics/bullying-prevention*
- *www.naesp.org/sites/default/files/images/as/PBIS_Bullying_TIPs.pdf*

Home/Community

Similar to the importance of examining the school, classroom, and social conditions that each student is experiencing, school teams should also consider the home and community conditions that may be negatively impacting the student. School teams should consider sudden and temporary changes in SEB needs not as an automatic Tier 2 referral. Instead, staff such as the school counselor should look into what is going on at home and in the community to determine if a sudden change (e.g., death in the family, divorce, racist acts in the community, caregiver overseas for military deployment) may be triggering a sudden SEB change in the student. For sudden and uncharacteristic changes, it is likely that something has dramatically shifted for the student at home or in the community. This is why part of the Tier 2 referral process should include discussions with the student and caregivers to determine what, if anything, has changed or could be at the root of the new SEB state. Seemingly small changes (e.g., late baseball practices, rising cost in groceries, transportation changes) can be responsible for serious changes in a student's ability to self-regulate and function as they typically do. These sudden changes should be addressed as signals to ask more questions, not automatically refer to Tier 2. Although the changes in context cannot be removed or fixed (e.g., divorces cannot be undone, deployments cannot be canceled, others' words cannot be controlled), once school staff become aware of these issues they can work in supporting the student temporarily, and even provide the student with additional temporary or Tier 2 coping skills and strategies to get through a difficult time and reframe the experience as an opportunity to learn and grow. It is also important to note that sometimes whole schools or communities experience trauma (e.g., global pandemics, school shootings, student death, community crime). The impacts of trauma may be visible immediately, or they can be delayed, showing up much later. In these cases, all students should be provided with the supports they need, and not all should receive Tier 2 supports.

PROMOTING GENERALIZATION

Aside from CICO and its variations, which is provided throughout the school day and includes an at-home component, many Tier 2 interventions are contextually specific, and the strategies taught and practiced in these contexts often do not naturally generalize to new settings, behaviors, or with new people without specific prompting and programming. That is, many social skills groups are conducted outside of the classroom, playground, or cafeteria, where students will most likely need to use the skills taught during these small groups. Or, self-regulation interventions often target a specific time of day, class period, or behavior, and students might not demonstrate self-regulation improvements outside of these targeted areas. Thus, it is important for the PST to implement generalization strategies once the student begins to display SEB improvements in the targeted context. Like all the strategies discussed in this book, there are a variety of generalization strategies that can range from simple to complex.

First, the adult working with the student can simply ask the student to try a new skill or strategy in a different setting or with different people. For example, if a student is in a social skills group where they are working on turn-taking during conversation, then the adult leading the group can simply ask the student to practice turn-taking while eating lunch in the cafeteria. Second, the PST might ask adults that the student interacts with to praise the student for using any strategies or replacement behaviors outside the context targeted in their Tier 2 intervention. To facilitate this generalization strategy, the PST should share information on the strategies or behaviors that the student is targeting in their Tier 2 intervention and offer examples of behavior-specific praise statements (e.g., "I noticed that you asked a question during your conversation with Joey. That's a great conversation strategy!"). Third, if the student does not generalize SEB improvements using the aforementioned strategies, the PST can implement the intervention in new settings, with new people, or target different behaviors. This might involve revising procedures to fit the new setting (e.g., identifying curriculum, storing materials, seating arrangements), training interventionists, and teaching the student how to apply the intervention in the new context. For example, if a student is demonstrating great improvements in their on-task behavior while self-monitoring in math, but their on-task behavior in reading has not improved, then they might benefit from implementing self-monitoring during reading, too. To implement self-monitoring during reading, the interventionist might need to tweak the operational definition of on-task to include reading-specific examples of on-task behavior (e.g., reading only assigned materials, using bean bag chairs for independent reading only, voices off during silent reading). Then, the student should practice role-playing these specific behaviors with the interventionist prior to implementing.

Data collection and progress monitoring for generalization should follow the same steps used in the original context, if possible. That is, if the teacher is collecting concurrent self-monitoring data during math, and the intervention is added to reading, then they should also collect concurrent self-monitoring data during reading. For students who are working on generalizing skills outside of the classroom context, then the PST should train the supervising adult (e.g., cafeteria or playground monitor) to collect data periodically. This might be a weekly DBR, an occasional frequency count of the targeted behavior (e.g., number of students conversed with, number of questions asked). If the context prohibits systematic data collection (e.g., supervising large numbers of students, cold weather during recess), the adult could simply record anecdotal notes related to the behavior or strategies of interest in a shared document. These generalization data should be reviewed alongside the data gathered in the original context to inform any necessary modifications or adaptations to generalization strategies. Figure 11.2 includes a tool to help the PST track the generalization strategies they are using with their student.

Directions: Record the date and type of generalization strategy in the table below. Make any notes regarding special considerations, who is involved with the generalization strategy, or modifications made to the intervention. Continue collecting and monitoring outcome and fidelity data.

Generalization Strategies:

1. Ask the student to try the new skill or strategy in a new setting.

2. Ask the student to try the new skill or strategy with a new person or group of people.

3. Ask the student's classroom teacher to reinforce the student for using the new skill or strategy.

4. Ask other adults interacting with the student to reinforce the student for using the new skill or strategy (e.g., cafeteria workers, bus driver, hall monitor).

5. Implement the intervention in a new setting.

6. Implement the intervention with new people.

7. Implement the intervention with new behaviors.

Date	Strategy	Notes

FIGURE 11.2. Generalization Tracking.

INTEGRATION WITH MENTAL HEALTH

In Chapter 8, we presented information regarding emotional needs, and evidence-based interventions that can address that area of need. For the sake of this book, we assume that the counselor serving on the Tier 2 PST will lead the management of services for students who have an identified emotional area of need. In this way, the school counselor serves as the "mental health liaison or lead" in deciding how best to address that need. The school counselor should work closely with school-based mental health staff, school psychologists, social workers, or outside mental health staff when necessary. The integration of school-based mental health is first important within Tier 1 levels of support to prevent mental health needs and promote wellness. This should extend into classwide strategies for emotion identification and emotion regulation (e.g., feelings charts, calm corners, fidget breaks, reflection or breathing opportunities). Then, when students are identified as requiring supports for Tier 2 emotional symptoms, those supports should be interconnected within the existing structure. At Tier 1, schools may also decide to provide universal social–emotional learning lessons, which can then be retaught in small-group or individual sessions for students needing Tier 2 supports. Regardless of what resources and experts are available in your schools, any mental-health-related professionals should be included during PST referral, intervention planning, and family communication, rather than existing on an isolated island, which is an inefficient, reactive, and siloed approach.

TIER 2 APPROACHES FOR MULTIPLE AREAS OF NEED

Throughout this book we have described approaches to address single areas of need (i.e., conduct, attention, social problem solving, emotional). Chapter 9 described an approach to integrating academic and SEB practices for students with co-occurring needs. Beyond a single area of need, or co-occurring academic need, many students will have needs across multiple SEB areas. In this case, PSTs should consider three options: (1) prioritizing one area, (2) layering multiple Tier 2 interventions, and (3) implementing a transdiagnostic Tier 2 intervention. In the first approach, the PST should consider which area of need is creating a concern for safety and the learning of that student and learning of others, and address that need first. Beyond those concerns, the PST could consider starting with an area of need that is more likely to change quickly, then build on that momentum to address a potentially more difficult area of need. In the second approach of layering two interventions from two different domains, there are several easy integrations of multiple areas. First, it is easy to integrate goal setting (self-regulation strategies) with CICO (conduct). Similarly, it is easy to add small-group test anxiety (emotional symptoms) with another intervention such as behavior contracts (social problem solving). Finally, you can adapt existing interventions to work for multiple areas as well. For example, adapting CICO (conduct) to include breaks from an academic task (academic) when students meet a work completion goal would cover both domains. The third approach to addressing multiple areas of need will require a new, and potentially less feasible intervention to be introduced to your Tier 2 system. Transdiagnostic interventions such as Coping Power are targeted interventions that have components primarily in one area (e.g., Coping Power is a cognitive-behavioral therapy for the emotional symptoms category) but also include components across other areas of need. Coping Power also has weekly goal setting, self-evaluation, daily check-in and point system, study skills and organization, and social-problem-solving lessons. One important note about transdiagnostic interventions is that they require more resources (i.e., time, materials) than simpler, one-area interventions presented in this book. However, this may still be a more efficient approach than layering multiple interventions if your school has a large number of students with co-occurring needs across multiple areas of need.

SECONDARY APPLICATIONS

Middle schools and high schools present unique challenges related to school size, organization, and student developmental level, which are important to consider when selecting and implementing Tier 2 interventions. First, secondary schools tend to be large buildings that support greater numbers of students, staff, and faculty than elementary schools do. As a result, practices that are adopted schoolwide must be suitable across more classrooms, often with larger class sizes, and may have to meet a diverse set of cultural and social needs. This increased diversity means that Tier 2 PSTs must ensure that a wide variety of evidence-based Tier 2 interventions are continuously available for any student referred to Tier 2.

Next, secondary schools are more organizationally complex than elementary schools are due to academic departmentalization and because students attend multiple classes taught by different teachers throughout the day. This complexity may result in challenges communicating Tier 2 implementation and data collection plans across teachers and maintaining treatment fidelity across multiple settings. To address this issue, many PSTs use technology for data tracking and communication. For example, Google Workspace for Education offers a suite of applications that offer users real-time editing, messaging, and documentation in a variety of formats. Researchers Yassine & Tipton-Fisler (2022) utilized Google Sheets to create electronic DPRs used in CICO for middle school students and compared completion, fidelity, and outcomes to traditional paper-and-pencil DPRs. Teachers completing the electronic DPRs were prompted with a phone call or email at the end of their class and completed their ratings within the Google Sheet while providing feedback to their student. The DPR ratings automatically populated graphs accessible to facilitators for data-based individualization and check-in and check-out sessions with students. Compared to traditional paper-and-pencil DPRs, Google Sheets yielded significantly higher fidelity and completion rates, and facilitators felt that the electronic graphs improved the quality of feedback provided to students. In addition, PSTs can create Google Forms (i.e., surveys) for collecting DBR data across multiple teachers, which may be particularly helpful when students engage in an intervention across multiple classes or to measure behavioral generalization.

Further, each academic department might have their own set of behavioral expectations and social norms, which may vary from the schoolwide expectations. Individual classrooms may have different expectations and norms as well as varying social structures due to different combinations of students. These class-by-class variations might create challenges for students who are working on generalizing behaviors across settings. As the PST designs interventions that will be implemented across multiple classrooms or settings, they should strongly consider inviting each teacher involved to help develop consistent language and expectations for their student. Additionally, all teachers and staff responsible for implementing or overseeing Tier 2 interventions should attend trainings until they can demonstrate 100% proficiency across all implementation considerations (e.g., providing feedback, collecting data, communicating across stakeholders).

Secondary students present different SEB challenges and considerations than elementary students present. As students enter adolescence, peer social structures (e.g., friendships, popularity, peer perception) become significantly more influential to student behavior than adult interactions are, particularly for students who struggle with antisocial behaviors (e.g., drug use, gang affiliation, defiance; Gardner et al., 2008). As a result, PSTs should consider utilizing interventions that include peer models or peer mediation to the greatest extent possible. Finally, adolescents thrive on opportunities to practice autonomy and independent decision making, so PSTs should involve students across intervention decision-making opportunities (Korinek, 2015). This may include reviewing Tier 2 referral data to match students to interventions, identifying and defining problem and replacement behaviors, reviewing response data, and assisting with data-based adaptations.

CONCLUDING THOUGHTS

As we conclude, we want to thank you for reading and centering what is best for students, families, and educators. We wrote this book after years of being asked how to go beyond readiness for Tier 2 or general Tier 2 systems or individual practices. It is our sincere hope that you have been able to expand your understanding of the complex, and sometimes interconnected, academic, social, emotional, and behavioral needs of students and how those needs are nested within systems and structures and policies that you can positively impact. We hope you are able to take these ideas and adapt them for your context, students, and community. We look forward to being in community with you and hearing from your experiences as we work together to improve the lives of all students and families. May your data be rich, your adaptations person-centered, your interventions implemented with fidelity, and your outcomes positive!

References

Alberto, P., & Troutman, A. (2012). *Applied behavior analysis for teachers* (9th ed.). Upper Merrill Prentice Hall.

Algozzine, B., Wang, C., & Violette, A. S. (2011). Reexamining the relationship between academic achievement and social behavior. *Journal of Positive Behavior Interventions, 13*(1), 3–16.

Algozzine, R. F., Barrett, S., Eber, L., George, H., Horner, R. H., Lewis, T. J., . . . Sugai, G. (2014). *SWPBIS Tiered Fidelity Inventory*. OSEP Technical Assistance Center on Positive Behavioral Interventions and Supports. Available from *www.pbis.org*.

Allison, A. C., & Ferreira, R. J. (2017). Implementing cognitive behavioral intervention for trauma in schools (CBITS) with Latino youth. *Child and Adolescent Social Work Journal, 34*, 181–189.

American Psychiatric Association. (2022). *Diagnostic and statistical manual of mental disorders* (5th ed., text rev.). Author.

Archer, A. L., & Hughes, C. (2011). *Explicit instruction: Effective and efficient teaching*. Guilford Press.

Arslan, S. (2014). An investigation of the relationships between metacognition and self-regulation with structural equation. *International Journal of Educational Sciences, 6*(3), 603–611.

Baer, D. M., Wolf, M. M., & Risley, T. R. (1968). Some current dimensions of applied behavior analysis. *Journal of Applied Behavior Analysis, 1*, 91–97.

Bandura, A., & Locke, E. (2003). Negative self-efficacy and goal effects revisited. *Journal of Applied Psychology, 88*(1), 87–99.

Barbrack, C. R., & Maher, C. A. (1984). Effects of involving conduct problem adolescents in the setting of counseling goals. *Child and Family Behavior Therapy, 6*(2), 33–44.

Bardhoshi, G., Cobb, N., & Erford, B. T. (2019). Determining evidence-based outcomes in school-aged youth: Free-access instruments for school counselor use. *Professional School Counseling, 22*(1b), 88–97.

Barrish, H. H., Saunders, M., & Wolf, M. M. (1969). Good Behavior Game: Effects of individual contingencies for group consequences on disruptive behavior in a classroom. *Journal of Applied Behavior Analysis, 2*, 119–124.

Beck, A. T. (1979). *Cognitive therapy and the emotional disorders*. Penguin.

Becker, S. P., Kerig, P. K., Lim, J.-Y., & Ezechukwu, R. N. (2012). Predictors of recidivism among delinquent youth: Interrelations among ethnicity, gender, age, mental health problems, and posttraumatic stress. *Journal of Child & Adolescent Trauma, 5*(2), 145–160.

Beidas, R. S., Benjamin, C. L., Puleo, C. M., Edmunds, J. M., & Kendall, P. C. (2010). Flexible applications of the Coping Cat Program for Anxious Youth. *Cognitive and Behavioral Practice, 7*(2), 142–153.

Berry Kuchle, L., Zumeta Edmonds, R., Danielson, L. C., Peterson, A., & Riley-Tillman, T. C. (2015). The next big idea: A framework for integrated academic and behavioral intensive intervention. *Learning Disabilities Research & Practice, 30*(4), 150–158.

Bitsko, R. H., Claussen, A. H., Lichstein, J., Black, L. I., Jones, S. E., Danielson, M. L., . . . Ghandour, R. M. (2022). Mental health surveillance among children—United States, 2013–2019. *MMWR Suppl, 71*(2), 1–42.

Bovend'Eerdt, T. J. H., Botell, R. E., & Wade, D. T. (2009). Writing SMART rehabilitation goals and achieving goal attainment scaling: A practical guide. *Clinical Rehabilitation, 23*, 352–361.

Boyd, J. R., & Anderson, C. M. (2013). Breaks are better: A Tier II social behavior intervention. *Journal of Behavioral Education, 22*(4), 348–365.

Briesch, A. M., Daniels, B., & Beneville, M. (2019). Unpacking the term "self-management": Understanding intervention applications within the school-based literature. *Journal of Behavioral Education, 28*, 54–77.

Bruce, C. D., Esmonde, I., Ross, J., Dookie, L., & Beatty, R. (2010). The effects of sustained classroom-embedded teacher professional learning on teacher efficacy and related student achievement. *Teaching and Teacher Education, 26*, 1598–1608.

Bruhn, A. L., Estrapala, S., Mahatmya, D., Rila, A., & Vogelgesang, K. (2020). Training teachers on data-based individualization: A mixed methods study. *Behavioral Disorders, 28*(1), 3–16.

Bruhn, A. L., Gilmour, A., Rila, A., Van Camp, A., Sheaffer, A., Hancock, E., . . . Wehby, J. H. (2020). Treatment components and participant characteristics associated with outcomes in self-monitoring interventions. *Journal of Positive Behavior Interventions*, 1–13.

Bruhn, A. L., & McDaniel, S. C. (2021). Tier 2: Critical issues in systems, practices, and data. *Journal of Emotional and Behavioral Disorders, 29*(1), 34–43.

Bruhn, A. L., McDaniel, S. C., Fernando, J., & Troughton, L. (2016). Goal-setting interventions for students with behavior problems: A systematic review. *Behavioral Disorders, 42*(2), 107–121.

Bruhn, A. L., McDaniel, S., Rila, A., & Estrapala, S. (2018). A step-by-step guide to Tier 2 behavioral progress monitoring. *Beyond Behavior, 27*(1), 15–27.

Bruhn, A. L., Wehby, J. H., & Hasselbring, T. S. (2020). Data-based decision making for social behavior: Setting a research agenda. *Journal of Positive Behavior Interventions, 22*(2), 116–126.

Bruhn, A. L., Wehby, J. H., Hoffman, L., Estrapala, S. E., Rila, A., Hancock, E., . . . Copeland, B. (2022). A randomized control trial on the effects of MoBeGo, a self-monitoring app for challenging behavior. *Behavioral Disorders, 48*, 29–43.

Bruhn, A. L., & Wills, H. (2018). The emerging research on and development of technology-based self-monitoring. In T. Landrum, B. Cook, & M. Tankersley (Eds.), *Emerging research and issues in behavioral disabilities* (Vol. 30, pp. 51–68). Emerald Group.

Brunwasser, S. M., Gillham, J. E., & Kim, E. S. (2009). A meta-analytic review of the Penn Resiliency Program's effect on depressive symptoms. *Journal of Consulting and Clinical Psychology, 77*(6), 1042–1054.

Burns, M. K., Riley-Tillman, T. C., & VanDerHeyden, A. M. (2012). *RTI applications: Academic and behavioral interventions*. Guilford Press.

Caldarella, P., Larsen, R. A. A., Williams, L., Downs, K. R., Wills, H. P., & Wehby, J. H. (2020). Effects of teachers' praise-to-reprimand ratios on elementary students' on-task behaviour. *Educational Psychology, 40*, 1306–1322.

Cannella-Malone, H. I., Sabielny, L. M., Jimenez, E. D., & Miller, M. M. (2013). Pick one! Conducting preference assessments with students with significant disabilities. *Teaching Exceptional Children, 45*, 16–23.

Carpenter, K. L. H., Baranek, G. T., Copeland, W. E., Compton, S., Zucker, N., Dawson, G., & Egger, H. L. (2019). Sensory over-responsivity: An early risk factor for anxiety and behavioral challenges in young children. *Journal of Abnormal Child Psychology, 47*(6), 1075–1088.

CASEL—Collaborative for Academic, Social, and Emotional Learning. (2021). *Focus Area 3 RUBRIC promote SEL for students*. Author.

Center on PBIS. (n.d.). What is PBIS? Retrieved from *www.pbis.org/pbis/what-is-pbis*.

Chafouleas, S. M. (2011). Direct Behavior Rating: A review of the issues and research in its development. *Education and Treatment of Children, 34*(4), 575–591.

Chafouleas, S. M., Briesch, A. M., Riley-Tillman, T. C., Christ, T. J., Black, A. C., & Kilgus, S. P. (2010). An investigation of the generalizability and dependability of Direct Behavior Rating Single Item Scales (DBR-SIS) to measure academic engagement and disruptive behavior of middle school students. *Journal of School Psychology, 48*, 219–246.

Chafouleas, S. M., Johnson, A. H., Riley-Tillman, T. C., & Iovino, E. A. (2021). *School-based behavioral assessment: Informing prevention and intervention*. Guilford Press.

Chafouleas, S. M., Kilgus, S. P., Jaffery, R., Riley-Tillman, T. C., Welsh, M., & Christ, T. J. (2013). Direct behavior rating as a school-based behavior screener for elementary and middle grades, *Journal of School Psychology, 51*(3), 367–38.

Chafouleas, S. M., Riley-Tillman, T. C., & Christ, T. J. (2009). Direct Behavior Rating (DBR): An emerging method for assessing social behavior within a tiered intervention system. *Assessment for Effective Intervention, 34*(4), 195–200.

Chaplin, T. M., Gillham, J. E., Reivich, K., Elkon, A. G. L., Samuels, B., Freres, D. R., . . . Seligman, M. E. P. (2006). Depression prevention for early adolescent girls: A pilot study of all-girls verses co-ed groups. *Journal of Early Adolescence, 26*, 110–126.

Chappuis, S., Chappuis, J., & Stiggins, R. (2009). Supporting teachers. *Educational Leadership, 66*(5), 56–60.

Cheney, D. A., Stage, S. A., Hawken, L. S., Lynass, L., Mielenz, C., & Waugh, M. (2009). A 2-year outcome study of the check, connect, and expect intervention for students at risk for severe behavior problems. *Journal of Emotional and Behavioral Disorders, 17*, 226–243.

Chiu, A., Falk, A., & Walkup, J. T. (2016). Anxiety disorders among children and adolescents. *Focus (American Psychiatric Publishing), 14*(1), 26–33.

Codding, R. S., Volpe, R. J., & Poncy, B. C. (2017). *Effective math interventions*. Guilford Press.

Cooper, J. O., Heron, T. E., & Heward, W. L. (2007). *Applied behavior analysis* (2nd ed.). Pearson Education.

Cooper, J. O., Heron, T. E., & Heward, W. L. (2020). *Applied behavior analysis* (3rd ed.). Pearson Education.

Copeland, W. E., Keeler, G., Angold, A., & Costello, E. J. (2010). Posttraumatic stress without trauma in children. *The American Journal of Psychiatry, 167*(9), 1059–1065.

Covington, M. V. (2000). Goal theory, motivation, and school achievement: An integrative review. *Annual Review of Psychology, 51*, 171–200.

Crawley, S. A., Kendall, P. C., Benjamin, C. L., Brodman, D. M., Wei, C., Beidas, R. S., . . . Mauro, C. (2013). Brief cognitive-behavioral therapy for anxious youth: Feasibility and initial outcomes. *Cognitive and Behavioral Practice, 20*(2), 123–133.

Cummings, C., Caporino, N., & Kendall, P. C. (2014). Comorbidity of anxiety and depression in children and adolescents: 20 years after. *Psychological Bulletin, 140*, 816–845.

Daly, E. J., III, Martens, B. K., Witt, J. C., & Dool, E. J. (1997). A model for conducting a functional analysis of academic performance problems. *School Psychology Review, 26*(4), 554–574.

Dane, A. V., & Schneider, B. H. (1998). Program integrity in primary and early secondary prevention: Are implementation effects out of control? *Clinical Psychology Review, 18*(1), 23–45.

Darney, D., Reinke, W. M., Herman, K. C., Stormont, M., & Ialongo, N. S. (2013). Children with co-occurring academic and behavior problems in first grade: Distal outcomes in twelfth grade. *Journal of School Psychology, 51*(1), 117–128.

Dobson, D., & Dobson, K. S. (2018). *Evidence-based practice of cognitive-behavioral therapy*. Guilford Press.

Dowdy, E., DiStefano, C., Greer, F., Moore, S., & Pompey, K. (2019). Examining the latent structure of the BASC-3 BESS Parent Preschool Form. *Journal of Psychoeducational Assessment, 37*(2), 181–193.

Dunlap, G., Iovannone, R., Wilson, K. J., Kincaid, D. K., & Strain, P. (2010). Prevent-teach-reinforce: A standardized model of school-based behavioral intervention. *Journal of Positive Behavior Interventions, 12*(1), 9–22.

Dunlap, G., & Kern, L. (2018). Perspectives on functional (behavioral) assessment. *Behavioral Disorders, 43*(2), 316–321.

Elliott, S. N., & Gresham, F. M. (2009). *Social Skills Improvement System intervention guide*. NCS Pearson.

Ellis, A. (1962). *Reason and emotion in psychotherapy*. Citadel.

Estrapala, S., Bruhn, A. L., & Rila, A. (2022). Behavioral self-regulation: A comparison of goals and self-monitoring for high school students with disabilities. *Journal of Emotional and Behavioral Disorders, 30*(3), 171–184.

Estrapala, S., Rila, A., & Bruhn, A. L. (2018). Don't quit cold-turkey: Systematic fading to promote sustained behavioral change. *Teaching Exceptional Children, 51*(1), 54–61.

Ezell, E. (2018). *Diagnostic accuracy of a universal behavior screener for identification of attention problems in first grade* [Unpublished master's thesis]. East Carolina University.

Farahmand, F. K., Grant, K. E., Polo, A. J., Duffy, S. N., & DuBois, D. L. (2011). School-based Mental health and behavioral programs for low-income, urban youth: A systematic and meta-analytic review. *Clinical Psychology: Science & Practice, 18*(4), 372–390.

Fuchs, L. S., Fuchs, D., & Malone, A. S. (2017). The taxonomy of intervention intensity. *Teaching Exceptional Children, 50*(1), 35–43.

Gardner, T. W., Dishion, T. J., & Connell, A. M. (2008). Adolescent self-regulation as resilience: Resistance to antisocial behavior within the deviant peer context. *Journal of Abnormal Child Psychology, 36*, 273–284.

Gettinger, M., Kratochwill, T. R., Eubanks, A., Foy, A., & Levin, J. R. (2021). Academic and behavior combined support: Evaluation of an integrated supplemental intervention for early elementary students. *Journal of School Psychology, 89*, 1–19.

Gillham, J. E., Hamilton, J., Freres, D. R., Patton, K., & Gallop, R. (2006). Preventing depression among early adolescents in the primary care setting: A randomized controlled study of the Penn Resiliency Program. *Journal of Abnormal Child Psychology, 34*, 203–219.

Goodman, R. (1997). The Strengths and Difficulties Questionnaire: A research note. *Journal of Child Psychology and Psychiatry, 38*, 581–586.

Goodman, R. (2001). Psychometric properties of the strengths and difficulties questionnaire. *Journal of the American Academy of Child & Adolescent Psychiatry, 40*(11), 1337–1345.

Gorski, P. (2010). Unlearning deficit ideology and the scornful gaze. Retrieved from *EdChange.org*.

Gresham, F. M., Van, M. B., & Cook, C. C. (2006). Social skills training for teaching replacement behaviors: Remediating acquisition deficits in at-risk students. *Behavioral Disorders, 31*(4), 363–377.

Hamilton, M. (1960). A rating scale for depression. *Journal of Neurology, Neurosurgery & Psychiatry, 231*, 56–62.

Harbour, K. E., McDaniel, S. C., Preast, J. L., & Buchanan, D. (2022). Integrating interventions for elementary students experiencing co-occurring academic and behavior needs. *Teaching Exceptional Children, 54*(5), 362–370.

Hawken, L. S., Adolphson, S. L., MacLeod, K. S., & Schumann, J. (2009). Secondary-tier interventions and supports. In G. Sugai, R. H. Horner, G. Dunlap, & W. Sailor (Eds.). *Handbook of positive behavior support* (pp. 395–420). Springer.

Hawken, L. S., Crone, D. A., Bundock, K., & Horner, R. (2020). *Responding to problem behavior in schools: The Check-In, Check-Out intervention* (3rd ed.). Guilford Press.

Hinshaw, S. P. (1992). Externalizing behavior problems and academic underachievement in childhood and adolescence: Causal relationships and underlying mechanisms. *Psychological Bulletin, 111*(1), 127–155.

Hirsch, S., Bruhn, A., McDaniel, S. C., & Stephens, H. (2021). A survey of educators serving students with emotional and behavioral disorders during the COVID-19 pandemic. *Behavioral Disorders, 47(* 2),

Hirsch, S. E., Macsuga-Gage, A., Park, K., & Dillon, S. (2016). A road map to systemically setting up a group contingency. *Beyond Behavior, 25*(2), 21–29.

Hoover, S. A., Sapere, H., Lang, J. M., Nadeem, E., Dean, K. L., & Vona, P. (2018). Statewide implementation of an evidence-based trauma intervention in schools. *School Psychology Quarterly, 33*, 44–53.

Horner, R. H., Todd, A. W., Lewis-Palmer, T., Irvin, L. K., Sugai, G., & Boland, J. B. (2004). The School-Wide Evaluation Tool (SET): A research instrument for assessing school-wide positive behavior support. *Journal of Positive Behavior Interventions, 6*(1), 3–12.

Hughes, C. A., Morris, J. R., Therrien, W. J., & Benson, S. K. (2017). Explicit instruction: Historical and contemporary contexts. *Learning Disabilities Research & Practice, 32*(3), 140–148.

Jaycox, L. H., Cohen, J. A., Mannarino, A. P., Walker, D. W., Langley, A. K., Gegenheimer, K. L., . . . Schonlau, M. (2010). Children's mental health care following Hurricane Katrina: A field trial of trauma-focused psychotherapies. *Journal of Traumatic Stress, 23*(2), 223–231.

Jaycox, L. H., Langley, A. K., & Dean, K. L. (2009). *Support for Students Exposed to Trauma: The SSET program—Lesson plans, worksheets, and materials.* RAND Corporation.

Jenkins, J. R., Hudson, R. F., & Johnson, E. S. (2007). Screening for at-risk readers in a response to intervention framework. *School Psychology Review, 36*(4), 582–600.

Kamphaus, R. W., & Reynolds, C. R. (2015). *Behavior Assessment System for Children—Third Edition (BASC-3): Behavioral and Emotional Screening System (BESS).* Pearson.

Kataoka, S., Jaycox, L. H., Wong, M., Nadeem, E., Langley, A., Tang, L., & Stein, B. D. (2011). Effects on school outcomes in low-income minority youth: Preliminary findings from a community-partnered study of a school-based trauma intervention. *Ethnicity and Disease, 21*(3, Suppl. 1), 71–77.

Kataoka, S. H., Stein, B. D., Jaycox, L. H., Wong, M., Escudero, P., Tu, W., . . . Fink, A. (2003). A school-based mental health program for traumatized Latino immigrant children. *Journal of the American Academy of Child and Adolescent Psychiatry, 42*(3), 311–318.

Kazdin, A. E., Rodgers, A., & Colbus, D. (1986). The hopelessness scale for children: Psychometric characteristics and concurrent validity. *Journal of Consulting and Clinical Psychology, 54*, 241–245.

Kelly, J. R., & Shogren, K. A. (2014). The impact of teaching self-determination skills on the on-task and off-task behaviors of students with emotional and behavioral disorders. *Journal of Emotional and Behavioral Disorders, 22*(1), 27–40.

Kendall, P. C., Crawley, S., Benjamin, C., & Mauro, C. (2013). *Brief Coping Cat: The 8-session therapist manual.* Workbook.

Kendall, P. C., & Hedtke, K. A. (2006). *Coping cat workbook* (Vol. 44). Ardmore, PA: Workbook.

Kilgus, S. P., Chafouleas, S. M., & Riley-Tillman, T. C. (2013). Development and initial validation of the Social and Academic Behavior Risk Screener for elementary grades. *School Psychology Quarterly, 28*, 210–226.

Kilgus, S. P., Izumi, J. T., von der Embse, N. P., Van Wie, M. P., Eklund, K., Taylor, C. N., & Iaccarino, S. (2019). Co-occurrence of academic and behavioral risk within elementary schools: Implications for universal screening practices. *School Psychology, 34*(3), 261–270.

Kilgus, S. P., Sims, W. A., von der Embse, N. P., & Taylor, C. N. (2016). Technical adequacy of the Social, Academic, and Emotional Behavior Risk Screener (SAEBRS) in an elementary sample. *Assessment for Effective Intervention, 42*, 46–59.

Kilgus, S. P., & von der Embse, N. P. (2014). *Social, academic, and emotional behavior risk screener.* Illuminate Education.

Kilgus, S. P., & von der Embse, N. P. (2015). *Social, Academic, and Emotional Behavior Risk Screener (SAEBRS).* Theodore J. Christ & Colleagues.

Klingbeil, D. A., Osman, D. J., Van Norman, E. R., Berry-Corie, K., Kim, J. S., Schmitt, M. C., & Latham, A. D. (2023). Universal screening with aimswebPlus reading in middle school. *Reading & Writing Quarterly, 29*(3), 192–211.

Korinek, L. (2015). Promoting self-determination through the FBA/BIP process. *Preventing School Failure, 59*(2), 98–108.

Kovacs, M., & MHS Staff. (2011). *Children's Depression Inventory 2nd Edition (CDI 2): Technical manual.* Multi-Health Systems.

Kratochwill, T. R., & Bergan, J. R. (1990). *Behavioral consultation in applied settings: An individual's guide.* Plenum.

Kruger, A. M., Strong, W., Daly, E. J., III, O'Connor, M., Sommerhalder, M. S., Holtz, J., . . . Heifner, A. (2016). Setting the stage for academic success through antecedent intervention. *Psychology in the Schools, 53*(1), 24–38.

Lane, K. L., Capizzi, A. M., Fisher, M. H., & Ennis, R. P. (2012). Secondary prevention efforts at the middle school level: An application of the behavior education program. *Education and Treatment of Children, 35*, 51–90.

Lane, K. L., & Menzies, H. M. (2009). Student Risk Screening Scale for Early Internalizing and Externalizing Behavior (SRSS-IE): Screening scale. Available at *Ci3t.org/screening.*

Lane, K. L., Menzies, H. M., Bruhn, A. L., & Crnobori, M. (2011). *Managing challenging behaviors in schools: Research-based strategies that work.* Guilford Press.

Lane, K. L., Oakes, W. P., Royer, D. J., Menzies, H. M., Brunsting, N. C., Buckman, M. M., . . . Lane, K. S. (2021). Secondary teachers' self-efficacy during initial implementation of comprehensive, integrated, three-tiered models. *Journal of Positive Behavior Interventions, 23*(4), 232–244.

Langberg, J. M., Epstein, J. N., Becker, S. P., Girio-Herrera, E., & Vaughn, A. J. (2012). Evaluation of the homework, organization, and planning skills (HOPS) intervention for middle school students with attention deficit hyperactivity disorder as implemented by school mental health providers. *School Psychology Review, 41*(3), 342–364.

Latham, G. P. (1988). Human resource training and development. In M. R. Rosenzweig & L. W. Porter (Eds.), *Annual review of psychology* (Vol. 39, pp. 545–582). Annual Reviews.

Lenz, A. S. (2015). Meta-analysis of the coping cat program for decreasing severity of anxiety symptoms among children and adolescents. *Journal of Child and Adolescent Counseling, 1*(2), 51–65.

Lewis, T. J., & Sugai, G. (1999). Effective behavior support: A systems approach to proactive schoolwide management. *Focus on Exceptional Children, 31*(6), 1–24.

Lloyd, B. P., Bruhn, A. L., Sutherland, K. S., & Bradshaw, C. P. (2019). Progress and priorities in research to improve outcomes for students with or at risk for emotional and behavioral disorders. *Behavioral Disorders, 44*(2), 85–96.

Maggin, D. M., Zurheide, J., Pickett, K. C., & Baillie, S. J. (2015). A systematic evidence review of the Check-In/Check-Out program for reducing student challenging behaviors. *Journal of Positive Behavior Interventions, 17*, 197–208.

Majeika, C., Bruhn, A. L., McDaniel, S. C., & Sterret, B. (2020). Reengineering Tier 2 interventions for responsive decision making: An adaptive intervention process. *Journal of Applied School Psychology, 36*(2), 111–132.

Majeika, C. E., Van Camp, A., Wehby, J. H., Kern, L., Commisso, C. E., & Gaier, K. (2020). An evaluation of adaptations made to Check-In Check-Out. *Journal of Positive Behavior Interventions, 22*, 25–37.

Markelz, A. M., Riden, B. S., Zoder-Martell, K. A., Miller, J. E., & Bolinger, S. J. (2021). Reliability assessment of an observation tool to measure praise characteristics. *Journal of Positive Behavior Interventions, 23*, 17–29.

Maynard, B. R., Kjellstrand, E. K., & Thompson, A. M. (2014). The effects of Check and Connect on attendance, behavior, and academics: A randomized effectiveness trial. *Research on Social Work Practice, 24*, 296–309.

McDaniel, S. C., Bruhn, A. L., & Mitchell, B. (2015). A tier 2 framework for identification and intervention. *Beyond Behavior, 24*(1), 10–17.

McDaniel, S. C., & Flower, A. (2015). Use of a behavioral graphic organizer to reduce disruptive behavior. *Education and Treatment of Children, 38*(4), 505–522.

McDaniel, S., Flower, A., & Cheney, D. (2011). Put me in, coach! A powerful and efficient Tier 2 behavioral intervention for alternative settings. *Beyond Behavior, 20*, 18–24.

McDaniel, S. C., Houchins, D. E., & Robinson, C. (2016). The effects of Check, Connect, and Expect on behavioral and academic growth. *Journal of Emotional and Behavioral Disorders, 24*, 42–53.

McDaniel, S. C., Scott, T., & Zaheer, I. (2018). Teaching social behaviors. In J. McLeskey, L. Maheady, B. Billingsley, M. Brownell, & T. J. Lewis (Eds.), *High-leverage practices for inclusive classrooms* (pp. 120–132). Routledge.

McIntosh, K., Gion, C., & Bastable, E. (2018). Do schools implementing SWPBIS have decreased racial and ethnic disproportionality in school discipline? Retrieved from *www.pbis.org/resource/do-schools-implementing-swpbis-have-decreased-racial-and-ethnic-disproportionality-in-school-discipline*.

McIntosh, K., & Goodman, S. (2016). *Integrated multi-tiered systems of support: Blending RTI and PBIS*. New York: Guilford Press.

McIntosh, K., & Goodman, S. (2020). *Multi-tiered systems of support: Integrating academic RTI and school-wide PBIS*. Guilford Press.

Mendelson, T., Tandon, S. D., O'Brennan, L., Leaf, P. J., & Ialongo, N. S. (2015). Brief report: Moving prevention into schools: The impact of a trauma-informed school-based intervention. *Journal of Adolescence, 43*, 142–147.

Miller, F. G., Cohen, D., Chafouleas, S. M., Riley-Tillman, T. C., Welsh, M. E., & Fabiano, G. A. (2015). A comparison of measures to screen for social, emotional, and behavioral risk. *School Psychology Quarterly, 30*(2), 184–196.

Miller, L. M., Dufrene, B. A., Sterling, H. E., Olmi, D. J., & Bachmayer, E. (2015). The effects of Check-In/Check-Out on problem behavior and academic engagement in elementary school students. *Journal of Positive Behavior Interventions, 17*(1), 28–38.

Mitchell, B. S., Adamson, R. M., & McKenna, J. W. (2017). Curbing our enthusiasm: An analysis of the Check-In/Check-Out literature using the Council for Exceptional Children's evidence-based practice standards. *Behavior Modification, 41*, 343–367.

Mitchell, B. S., Bruhn, A. L., & Lewis, T. J. (2015). Essential features of Tier 2 & 3 school-wide positive behavioral supports. In S. R. Jimerson, M. K. Burns, & A. M. VanDerHeyden (Eds.), *Handbook of response to intervention: The science and practice of assessment and intervention* (2nd ed., pp. 539–562). Springer.

Park, E.-Y., & Blair, K.-S. C. (2020). Check-in/Check-out implementation in schools: A meta-analysis of group design studies. *Education and Treatment of Children, 43*(4), 361–375.

Powers, K., Hagans, K., & Linn, M. (2017). A mixed-method efficacy and fidelity study of Check and Connect. *Psychology in the Schools, 54*, 1019–1033.

Reback, R. (2010). Schools' mental health services and young children's emotions, behavior, and learning. *Journal of Policy Analysis and Management, 29*(4), 698725.

Reinke, W. M., Herman, K. C., Petras, H., & Ialongo, N. S. (2008). Empirically derived subtypes of child academic and behavior problems: Co-occurrence and distal outcomes. *Journal of Abnormal Child Psychology, 36*(5), 759–770.

Restorative Justice Exchange. (n.d.). What is restorative justice? Retrieved from *https://restorativejustice.org/what-is-restorative-justice*.

Reynolds, S., Wilson, C., Austin, J., & Hooper, L. (2012). Effects of psychotherapy for anxiety in children and adolescents: A meta-analytic review. *Clinical Psychology Review, 32*, 251–262.

Riley-Tillman, T. C., Chafouleas, S. M., Sassu, K. A., Chanese, J. A. M., & Glazer, A. D. (2008). Examining the agreement of Direct Behavior Ratings and Systematic Direct Observation Data for on-task and disruptive behavior. *Journal of Positive Behavior Interventions, 10*(2), 136–143.

Romer, N., von der Embse, N., Eklund, K., Kilgus, S., Perales, K., Splett, J. W., . . . Wheeler, D. (2020). Best practices in social, emotional, and behavioral screening: An implementation guide. Version 2.0. Retrieved from *smhcollaborative.org/universalscreening*.

Royer, D. J., Lane, K. L., Dunlap, K. D., & Ennis, R. P. (2019). A systematic review of teacher-delivered behavior-specific praise on K–12 student performance. *Remedial and Special Education, 40,* 112–128.

Sanetti, L. M., & Fallon, L. M. (2011). Treatment integrity assessment: How estimates of adherence, quality, and exposure influence interpretation of implementation. *Journal of Educational and Psychological Consultation, 21*(3), 209–232.

Santesteban-Echarri, O., Hernández-Arroyo, L., Rice, S. M., Güerre-Lobera, M. J., Serrano-Villar, M., Espín-Jaime, J. C., & Jiménez-Arriero, M. Á. (2018). Adapting the Brief Coping Cat for children with anxiety to a group setting in the Spanish public mental health system: A hybrid effectiveness–implementation pilot study. *Journal of Child and Family Studies, 27,* 3300–3315.

Scarborough, H. S. (2001). Connecting early language and literacy to later reading (dis)abilities: Evidence, theory, and practice. In S. Neuman & D. Dickinson (Eds.), *Handbook of early literacy research* (Vol. 1). Guilford Press.

Seligman, M. E. P., Kaslow, N. J., Alloy, L. B., Peterson, C., Tanenbaum, R. L., & Abramson, L. Y. (1984). Attributional style and depressive symptoms among children. *Journal of Abnormal Psychology, 93,* 235–238.

Shapiro, E. S., & Clemens, N. H. (2023). *Academic skills problems* (5th ed.). Guilford Press.

Sinclair, M. F., Christenson, S. L., Evelo, D. L., & Hurley, C. M. (1998). Dropout prevention for high-risk youth with disabilities: Efficacy of a sustained school engagement procedure. *Exceptional Children, 65,* 7–21.

Spitzer, R. L., Kroenke, K., Williams, J. B. W., & Löwe, B. (2006). A brief measure for assessing generalized anxiety disorder: The GAD-7. *Archives of Internal Medicine (1960), 166*(10), 1092–1097.

Stage, S. A., & Galanti, S. B. (2017). The therapeutic mechanisms of Check, Connect, and Expect. *School Psychology Review, 46,* 3–20.

Stein, B. D., Jaycox, L. H., Kataoka, S. H., Wong, M., Tu, W., Elliott, M. N., & Fink, A. (2003). A mental health intervention for schoolchildren exposed to violence: A randomized controlled trial. *Journal of the American Medical Association., 290*(5), 603–611.

Sterret, B., McDaniel, S. C., Majeika, C., & Bruhn, A. L. (2020). Using evidence informed strategies to adapt Tier 2 interventions. *Journal of Applied School Psychology, 36*(2), 133–154.

Substance Abuse and Mental Health Services Administration. (2020). *2019 National Survey on Drug Use and Health: Methodological summary and definitions.* Author.

Swoszowski, N. C., McDaniel, S. C., Jolivette, K., & Melius, P. (2013). The effects of tier II check-in/check-out including adaptation for non-responders on the off-task behavior of elementary students in a residential setting. *Education and Treatment of Children, 36,* 63–79.

Tilly, W. D. (2008). The evolution of school psychology to science-based practice: Problem-solving and the three-tiered model. In A. Thomas & J. P. Grimes (Eds.), *Best practices in school psychology* (Vol. 5, pp. 17–36). National Association of School Psychologists.

U.S. Department of Education, Institute of Education Sciences, What Works Clearinghouse. (2015, May). Dropout Prevention intervention report: Check & Connect. Retrieved from *http://whatworks.ed.gov*.

Van Norman, E. R., Nelson, P. M., & Parker, D. C. (2018). Curriculum-based measurement of reading decision rules: Strategies to improve the accuracy of treatment recommendations. *School Psychology Review, 47*(4), 333–344.

Vaughn, S., Grills, A. E., Capin, P., Roberts, G., Fall, A. M., & Daniel, J. (2022). Examining the effects of integrating anxiety management instruction within a reading intervention for upper elementary students with reading difficulties. *Journal of Learning Disabilities, 55*(5), 408–426.

von der Embse, N. P., Eklund, K., & Kilgus, S. P. (2022). *Conducting behavioral and mental health assessments in MTSS.* Taylor & Francis.

Walker, H. M., Ramsey, E., & Gresham, F. M. (2004). *Antisocial behavior in school: Evidence-based practices* (2nd ed.). Thomson/Wadsworth Learning.

Walker, H. M., & Severson, H. H. (1992). *Systematic screening for behavior disorders (SSBD)*. Sopris West.

Weist, M. D., Eber, L., Horner, R., Splett, J., Putnam, R., Barrett, S., . . . Hoover, S. (2018). Improving multitiered systems of support for students with "internalizing" emotional/behavioral problems. *Journal of Positive Behavior Interventions, 20*(3), 172–184.

Weisz, J. R., Vaughn-Coaxum, R. A., Evans, S. C., Thomassin, K., Hersh, J., Ng, M. Y., . . . Mair, P. (2020). Efficient monitoring of treatment response during youth psychotherapy: The behavior and feelings survey. *Journal of Clinical Child & Adolescent Psychology, 49*(6), 737–751.

Whiston, S. C., Tai, W. L., Rahardja, D., & Eder, K. (2011), School counseling outcome: A meta-analytic examination of interventions. *Journal of Counseling and Development, 89*, 37–55.

Wills, H. P., & Mason, B. A. (2014). Implementation of a self-monitoring application to improve on-task behavior: A high-school pilot study. *Journal of Behavioral Education, 23*, 421–434.

Wills, H., Wehby, J. H., Caldarella, P., Kamps, D., & Romine, R. S. (2018). Classroom management that works: A replication trial of the CW-FIT program. *Exceptional Children, 84*(4), 437–456.

Witt, J. C., & Elliott, S. N. (1985). Acceptability of classroom intervention strategies. In T. R. Kratochwill (Ed.), *Advances in school psychology* (Vol. 4, pp. 251–288). Erlbaum.

Wolpe, J. (1969). *The practice of behavior therapy*. New York: Pergamon Press.

Yassine, J., & Tipton-Fisler, L. A. (2022). Check-In/Check Out: Electronic adaptation and individual progress monitoring. *Journal of Special Education Technology, 37*(2), 215–224.

Yeaton, W. H., & Sechrest, L. (1981). Critical dimensions in the choice and maintenance of successful treatments: Strength, integrity, and effectiveness. *Journal of Consulting and Clinical Psychology, 49*(2), 156–167.

Index

Note. *f* or *t* following a page number indicates a figure or a table.